Prime Minister Gyula Andrássy's Influence on Habsburg Foreign Policy

During the Franco-German War of 1870–1871

JÁNOS DECSY

EAST EUROPEAN QUARTERLY, BOULDER
DISTRIBUTED BY COLUMBIA UNIVERSITY PRESS
NEW YORK

1979

EAST EUROPEAN MONOGRAPHS, NO. LII

János Decsy is Professor of History at
Greater Hartford Community College

BROOKLYN COLLEGE

OF

THE CITY UNIVERSITY OF NEW YORK

SCHOOL OF SOCIAL SCIENCE

STUDIES ON SOCIETY IN CHANGE, No. 8

EAST EUROPEAN MONOGRAPHS

The *East European Monographs* comprise scholarly books on the history and civilization of Eastern Europe. They are published by the *East European Quarterly* in the belief that these studies contribute substantially to the knowledge of the area and serve to stimulate scholarship and research.

19. *The Radical Left in the Hungarian Revolution of 1848.* By Laszlo Deme. 1976.
20. *Hungary between Wilson and Lenin: The Hungarian Revolution of 1918–1919 and the Big Three.* By Peter Pastor. 1976.
21. *The Crises of France's East-Central European Diplomacy, 1933–1938.* By Anthony J. Komjathy. 1976.
22. *Polish Politics and National Reform, 1775–1788.* By Daniel Stone. 1976.
23. *The Habsburg Empire in World War I.* Robert A. Kann, Bela K. Kiraly, and Paula S. Fichtner, eds. 1977.
24. *The Slovenes and Yugoslavism, 1890–1914.* By Carole Rogel. 1977.
25. *German-Hungarian Relations and the Swabian Problem.* By Thomas Spira. 1977.
26. *The Metamorphosis of a Social Class in Hungary During the Reign of Young Franz Joseph.* By Peter I. Hidas. 1977.
27. *Tax Reform in Eighteenth Century Lombardy.* By Daniel M. Klang. 1977.
28. *Tradition versus Revolution: Russia and the Balkans in 1917.* By Robert H. Johnston. 1977.
29. *Winter into Spring: The Czechoslovak Press and the Reform Movement 1963–1968.* By Frank L. Kaplan. 1977.
30. *The Catholic Church and the Soviet Government, 1939–1949.* By Dennis J. Dunn. 1977.
31. *The Hungarian Labor Service System, 1939–1945.* By Randolph L. Braham. 1977.
32. *Consciousness and History: Nationalist Critics of Greek Society 1897–1914.* By Gerasimos Augustinos. 1977.
33. *Emigration in Polish Social and Political Thought, 1870–1914.* By Benjamin P. Murdzek. 1977.
34. *Serbian Poetry and Milutin Bojic.* By Mihailo Dordevic. 1977.
35. *The Baranya Dispute: Diplomacy in the Vortex of Ideologies, 1918–1921.* By Leslie C. Tihany. 1978.
36. *The United States in Prague, 1945–1948.* By Walter Ullmann. 1978.
37. *Rush to the Alps: The Evolution of Vacationing in Switzerland.* By Paul P. Bernard. 1978.
38. *Transportation in Eastern Europe: Empirical Findings.* By Bogdan Mieczkowski. 1978.
39. *The Polish Underground State: A Guide to the Underground, 1939–1945.* By Stefan Korbonski. 1978.
40. *The Hungarian Revolution of 1956 in Retrospect.* Edited by Bela K. Kiraly and Paul Jonas. 1978.
41. *Boleslaw Limanowski (1835–1935): A Study in Socialism and Nationalism.* By Kazimiera Janina Cottam. 1978.
42. *The Lingering Shadow of Nazism: The Austrian Independent Party Movement Since 1945.* By Max E. Riedlsperger. 1978.
43. *The Catholic Church, Dissent and Nationality in Soviet Lithuania.* By V. Stanley Vardys. 1978.

44. *The Development of Parliamentary Government in Serbia.* By Alex N. Dragnich. 1978.
45. *Divide and Conquer: German Efforts to Conclude a Separate Peace, 1914–1918.* By L. L. Farrar, Jr. 1978.
46. *The Prague Slav Congress of 1848.* By Lawrence D. Orton. 1978.
47. *The Nobility and the Making of the Hussite Revolution.* By John M. Klassen. 1978.
48. *The Cultural Limits of Revolutionary Politics: Change and Continuity in Socialist Czechoslovakia.* By David W. Paul. 1979.
49. *On the Border of War and Peace: Polish Intelligence and Diplomacy in 1937–1939 and the Origins of the Ultra Secret.* By Richard A. Woytak. 1979.
50. *Bear and Foxes: The International Relations of the East European States 1965–1969.* By Ronald Haly Linden. 1979.
51. *Czechoslovakia: The Heritage of Ages Past.* Edited by Ivan Volgyes and Hans Brisch. 1979.
52. *Prime Minister Gyula Andrássy's Influence on Habsburg Foreign Policy.* By János Decsy. 1979.

BROOKLYN COLLEGE STUDIES ON SOCIETY IN CHANGE

Distributed by Columbia University Press (except as noted)

— EDITOR IN CHIEF BÉLA K. KIRÁLY —

1. *Tolerance and Movements of Religious Dissent in Eastern Europe.* Edited by B. K. Király. Boulder: East European Quarterly, 1975.
2. *The Habsburg Empire in World War I.* Edited by R. A. Kann, B. K. Király, P. S. Fichtner. Boulder: East European Quarterly, 1976.
3. *The Mutual Effects of the Islamic and the Judeo-Christian Worlds: The East European Pattern.* Edited by A. Ascher, T. Halasi-Kun, B. K. Király. New York: Brooklyn College Press, 1978.
4. *Before Watergate: Problems of Corruption in American Society.* Edited by A. S. Eisenstadt, A. Hoogenboom, H. L. Trefousse. New York: Brooklyn College Press, 1978.
5. *East Central European Perceptions of Early America.* Edited by B. K. Király, G. Barany. Lisse (Netherlands): Peter de Ridder Press, 1977. Distributed by Humanities Press, Atlantic Highlands, N.J.
6. *The Hungarian Revolution of 1956 in Retrospect.* Edited by B. K. Király, P. Jónás. Boulder: East European Quarterly, 1978.
7. *Brooklyn, U.S.A.: The Fourth Largest City in America.* Edited by R. S. Miller. New York: Brooklyn College Press, 1979.
8. *Prime Minister Gyula Andrássy's Influence on Habsburg Foreign Policy.* By J. Decsy. Boulder: East European Quarterly, 1979.
9. *The Great Impeacher: A Political Biography of James M. Ashley.* By R. F. Horowitz. New York: Brooklyn College Press, 1978.
10. *War and Society in East Central Europe.* Edited by B. K. Király, G. E. Rothenberg. In preparation.

Csíkszentkirályi krasznahorkai
GRÓF ANDRÁSSY GYULA
OSZTRÁK-MAGYAR KÖZÖS KÜLÜGYMINISZTER

To my family and to the memory of my late father

Preface

The "Brooklyn College Studies on Society in Change" was established as a series for the publication primarily of the proceedings of scholarly conferences held by the School of Social Sciences of our college, either alone or in conjunction with the Center for European Studies of the Graduate School and University Center of the City University of New York. From its inception, however, we intended also to publish monographs. The prerequisites have been archival research, innovative interpretation, revision of obsolete concepts and work that pioneers in fields not yet plowed by academe. Professor János Decsy's present monograph, the first in our series, meets these standards very well. The book is based, in Professor Robert A. Kann's words, on "sophisticated research," and Professor István Deák called it "sophisticated and amazingly well researched. I doubt that anything better will be written on the subject for a long time to come."

The present study is not a biography of Gyula Andrássy; the title does not call it that nor did the author intend it to be. Professor Decsy would in fact do a great service to the field should he later decide to write one. Without being a full account of the statesman's life and deeds, the present monograph truly fills a gap in the literature in Western languages. It puts Andrássy into proper historical perspective, and so complements the efforts of other American scholars to expound nineteenth-century Hungarian history through the mirror of the statesmen who made it.

Professor George Barany took the first step with his well-received volume on the father of Hungarian liberalism, *Stephen Széchenyi and the Awakening of Hungarian Nationalism, 1791–1841* (Princeton University Press, 1968). This, too, is not a complete biography, but it contains enough material and judgment to understand Széchenyi and the origins of Hungarian liberalism. Professor Paul Bödy followed with his *Joseph Eötvös and the Modernization of Hungary, 1840–1870: A Study of Ideas of Individuality and Social Pluralism in Modern Politics* (American Philosophical Society, 1972). This penetrating account illumines mature Hungarian liberalism and Eötvös, its theoretician, the advocate of compulsory, free popular education and full equality for all Hungary's nationalities. My own *Ferenc Deák* (Twayne Publishers, 1975) examines nineteenth-century Hungary's remarkable practitioner of realpolitik, who reestablished the country's self-government through the Compromise of 1867 without ever compromising his own high liberal ideals. Professor István Deák's biography of Lajos Kossuth, Hungary's man of destiny, recently went to press and will be published by Columbia University Press. Deák's and Decsy's books thus complete the cycle. Together the five books give the Western academic world the gist of the history of Hungary in the nineteenth century.

"Brooklyn College Studies on Society in Change" is gratified to be a part of that endeavor.

Highland Lakes, N.J.   Béla K. Király
March 15, 1978   Editor in Chief

Acknowledgments

In refining my doctoral dissertation, written at Columbia University, into this monograph, I have been given willing help by many. Particularly I wish to express my debt and heartfelt thanks to my fatherly friend, Prof. Béla K. Király, who has been most responsible, both in the army and in academia, for molding my intellect and character. It is he who has been instrumental in making this book a reality. He has been an unfailing source of encouragement, and without his constant advice, sound judgment and unvarnished criticism this work never would have been completed.

I am also deeply grateful to my dissertation advisor, Prof. István Deák, director of the Institute on East Central Europe, who encouraged me to persist in my labors, and aided me greatly by reading the manuscript in all its stages of preparation and suggesting improvements in emphases and interpretation. I have drawn heavily upon his learning, advice and time. He has also been responsible for providing funds for the acquisition of contemporary newspapers in various languages. Among my other creditors is Prof. Robert A. Kann of the University of Vienna, who was kind enough to prepare a searching, systematic critique and suggestions for additions and revisions to the manuscript. To him I shall always be grateful.

Special gratitude is due to a host of friends and scholars who have given me the benefit of their knowledge and of their counsel. These include Prof. János Bak of the University of British Columbia, Prof. Joseph Held of Rutgers University, Prof. Douglas W. Houston of Fordham University, Prof. Peter Pastor of Montclair State College and Prof. Gunther E. Rothenberg of Purdue University. Dr. Arthur C. Banks, Jr., president of Greater Hartford Community College, deserves a special word of thanks both for his useful comments on contemporary statesmen and suggestions on source material, and for the financial aid that enabled me to acquire microfilms and diplomatic documentary collections. My colleagues in the Department of History, especially Prof. Cornelius A. Moylan and Prof. Nicholas J. Costa, have frequently helped in conversation, often without realizing that they were doing so. Dr. Frank Patella and Prof. Samuel Goldberger did me an inestimable service by correcting and helping me with my Italian, German and Hungarian translations.

Mr. Jean F. Hart, director of Library Services at our college, and his executive secretary, Mrs. Catherine Hermanowski, merit my warm gratitude for securing for me the needed documentary material from the *Geheim Staatsarchiv* in Munich, *Staatsarchiv* in Darmstadt, *Hauptstaatsarchiv* in Stuttgart, *Deutsches Hauptarchiv des Auswärtigen Amts* in Bonn, *Ministero degli Affari Esteri, Archivo Storico* in Rome, *U.S. State Department, National Archives* in Washington, D.C., and *Magyar Országos Levéltár* and *Országos Széchenyi Könyvtár kézirattár* in Budapest. Prof. Ingrun Lafleur did valuable service for me by arranging the typing or microfilming of the material that I requested from the *Haus-, Hof-, und Staatsarchiv* in Vienna. Equally appreciative am I to the directors and staff of the above archives for their prompt and courteous responses.

Appreciation is due to Mr. Peter Beales for editorial help and to my typist Mrs. Shirley Lerman for her expeditious and precise work. My warmest thanks go to my wife, Dr. Mária Decsy, who helped me greatly by reading, checking and commenting on what I had written, but even more for her unflagging encouragement and support. My three little children, real sources of my ambition, left periodically their marks of approval on my manuscript, which recognition is lovingly acknowledged.

Bolton, Conn.   János Decsy
January 17, 1978

Contents

Introduction

More than a half-century has passed since the collapse of the Habsburg monarchy. Yet the foreign policy of Austria-Hungary is not a closed chapter. Time has not reduced the number of historical problems associated with its diplomacy and its principal statesmen. One of the most intriguing problems still not thoroughly explored and objectively analyzed is the part played by Count Gyula Andrássy (the Elder) as prime minister of dualist Hungary in the foreign-policy decisions of the Danubian empire before and during the Franco-German War of 1870–71.[1] No detailed, balanced study has been written on this complex question. There are, of course, many biographies and histories, essays and monographs about Andrássy and other contemporary statesmen with whom his career was closely identified, such as Friedrich von Beust and Otto von Bismarck. Some Andrássy biographies are popular, others scholarly, some are adulatory, others hostile, but most are propagandistic and less than trustworthy. This is not to disregard the researches of Manó Kónyi, Ede Wertheimer, István Diószegi, Imre Gonda, Richard Charmatz, Hermann Oncken, Heinrich Ritter von Srbik and Heinrich Potthoff, but they all had a political axe to grind: they were all anxious to prove that Andrássy succeeded or failed, that he was "innocent" or "guilty." The reason lies in the political vicissitudes of Hungary and the monarchy after Andrássy's death in 1890. The whole story of Andrássy's foreign policy, however, has never been told and certain aspects have still to be discovered among his obviously rich achievements.

What concepts and aims motivated Andrássy's foreign policy as prime minister of Hungary? What influence did he exert on the Dual Monarchy's foreign policy? Did he make Hungary's wishes respected in external affairs? Did he place the narrow interests of Hungary before those of the empire as a whole? What role did he play in the diplomatic crisis that accompanied the Franco-German War?

This study will attempt to answer these questions and expose the elements that determined his actions, the means and ways by which he strove for their achievement, and the ultimate consequences of both for the development of Austro-Hungarian foreign policy. The purpose is to explore how Andrássy viewed and dealt with the issues he faced. During his lifetime Andrássy was uncritically acclaimed by contemporary Hungarian, Austrian and German historians. Subsequent historians of the Dual Monarchy continued to write in the afterglow cast by his imposing figure. The most significant and influential was Ede Wertheimer, a Hungarian historian of German descent, and author of a lengthy and authoritative biography of Andrássy.[2] This work contains a maze of detail, juxtaposing supposition and fact, the germane and the irrelevant, the marginal and the essential. A Hungarian historian recently remarked that Wertheimer's work was written from the point of view of maintaining the Great Power position of the Dual Monarchy. This consideration eclipsed all others. Yet Wertheimer's access to Andrássy's private and public papers could have resulted in a work much broader in scope.[3] Since the family library housing these papers was destroyed during the Second World War,[4] the material Wertheimer brought to light is indispensable, but judicious analysis is required to sift out the primary sources from the author's biased interpretive framework.

Wertheimer used this rich collection of documents to lay the scholarly foundation of a historical legend of Andrássy. In his view Andrássy was a giant in the art of politics, both domestic and external, who could do nothing wrong or even be mistaken. Andrássy emerged as a fervent Magyar nationalist, a successful promoter of exclusive Magyar interests in the conduct of the monarchy's foreign policy, an unquestioning partisan of Bismarckian Germany, and an unrelenting foe of Russia and Pan-Slavism.

Wertheimer credits Andrássy with having almost single-handedly prevented the monarchy's intervention on the side of France in the crisis surrounding the Franco-German War. He frustrated the revanchist policy of Beust and the emperor as well as that of the military circles headed by Archduke Albrecht.[5] Although the opening of Austrian archives to researchers after the First World War allowed Wertheimer to round out his earlier work, his two studies on Austro-French cooperation reflect essentially the same conclusions.[6]

Wertheimer's views followed the example set by Manó Kónyi who, in his work on Beust and Andrássy,[7] had already furnished the blueprint for such an interpretation. Other works by Imre Halász and Adolf Kohut, the latter a German historian of Hungarian descent, reiterated the same theme.[8] These writers reveal their ardent admiration for Andrássy and Bismarck and their dislike for Beust. Their idolization precluded the possibility of any critical judgment of their heroes' actions. By the beginning of the twentieth century the Hungarian historians' views completely dominated writing about Andrássy. Considerations of realpolitik prompted these historians to create and propagate the "Andrássy legend." Instead of explaining fully the complex issues Andrássy faced, they felt it necessary to expurgate systematically from the record of the cocreator of the Dual Alliance of 1879, and the friend of Bismarck, every trace of his earlier hesitations and intermittent distrust of the great chancellor. This myth of "Andrássy orthodoxy" was faithfully reflected in the dominant schools of Austrian and German historiography. Endorsement of the Dual Alliance brought together the members of the Austrian liberal school and the Hungarian interpreters of dualism. Surveying the events of the early summer of 1870, both Heinrich Friedjung and Charmatz[9] agreed either with the younger Andrássy's[10] or with Wertheimer's presentations.

Contemporary German historians propagated views similar to those of Kónyi and Wertheimer. Heinrich von Sybel, the head of the *kleindeutsch* national-liberal school, claimed in his monumental work on the foundation of the German Empire[11] that Beust's aim throughout the long negotiations for an alliance with France was to maintain a balance between France and Prussia. Sybel felt that Napoleon III started the negotiations only with the aim of making Prussia uneasy, not of actually going to war. According to him, the French passion for war in 1870 was the work not of the emperor but of Bonapartist fanatics. In reviewing the record of the Austro-Hungarian Council of Ministers for Common Affairs, Sybel implies Beust's willingness to intervene at a later date and portrays Andrássy as solely responsible for the declaration of neutrality.[12] Hans Delbrück, on the other hand, most emphatically rejected Sybel's thesis and claimed that Napoleon was seriously preparing for war. Delbrüch saw Beust and Francis Joseph as eager for war and felt that only the success of the Prussian armies deterred them from intervention on the French side.[13] Erich Brandenburg shared Sybel's view of Andrássy and Delbrück's of Beust and Francis Joseph.[14]

While the situation after the collapse of the Dual Monarchy in 1918 should have discouraged the mere eulogies typical of the recent past, Hungarian historians continued to cite Andrássy to refute accusations of chauvinism or sterile realpolitik. Certainly Andrássy never overrated what he achieved and never believed that anything definite could be settled by power alone. There is ample documentary evidence that even in his most heated moments reason and not impulse guided him. During his long years of service he had consciously sought to check irrational forces, but it cannot be overlooked that Andrássy, by concentrating his great abilities on problems of foreign policy, failed to attend to the sources of some fatal domestic trends, which had been evident in the development of the monarchy at least since 1848 and were to bring about its eventual collapse.

Despite the opening of the Austrian foreign archives after the war, Wertheimer's views remained, if no longer predominant, the most influential in works on the Dual Monarchy. Postwar Hungarian historians, whether liberal or conservative, oriented toward *Geistesgeschichte*[15] or positivist, were influenced by the "war guilt" of the 1920s and adopted an even more extreme position than their prewar predecessors. Disregarding any other consideration, they credited Andrássy alone with keeping the monarchy out of the Franco-German War. According to Gyula Szekfű, "He [Andrássy] also served the common German-Hungarian interest when by his personal intervention [he] prevented the Austrian statesmen in 1870 from falling on Prussia from the rear in revenge for Königgrätz."[16] This is also the position of Jenő Horváth, Gusztáv Gratz and Dominic Kosáry.[17] It is not surprising that publicists followed the example of such serious scholars.[18] Hungarian historians of the interwar years never engaged in a critical reappraisal of the past, a reappraisal that ought to have led to needed Hungarian self-criticism.

The Austrian nationalist and liberal historians after 1918 seemed to be equally determined to uphold the traditional view.[19] It is true that Victor Bibl, a nationalist historian, while holding to the old interpretation, could not suppress his doubts. He said: "Even the Hungarian prime minister, Count Andrássy, who fought with the utmost determination at the decisive Crown Council of July 18 against the lust for revenge, gave cause for reflection."[20] But Bibl failed to enlarge on this remark.

During the 1920s, Herman Oncken, a noted German historian, collected and published three volumes of documents from German and Austrian archives. His purpose was to prove that the war of 1870 resulted from centuries-old French ambition to annex the German Rhineland. He was clearly influenced in his judgment of French policy by his concern over the "war guilt" question and the Rhineland clauses. Although Beust's activities emerge distinctly from the documents, Oncken, in his short but militant introduction, draws his sword in favor of Andrássy: "The considerations of domestic and foreign policy, which in the Austrian Council of War of July 18 were opposed to Austria's declaration of war, are well known. They were primarily Andrássy's opposition and the menacing attitude of Russia."[21]

One of Oncken's disciples, Ernst Erichsen, who produced the first major study of Beust's German policy, shares Oncken's views on Beust's revanchism and Andrássy's firm opposition to it.[22] Alfred Stern, another German historian, is equally hostile to the Austrian chancellor.[23] It is evident that these pioneers of the neonationalist German historical trend could not implicate Bismarck's ally, Andrássy, in any wrongdoing. Equally, they could not view Beust, the Iron Chancellor's most capable German opponent, favorably. They believed that Beust committed a "cardinal sin" against Bismarck. The fact was that Beust had policies and interests of his own and these conflicted with the designs of Prussian-dominated Germany.

It cannot be overlooked, however, that some German historians questioned Andrássy's Germanophilism. In one of his articles, Walter Platzhoff, the noted postwar German historian, remarked: "He [Andrássy], whose concern 'day and night'[24] was Russia, wanted to prevent a German-Russian alliance at any price. His policy was and remained Hungarian-oriented and it is a very mistaken notion to represent him as an absolutely reliable friend of Germany."[25] A similar opinion was expressed by Erich Eyck, the liberal biographer of Bismarck. Viewing the Dual Monarchy's attitude at the beginning of the Franco-German war, Eyck emphasized that "Andrássy, who later was to become the staunchest supporter of Bismarck's international policy, was then by no means a friend of Prussia; he even called Prussia's eventual victory undesirable."[26] Both Platzhoff and Eyck arrived at their conclusions by reading Andrássy's anti-Prussian statements in the Council of Ministers for Common Affairs on July 18, 1870. Yet neither of them felt it necessary to probe the problem in depth. They failed to inquire whether Andrássy had a legitimate reason for his anti-Prussian sentiments.

In the past two decades a drastic reappraisal of Andrássy's policy has been undertaken by representatives of two widely divergent historical trends, conservative and Marxist, both bent on destroying the "Andrássy myth."

The opening salvo had been fired by Heinrich Ritter von Srbik, a leading interwar Austrian conservative historian. Trying to demonstrate that nineteenth-century *grossdeutsch* dreams were being realized by the Third Reich, Srbik could view Andrássy's activities only through his own prejudices.[27] Familiar with Andrássy's policies, Srbik concentrated his attack on Andrássy's motives during the July crisis of 1870. In explaining his reinterpretation, Srbik said: "We must finally put an end to idealization of the Hungarian premier. His prime guiding principle was his special interest in Hungary's newly attained statehood, not the *Gesamtmonarchie*. The German tradition did not matter to him and the reinstatement of the Habsburgs' German primacy he repudiated."[28]

This last sentence suggests that Andrássy was to be condemned because he did not share Srbik's dreams of a Germanic *Mitteleuropa*. Srbik studied and analyzed the minutes of the council of ministers of July 18, and correctly reproduced the viewpoints of Beust and the members of the Court party, but, as might be expected, he denounced Andrássy's concept as narrow and exclusively Hungarian-oriented. Srbik declared himself in favor of Beust's policy, although he condemned the Austrian statesman for the *Ausgleich*. Surprisingly, the controversial British historian A.J.P. Taylor agrees with this conservative view.[29]

Srbik's ideas did not go unchallenged. A Hungarian Marxist historian, István Diószegi, in a painstaking work on the Dual Monarchy's reaction to the Franco-German War,[30] rejected the Austrian historian's "surprising thesis." Unlike Srbik, Diószegi believed that Andrássy had independent and purposeful foreign-policy ideas. He contended that Beust's and Andrássy's policies were similar at the end of July and the beginning of August 1870. Nevertheless, he agreed with Srbik that Andrássy desired a French victory (a view neither historian can substantiate), and wanted to march against Russia with a victorious France. Diószegi considered Austro-Hungarian foreign-policy tendencies from a party-political standpoint. He stressed the general Francophile sentiments of the Deák party but failed to discern that Andrássy's was not a party but a personal policy. His policy undoubtedly enjoyed the support of Francis Deák and Joseph Eötvös as well as of Kálmán Tisza's Left-Center party. The Deák party was not homogeneous. It was mainly its conservative wing, with which Menyhért Lónyay can probably be counted, that favored a French orientation in foreign policy. Although Diószegi consistently criticized Andrássy's actions, he conceded that his ideas were sound and acknowledged his remarkable abilities, denied by Srbik. The figure of Beust gains much in Diószegi's close scrutiny. He saw Beust not only as a shrewd tactician but also as a man of vision, aware of the Russian danger to the monarchy and of the inevitability of a Franco-German war.

In spite of their obvious biases, both Srbik's and Diószegi's works are useful guides for the researcher. In the present analysis of Andrássy's foreign policy prior to and during the Franco-German War, some of the same ground has necessarily to be surveyed, but from a different standpoint. The emphasis of this study is exclusively on Andrássy's position.

From a welter of evidence a number of facts emerge quite clearly. One is that Andrássy secured a decisive voice for Hungary in the monarchy's foreign-policy formulation. This was due to Andrássy's resolute advocacy of a policy that enjoyed mass support in Hungary; and, more important, it corresponded to the ambitions of the Austro-German liberals. Furthermore, he had the prestige and ability to convince the emperor of the soundness of the policy he suggested. At the same time, Andrássy was always guided equally by Hungarian and imperial considerations, and this was well known to the emperor.

The bases of Andrássy's foreign policy appear to have been straight-forward. One fundamental principle was that Austria should remain excluded from Germany in accordance with the logic of the Compromise of 1867.[31] Andrássy apparently feared that a revival of Austrian domination in Germany would enable Vienna to undo dualism. Prussian preeminence in Germany seemed the best insurance against such a development. The Hungarian statesman evidently felt the chief dangers were aggressive Russian expansionism and the encroachments of the national movements of the Slavic peoples in the Dual Monarchy and the Balkans. From this came the second principle of Andrássy's foreign policy. Austria's energies should be turned to the east to defend the territorial integrity of the Dual Monarchy against Russia and to prevent a coalition of the latter with the South Slav national movements in the Balkan area. Owing to its geographical distance and over-whelming interest in an Austro-French offensive alliance against Prussia, France as an ally appeared to present only danger to Hungary's own national interests. Friendship and alliance with Bismarck-ian Germany seemed the best guarantee against Russian aggression. This conveniently paralleled Bismarck's ideas and was why he endeavored to strengthen Hungary's influence in the foreign policy of the Dual Monarchy. For similar reasons, the preservation of the Ottoman Empire suited Andrássy's policy.

These appear to have been the considerations behind Andrássy's position on all important questions faced by the Dual Monarchy during the Franco-Prussian War of 1870–1871.

Andrássy's idea of an eastern-oriented policy coincided with that of the Austro-German liberal bourgeoisie. Beust and the conservatives also wanted an active eastern policy, but not at that time.[32] For them first priority went to the German policy; once it had succeeded, then they would look to Austrian expansion into the Balkans. This difference in priorities was one of the principal elements of conflict between Andrássy and Beust. The outcome of the wars of 1859 and 1866 had already made it clear that, if the Habsburgs were to survive as a Great Power in the context of the nineteenth century, a "drive toward the east" was the only policy open to them. In view of all this, Austrian historians' accusations that the Hungarians were solely responsible for the monarchy's turning to the east cannot be accepted.

I

Dualism: Changed Conditions in the Formulation of Foreign Policy

Prussia's victory over Austria in 1866 deprived the Habsburg Empire of its centuries-old primacy in Germany and most of its remaining possessions in Italy.[1] The political order created by the Congress of Vienna had been badly shaken by the revolutionary storms of 1848, irreversibly damaged by the Crimean War, and largely demolished by the Schleswig-Holstein crisis of 1863; Königgrätz and the resultant Treaty of Prague completed its destruction. The end of the congress system signaled the triumph of several national movements in Europe. On the eve of the Austro-Prussian contest, the Rumanians, with the quiet approval of Napoleon III and Bismarck, elected Charles Hohenzollern-Sigmaringen as ruling prince of the United Principalities.[2] With the establishment of the North German Confederation, Prussia took a giant step toward the realization of the *kleindeutsch* concept of German unity under Hohenzollern leadership. Venetia was incorporated into the kingdom of Italy after a plebiscite, leaving only the Roman question unresolved. In the Habsburg Empire, Magenta and Solferino made advisable, and Königgrätz made mandatory, the appeasement of Hungarian aspirations.

The disastrous defeat of the Austro-Prussian war[3] dramatized the bankruptcy of Habsburg neoabsolutism. Prince Felix Schwarzenberg's and Anton Ritter von Schmerling's idea of a centralized and germanizing Greater Austria was beyond recall. Heinrich von Gagern, the ambassador of Hesse-Darmstadt in Vienna, declared: "Vienna is no longer an important center of German politics."[4] This view was even more clearly expressed by a German-Austrian: "Austria has ceased to exist as a German and hence as a European power."[5] In the highest political circles in Vienna, grief at Austria's loss of German primacy was felt widely. Austria had been kicked out of the door,[6] the Austrian writer and politician Count Anton Alexander Auersperg complained bitterly.[7] Ludwig von Biegeleben, head of the German affairs department in the foreign ministry and one of Prussia's most determined foes, broke into tears as he reported the terms of the Treaty of Prague.[8] He was convinced that "the treaty that forced Austria's withdrawal from Germany would be the first Austria would not keep because it could not."[9] The atmosphere in the diets of the late fall was one of resignation and loss of self-confidence. It seemed that "Austria was not far from a state of despair."[10] According to Friedrich von Varnbüler, the Württemberg foreign minister, "The people crawl like wretches, a sickening sight to those of strong character."[11]

The empire's future looked hopeless. Many asserted that *Autriche n'a pas raison d'être* and that the collapse of the monarchy was inevitable. A few days after conclusion of the preliminary peace of Nikolsburg, Karl Giskra, mayor of Brünn (Brno), reacted to the news of Austria's exclusion from Germany by telling the Prussian crown prince: "Austria cannot make that concession without signing its own death warrant. Austria exists only through Germany."[12] To justify the French refusal to support Austria against Prussia, Empress Eugénie expressed similar feelings about the monarchy's future. "Unfortunately the news reaching here," she said, "provides powerful encouragement for those anxious to justify their policy of nonintervention. 'What a mistake we would be making,' they say, 'if we were to involve ourselves in a quarrel on the side of an empire on the verge of collapse'."[13] About the same time, the French military attaché rhetorically asked in a report to Paris: "Is Austria in decay?"[14] The affirmative seemed the only reasonable answer. During the hostilities Prussian intelligence had found it easy to secure information of great value from the treason of Austrian citizens. The number of Austrian troops captured was exceedingly high; among the officers who surrendered five hundred were unwounded. In spite of the defeat there was an air of general gaiety in the capital; on the evening the news of Königgrätz was received thousands of Viennese flocked to a summer carnival as if nothing had happened.[15] Thus only official Austria had seemed distressed.

Among the subject nationalities, the Czechs considered the empire's exclusion from Germany as the "happiest outcome of our unlucky days."[16] In Hungary, most of the moderate liberal leaders agreed with Andrássy that Austria's loss of position in Germany and Italy freed it of a twofold burden that demanded sacrifices without yielding any advantages.[17] The sentiments of ordinary Hungarians were similar, and there was some restlessness. Italian prisoners of war were enthusiastically welcomed by thousands in the central Hungarian city of

Kecskemét. In Pest students demonstrated their feelings by wearing red-feathered hats. In many parts of the country young people determined to take to the forests rather than fight.[18] Realizing the seriousness of the situation, on the eve of the war the Viennese government had issued a series of ordinances to deal with any eventualities.[19] It feared the effect of revolutionary agitation by underground representatives of the Hungarian emigration and by agents of Bismarck, who had approved and supported the organization of a Hungarian Legion in Prussia.[20] Under the command of General György Klapka, one of the military leaders of the revolution and war of independence of 1848/49, the legion had been prepared to invade Hungary.[21]

But in early 1867, the prophecies of the immediate disintegration of the Habsburg Empire were confounded by the conclusion of an *Ausgleich*,[22] a compromise, with the Hungarians, which restructured the empire on the basis of constitutional dualism.[23] R. A. Kann, the noted American-Austrian historian, deduced from this development that "the Compromise served its purpose of prolonging the existence and in fact the Great Power position of the Empire."[24]

On May 29, 1867, the Hungarian Parliament accepted the results of the compromise negotiations as Law XII of 1867,[25] adopting it by the comfortable majority of 209 votes to 89 with 83 abstentions. On June 8 Francis Joseph was crowned king of Hungary with all the traditional pomp, and on July 28 he gave royal assent to Law XII.

By virtue of the Compromise, Austria[26] and Hungary enjoyed full equality of rights in their mutual relations. In domestic matters, both halves of the Dual Monarchy became sovereign with responsible ministries and separate legislative assemblies and enforcement agencies. Beyond the person of their common sovereign, they were connected only in the area of so-called common affairs. These were derived in part from the Pragmatic Sanction of 1722/23 and Law XVII of 1790, and consisted primarily of foreign affairs, defense and common finances,[27] the last of which were to meet the expenses of the former two.[28]

It was during the final stage of the protracted negotiations over the Compromise that the paths of Beust, the new foreign minister, and of Andrássy, the future prime minister of Hungary, first crossed. Both Beust and Andrássy played particularly important roles in the negotiations. They were the driving force that overcame the wariness of Francis Deák[29] and the hesitations of Francis Joseph. Erich Zöllner observed that during the negotiations Beust and Andrássy "understood each other's aims well."[30] At this stage they could work well together because both thought in terms of foreign policy; their common goal was to restore the empire to its position as a Great Power. Beyond this the seeds of conflict between the two statesmen were present from the beginning.

The inauguration of dualism, which significantly modified the internal composition of the Habsburg Empire, required corresponding changes in the structure of foreign policy. The common ministers, including the foreign minister, were made responsible to the monarch but were also obliged to take into account the views of the two parliaments and the two cabinets. The device for coordinating the two parliaments was the delegations. They were a proposal of Andrássy, who regarded them as an "international committee" symbolizing the absolute equality of Austria and Hungary.[31] Both delegations consisted of sixty members from each parliament: twenty from each upper house and forty from each lower house. To prevent their development into a central parliament, on the insistence of Deák and Andrássy, the two bodies were selected annually and met separately in Vienna and Budapest in alternate years, exchanging views by notes.[32] If three exchanges of notes failed to bring about agreement, the delegations met jointly and without debate decided the matter at issue by majority vote; in the event of deadlock, the monarch decided. Through their debates, votes on the common budget, and rights to question and impeach a common minister[33] the delegations could, in theory at least, exert control over the Dual Monarchy's foreign policy.[34] But since they were deliberative, met infrequently for short periods only and debated separately, their influence on the formulation of foreign policy was in fact weak. Besides, their advice was rarely sought.[35]

In external affairs the political parties of the two halves of the monarchy could similarly make themselves heard and felt through the parliaments. The most important political parties in the Dual Monarchy were the Hungarian Deák party,[36] Kálmán Tisza's Left-Center party,[37] and the Austrian *Verfassungspartei* (Constitution party).[38] Outside the parliaments but with great influence on foreign affairs through the emperor was the "Court party."[39] In analyzing the inner motives and aims of the monarchy's foreign policy, the goals of these parties have to be considered.[40] With the advent of a parliamentary system, the press, or more precisely the "great press" of Vienna and the leading journals of Budapest, also gained some influence over Austro-Hungarian diplomacy.[41]

Under dualism the Council of Ministers for Common Affairs acquired considerable power in deciding the basic questions of foreign policy. No such body had been mentioned in Law XII, 1867, only common ministers and ministries, but since no common Austro-Hungarian[42] government existed, establishment of the Council of Ministers for Common Affairs as a supreme governmental organ became a necessity. Its functions had never been regulated and it generally followed the procedures of the former Imperial Crown Councils. The term Council of Ministers for Common Affairs (*Ministerrath für gemeinsame Angelegenheiten*) was used first on February 9, 1868.[43] The council was composed of the common ministers, the two prime ministers and, depending on the matter in hand, other ministers and military leaders. The monarch often presided over its sessions.

It would require a substantial study to provide an objective view of Hungary's weight in each area of common affairs.[44] The present study will concentrate on the Hungarians' opportunities to influence foreign-policy decisions only.

Article 8 of the Compromise law[45] stipulated that the foreign affairs "of all countries under His Majesty's rule" required common management. A common foreign minister, who inherited the office of the imperial chancellor, was therefore appointed. Diplomatic missions and trade delegations as well as matters of international agreements were entrusted to his care. The foreign minister, like the other common ministers, was appointed by the monarch and was responsible to him and the delegations. The procedural rules of the delegations, however, made their effective control over the foreign minister's actions almost impossible.[46] Had the two parliaments of the monarchy exercised influence over the conduct of foreign policy only through the delegations, foreign affairs would have amounted to an exclusive prerogative of the sovereign.[47]

In a formal sense it is true that Francis Joseph, through the peculiar constitutional arrangement of the Dual Monarchy, preserved many of his absolutist prerogatives in the actual conduct of foreign policy. But Article 8 contained a further limitation: the foreign minister had to carry out his duties "in accordance with the ministries of both halves [of the monarchy] and with their consent."[48] This imposed on him the obligation to consult and reach prior agreement with both prime ministers about the course to be followed in foreign policy. Because of the fictitious nature of the delegations' supervisory rights, this stipulation later acquired great importance. As Péter Hanák rightly remarked: "Even though this regulation did not bind the foreign minister's hands in supervising the details of his office or in taking certain actions, it did give the Hungarian government the right to voice its wishes in essential matters."[49] Thus it was possible for the Hungarian government and hence parliament to participate in the formulation of the Dual Monarchy's foreign policy.

The prime ministers of the Hungarian governments in power always exercised this important right, though to varying degrees. The most important foreign-policy questions were discussed in the Council of Ministers for Common Affairs. The minutes of them show that the Hungarian prime ministers in most instances participated actively in their debates. Without their cooperation not a single important move could be made. As István Burián, a former common foreign minister, wrote:

> The Prime Ministers . . . had a very considerable voice in foreign policy, for they assisted not only in determining its general lines but were also the leaders of the two parliaments or delegations and . . . provided the Minister of Foreign Affairs . . . with the necessary majority. If he could not arrive at agreement with either one of the Prime Ministers, the position of the joint minister became untenable. A good understanding with the two Prime Ministers was, therefore, of primary importance in the conduct of foreign affairs.[50]

In May 1869, Andrássy told Wäcker-Gotter, the Prussian consul in Pest, that, "without his knowledge and consent, no action would be possible" in foreign affairs.[51] During a session of the Hungarian delegation, he declared: "The Hungarian prime minister is directly responsible for what is happening in the field of foreign policy."[52] Andrássy, referring to Article 8, even claimed that "he was quite justified, as Hungarian prime minister, in maintaining direct communications with the representatives of foreign powers, and he was certain that no one in Vienna could or would object to this."[53]

The common foreign minister was responsible only to the monarch and the delegations. The Hungarian prime minister, on the other hand, was required to carry out his duties in accordance with Article 8, that is, he was to make sure the foreign minister acted in consultation with him and with his consent.[54] To be assured of this, the parliament could summon the prime minister to answer for his conduct. Thus the Hungarian parliament could, and in fact did, also deal indirectly with foreign-policy matters. It was possible for the members of parliament to raise any question about foreign relations with the prime minister. In addition, the parliament had further opportunities to debate foreign policy when it discussed the response to be made to speeches from the throne, considered the budget, and weighed ratification of compacts concluded with foreign powers. Although these debates were legally binding only on the Hungarian government, they could not be ignored by the common leadership.[55] The Hungarian parliament was in a particularly strong position, for it could reject bills and vote down a government. The king could suspend sessions or prorogue the parliament at will, but he could not leave it in abeyance indefinitely. He was required to summon it again within three months, and even sooner if the annual budget for the next fiscal year had not been passed. The Hungarian constitution, unlike Austrian Law 146 of 1867,[56] contained no emergency provision empowering him to rule by decree.[57] Thus the idiosyncrasies of dualism prevented Austria from imposing its foreign-policy aims on Hungary. Conversely, there was even less opportunity for Hungary to impose its policy on Austria. The peculiar structure of the dual system called for common agreement and consideration of the interests of the ruling strata of both Austria and Hungary in foreign affairs. Only a policy that rested on common interest could function without seriously upsetting the whole system.

Andrássy, from the very beginning of his prime ministry, devoted himself to placing and maintaining Hungary in a position of weighty influence in the external affairs of the monarchy. By taking full advantage of the constitutional opportunities, he succeeded in realizing Hungary's right to parity as set out in the Compromise law of 1867. His efforts were well planned, single-minded and aggressive, qualities that ensured their success. To appreciate the magnitude of his achievement, one must understand the tremendous opposition Andrássy had to combat at every turn from the powerful anti-Hungarian conservative forces around the court.[58] A brief look at his background and character will help to reveal the secret of his success.

Andrássy was a descendant of one of the oldest Hungarian noble families belonging to the most exclusive branch of the aristocracy.[59] He was born in North Hungary, at Kassa (now Košice in Slovakia) on March 3, 1823. After formal education which included the study of law,[60] Andrássy visited several foreign countries, and on his return joined the struggle to secure Hungary's constitutional freedom.[61] He was elected one of the radical liberal deputies to the diet of 1847/48 and played an important role in its proceedings.[62] In the subsequent revolution and war of independence, Andrássy commanded a National Guard battalion[63] and was then sent in May 1849 as ambassador to the Ottoman Empire, in the hope of persuading the Sublime Porte to declare war on Austria and Russia.[64] The mission failed, but the young diplomat did achieve success insofar as the Porte declined to extradite the Hungarian political refugees of 1849 and permitted their departure to western Europe, mostly to France and England. Andrássy himself emigrated first to London and then to Paris; he was condemned to death in absentia and on September 21, 1851, was hanged in effigy by the Austrian government for his part in the revolution.

His experiences in 1848/49 and the movements among the Slovaks and Ruthenians in his native North Hungary made Andrássy keenly alive to the Russian-Slav danger. All this, coupled with the malevolence of the Russian-Pan-Slavists[65] and certain pronouncements by František Palacký,[66] one of the most important leaders of the Old Czech party, developed in him a conviction, which afterwards determined his whole domestic and foreign policy, that Hungary would not survive except as part of a Great Power. In other words, Hungary's security lay in a close connection with Austria. In his view, this was feasible only if Austria changed its centralized system of government for a federative one that would "restore to Hungary its independence and national rights." Andrássy put forward these ideas in a study published in *The Eclectic Review* (England) in 1850.[67] To be sure, this interesting piece of political journalism bitterly condemned Habsburg absolutism and its cooperation with and reliance on the reactionary forces of tsarist Russia. Both the conservative Wertheimer and the marxist Gonda have considered this essay evidence of Andrássy's devotion to the dynasty, renunciation of the revolution and insistence on reconciliation. Their interpretation does not hold water, however. At this time Andrássy had not yet turned his back on Lajos Kossuth's policy. In fact, he was a radical among the prominent exiles. For years he turned a deaf ear to his mother's pleas that he ask for clemency. Andrássy remained loyal to the policy based on Hungary's declaration of independence of 1849[68] even after Kossuth's visit to the United States in 1851–52.[69] His next nine years' experience in exile, however, had a sobering influence on him. Owing largely to the realities of international developments, instead of becoming more extreme Andrássy grew in moderation. The events in Hungary, Austria and the world, above all the Crimean War, made him realize the futility of the Hungarian émigrés' schemes to overthrow the Habsburgs with foreign help. Andrássy became ever more convinced of the need to subordinate Hungarian aspirations for full independence to the exigencies of the Habsburg monarchy as a Great Power. As a result he obtained an amnesty in 1857 and returned to Hungary the following year with his bride of two years, Countess Katinka Kendeffy.[70]

There he joined forces with Deák, becoming his chief lieutenant in demanding the restoration of 1848 legislation and acting as a mediator between Deák and the court.[71] Although far less versed in constitutional law than Deák, Andrássy had more appreciation of nonlegal, political matters. Louis Eisenmann correctly stressed that "the form and legal tenour of the Compromise were due to Deák, its political tone to Andrássy."[72] From the very beginning, Andrássy supported the principle of liberal government for both Austria and Hungary. "Hungary can be free, the whole empire can be strong, only if both according to their own forms are equally free and constitutional,"[73] he emphasized in a telling speech on September 27, 1865. On Deák's recommendation,[74] Francis Joseph on February 17, 1867, entrusted Andrássy to form a Hungarian government.[75]

In Hungary the inauguration of dualism introduced a period of significant and sustained political development.[76] In the face of stubborn opposition, Andrássy organized a national militia, the *Honvéd*,[77] and preserved the territorial integrity of the kingdom through the Croatian-Hungarian Compromise of 1868, also known by its Croatian name *Nagodba*.[78] Of no less importance was the reincorporation into Hungary in 1869 of the military border districts. Created in the sixteenth century by the Habsburgs along the southern rim of Hungary and in Croatia to resist the expanding Ottoman Empire, the military border had been governed by the ministry of war in Vienna, though it had local autonomy.[79] Hungary's political administration was modernized, and a number of truly liberal laws were enacted, of which the most important was the nationality law of 1868.[80] This law bore the stamp of Baron József Eötvös's liberalism and was a tribute to Deák's sense of justice and Andrássy's political intelligence.[81] Other progressive acts of the Andrássy ministry eased arbitrary censorship of the press and granted full civil equality to Hungary's Jews.[82] The future of the country looked bright and its problems soluble. The failures of this altogether optimistic period should not be overlooked, however, especially the neglect of social problems. Furthermore, the nationality law of 1868 became virtually a dead letter after Eötvös and Deák died and Andrássy moved to Vienna as foreign minister.

Andrássy was unquestionably one of the outstanding statesmen of the nineteenth century. From the opinions of his contemporaries, both friends and foes, Andrássy emerges as neither hero nor villain, but as an honorable man of strong character and great ability. He was high-spirited and warm-hearted with an unfailing courtesy and charm that combined the Hungarian magnate and the modern gentleman. In 1866 at their first official meeting, Andrássy appeared to Francis Joseph as "a good, honorable and highly gifted man."[83] The subsequent twenty-three years of association with Andrássy more than confirmed the monarch's first estimate: "He was just as much an extraordinarily gifted and good man as an agreeable companion."[84] Moritz von Kaiserfeld, the liberal Austrian politician, expressing similar sentiments in a letter to his wife, exclaimed: "I wish we had this kind of man."[85]

Although his liberal views and broad European outlook placed him head and shoulders above most of his fellow magnates absorbed in their exclusive world, Andrássy never completely freed himself from their milieu.[86] Andrássy cared perhaps less than most Hungarian politicians about public opinion and the press. This is not to imply that he ignored the need to cultivate public confidence; it was popularity that he refused to seek. "Public confidence," he said, "is not only the highest reward but at the same time also the strongest mandate, for real confidence is a treasure even the most egocentric would not put up for sale."[87] Lord Robert Lytton, a British diplomat in Vienna, wrote of Andrássy: "He has a sincere belief in the principles of parliamentary government."[88] But Andrássy shared the general view of statesmen of his time that political and especially foreign affairs were not a subject for general discussion. Understandably, such a statesman, although he commanded general respect, could not evoke warm emotion and popular adulation.

Andrássy was an ardent Hungarian nationalist but not a chauvinist. Alarmed by the growing militancy of Hungarian nationalism, Andrássy devoted one of his last speeches in the upper house to a denunciation of the perils of "national chauvinism."[89] He possessed precisely those qualities of moderation and reason that were lacking in many contemporary East Central European statesmen. He never preached doctrines of racial superiority or conquest of others' lands.

A broad knowledge of Europe and of the problems of European politics, great linguistic ability, breadth of view, swift resourcefulness, and excellent judgment of men[90] and situations were the distinguishing features of his statesmanship. To Lord Augustus Loftus, the British ambassador in St. Petersburg, Andrássy "was gifted with great perspicacity, large-minded and liberal views, and the decision of character so necessary to be a ruler of men. . . . He was ever governed by a feeling of justice and honour in the performance of duty."[91] Lord Lytton regarded Andrássy as "a man of unquestionable energy and courage who has . . . talents and natural political tacts which are remarkable. . . . He is fully capable of combining prudence with promptitude and forethought with firmness. If the internal conditions of the Empire were settled, I should feel no doubt of Andrássy's ability to deal most efficiently with any great crisis in its foreign relations."[92]

Although he had a good opinion of his own abilities, he was free of the kind of vanity that made the Russian Chancellor Aleksander Gorchakov ludicrous. Hans Lothar von Schweinitz, the ambassador of the North German Confederation in Vienna, reported of Andrássy that he was "gifted, brave and sly, more proud than vain"; he added, "Count Andrássy has the power to charm me."[93] Andrássy respected and readily recognized men of talent and knowledge. Himself not an academician, Andrássy refused to accept the presidency of the prestigious Academy of Sciences. When a fellow aristocrat reproached him for his friendship with the renowned Hungarian artist Mihály Munkácsy, a man of simple origin, Andrássy quipped: "Tell me, please, are you familiar with Raphael?" "Naturally," came the answer. "Well, and who was foreign minister in Raphael's time?"[94]

Andrássy had a passionate nature but that was exactly what gave stimulus to his constant activities. He could always keep his internal fires in check while dealing with state affairs or conducting foreign policy. He believed that "passion is only an obstacle in politics and reason dictates that it should be disregarded."[95] To a great extent Andrássy's passion took the form of wholehearted commitment to the office he held, the cause of his nation and the monarchy. His actions were animated by a deep sense of responsibility, which had its roots in his patriotism and highly sensitive conscience.[96]

Above all, Andrássy was distinguished as a statesman by his realism. Contemptuous of abstract speculation, theories and ideologies, he always aimed at the practical in dealing with problems of politics. When asked to autograph a lady's album with "what he sought in art," he wrote: "What I despise most in politics — the ideal."[97] Andrássy knew what he wanted and understood the "art of the possible." Throughout his career, he was conscious of the limitations imposed on practitioners of politics. His sense of proportion enabled him to understand that a statesman can only rarely do what he wants to do. Therefore, in charting his courses of action, he refused to rely on theories, for he knew that circumstances made their practical application impossible. "Books prevent scholars from perceiving ultimate goals,"[98] he used to say. The best program in any contingency, as he himself put it most succinctly, was: "Avoid stupidities."[99] His considerable intuition and experienced enabled him to discern the factors that would limit his freedom of choice and action.[100]

In addition, Andrássy had a most persuasive tongue and a good sense of timing, knowing when to restrain himself and when to push forward. He knew how to win over the men he needed to attain his aims: Deák, Eötvös, Francis Joseph, the parliamentary leaders and the delegations. Eötvös, who highly admired these qualities in Andrássy, remarked: "This Andrássy has a magic power over me, he succeeds in everything."[101] Deák, who was so grudging of praise, once wrote to Andrássy: "God has given you to us in benevolence; the only trouble is that He did not make a duplicate, for we need two of you, one in Vienna and the other here [in Budapest]."[102]

But M. G. de Blowitz, the Paris correspondent of *The Times* (London), provided the most illuminating sketch of Andrássy:

> His physiognomy is a faithful reflection of the peculiar cast of Andrássy's mind. The sharp lines of his head, his bright and restless eye, his vigorous chin, his nervous gait and vivacity of his expression, all indicate an irresistible will at the service of a fertile and indefatigable imagination. He is at the same time a man of great suppleness and patience, something like one of these Zingary hunters who, not daring to fire a gun for fear of the echo, watch for whole days to throw the lasso round the neck of the wild horse they have determined to capture.[103]

Andrássy could also be very cautious and patient, on occasions too much so, for fear of excess. As Lord Lytton observed, Andrássy as a practical politician "has perhaps the defect of too great anxiety to convince and sometimes argues, when it would suffice to affirm."[104] In a fluid situation, he felt it unwise to commit himself to a definite course too early,[105] and he held to this all the more because he knew that this was a weakness to which his countrymen were susceptible. "We Hungarians get excited easily,"[106] he observed. Therefore, "it must be our leaders' concern to point out the whirlpool toward which we are running." Then, with his usual optimism, he added: "Once we perceive it, we do not have to be restrained by force, we turn back by ourselves."[107] To the end of his career, Andrássy set his face steadfastly against delusions. It is a tragedy that he was succeeded by epigones who lacked his insight.

Other marks of the statesmanship to which he largely owed his success were, first, his ability to keep control of a fluid situation, and second, his honesty, which was a passion with Andrássy in politics. He denounced the fraud and intrigue so characteristic of his colleague and rival, Beust. In contrast to Talleyrand who said that "words — especially those of statesmen — are to conceal thoughts," he displayed blunt candor in meeting people and in the councils of the monarchy and of Europe. For all these reasons, foreign diplomats found dealing with him pleasant, even stimulating, and often reached the point of letting him into their full confidence.[108]

Prince Bernhard von Bülow, the former German chancellor, noted that Andrássy "possessed the 'chevalier perspective' that Bismarck demanded of the leader of a great state."[109] Bismarck came to appreciate him as "the straightforward man, the downright states-man." "I am satisfied with him, he is all I would wish,"[110] he said to the British ambassador. The confidence Andrássy displayed in him when they met in Salzburg on September 18, 1877, prompted the apparently flattered German chancellor to coin his famous phrase: "They treat me like a fox, a cunning fellow (*Schlaukopf*) of the first rank. But the truth is that with a gentleman I am always a gentleman and a half, and when I have to deal with a pirate, I try to be a pirate and a half."[111] At their first meeting in Berlin in 1872, Gorchakov found Andrássy to be "an honest, straightforward, sensible and earnest patriot with whom he could establish a perfect understanding."[112] Emperor Alexander II also formed a very high opinion of Andrássy's probity. "Andrássy is too proud to deceive," he believed.[113]

There is much truth in the charge that, owing to his easygoing nature, Andrássy often preferred to defer decisions on troublesome questions, which then worsened for lack of immediate action. Meny-hért Lónyay, the Hungarian finance minister, noted in his diary:

> Generally one can say that our ministry is lacking in energy. Andrássy speaks always of firmness, of acting without delay and of sweeping measures, but when it is time to act, he stops and it gives him pleasure if he can defer something. . . . Gyula is a man of brilliance, sound judg-ment and diplomatic ability with moral courage, particularly toward higher authorities — but he is a miserable premier and vacillating worker.[114]

In view of Andrássy's achievements as prime minister, Lónyay in his exasperation may have exaggerated the situation. It is nonetheless correct that Andrássy shuddered at the daily routine of domestic administrative work. Szekfű pointed out correctly that "work, glori-fied with such hypocrisy as much in the practical philosophy of the bourgeois as in that of the socialist, was never his [Andrássy's] ambi-tion and he felt no shame when he had none to do."[115] But, as Szekfű rightly emphasized, Andrássy gave his country something else — "his energy, perhaps the most dynamic and successful generated last century in Hungary, besides Kossuth's."[116]

His major concern, as already noted, was foreign policy and his whole career was devoted to putting Hungary into a position where it could have decisive influence on the external affairs of the monarchy, and to restoring the latter to Great Power status in Europe.[117] Well informed on the internal and external peculiarities of the multinational Austro-Hungarian Empire, he professed the view that, since the geopolitical situation of the monarchy left it open to unremitting pressure from without, foreign policy had to have priority over domestic. This, he believed, required a vigilant and active policy. "There scarcely exists a state," Andrássy maintained, "that by virtue of its makeup and geographical location is interested in so many significant European questions as is the Austrian Empire." Therefore, "Austria cannot shirk the need to make its influence felt on certain issues."[118]

In any case, if Andrássy's hesitancy in certain matters led him into difficulties, he always managed to extricate himself with swift and impressive ingenuity. His fund of expedients was rarely found wanting.[119] It should also be noted that, while after thorough deliberation he dealt very efficiently and energetically with major problems, he neglected details, and little things perplexed him. "A court councillor can do these, too,"[120] he used to say. He himself admitted, "In politics, and it is perhaps a fault of mine, I have always considered the goal, and even this in a broad manner, rather than the details and forms."[121] All this may have occasionally reduced the efficiency of his work, but it cannot diminish his many outstanding qualities and the notable results of his labor.

II

Austria at the Crossroads

In the years immediately after 1867, the security of the new dualist system was threatened by conservative forces in Vienna that were not averse to a French attack on Prussia. To realize what he thought the monarchy's foreign policy should be and so safeguard the interests of Hungary and the empire, Andrássy had a constant struggle with these elements and especially with Foreign Minister Beust, who seemed to favor a decidedly anti-Prussian and pro-French policy. Revenge and hatred of Prussia were very marked in Viennese court circles after the Austro-Prussian War of 1866.[1] Emperor Francis Joseph and the military and court circles seemed determined to reverse the outcome of Königgrätz and restore Habsburg power in Germany.[2]

The result of the war had left the Austrian emperor disillusioned, bitter and on the verge of a nervous breakdown.[3] He felt himself to be a victim of deceit and was convinced the Prussians meant to destroy his realm entirely.[4] The incorporation of Saxony into the North German Confederation on October 21, 1866, only deepened his bitterness.[5] He could not forgive Bismarck's alliance with Italy[6] and was shocked by the creation and deployment of General György Klapka's legion. He did not hide his intense resentment when the Prussian ambassador had his first audience with him after the war was over.[7] His statement to the council of ministers on May 22, 1867, that "it is not the secret idea of revenge that inspires our steps"[8] gives the impression that he accepted the verdict of the war. So do his words: "It will be Austria's mission for a long time to come to disclaim any thoughts of war."[9] But his close associates knew his real feelings. "The Emperor desires war to make up for Königgrätz,"[10] Andrássy confided to Kállay. Beust himself admitted in the fall of 1870 that "the emperor, the army, Austria even, wished to have their revenge."[11]

Revanchism was rampant in the Court party. The irreconcilables gathered around Archduke Albrecht, the victor of Custozza, and Count Franz Folliot de Crenneville.[12] Franz von Kuhn, the minister of war, even made plans for a final, decisive battle in his memoranda and diary.[13] The most unyielding member of the group was Baron Ludwig

Maximilian von Biegeleben, head of the German bureau of the state chancellery. He declared openly that peace could not be kept between Austria and Prussia; "he wants to start turning the clock back immediately and would not even wait till domestic matters have somehow been settled," noted Gagern.[14] His advisers' anti-Prussian sentiments apparently surpassed the emperor's own.

Although Bismarck between 1866 and 1870 reckoned with Austria's desire for a war of revenge, he consistently sought its friendship after Königgrätz.[15] He commented in his memoirs: "We had to avoid wounding Austria too severely; we had to avoid leaving it any unnecessary bitterness of feeling or desire for revenge; rather had we to preserve the possibility of becoming friends again with our adversary of the moment, and in any case to regard the Austrian state as a piece on the European chessboard and the renewal of friendly relations with it as a move open to us."[16]

The Prussian statesman felt that, "if Austria were severely injured, it would become the ally of France and all our opponents for the sake of revenge on Prussia."[17] He laid great stress on the desirability of good relations with Austria. "We shall need Austria's strength in the future for ourselves,"[18] he remarked to a Prussian general shortly after Königgrätz.

Bismarck considered a strong Habsburg Empire a European necessity and recognized the value of Austrian cooperation in the event of a German war with France.[19] He believed that a German bloc, as it existed before 1866 under the German confederation, should in some way be restored, if only to serve as a counterweight to the growing power of Russia in the east. An alliance of the North German Confederation with the reorganized Habsburg Monarchy would not only reestablish the old cooperation for defense but would also strengthen German influence in Europe. Yet in spite of Bismarck's gestures of goodwill, Francis Joseph dismissed his ministers who advised reconciliation and friendship with Prussia, and appointed Beust,[20] an enemy of the chancellor, as foreign minister of Austria.

Beust was regarded as one of the most able of his country's statesmen.[21] He was named to his new post in mid-September but at his own wish the nomination was kept secret until October 30, after the peace between Saxony and Prussia had been finally concluded.[22] His highly controversial appointment seemed more indicative of Austrian defiance than resignation.[23] Whatever additional reasons the emperor might have had in appointing the Saxon, to the outside world it "announced a policy of revenge against Prussia."[24]

That the press in Germany was shocked and greeted Beust's entry into Austrian service with suspicion and distrust, and that the Prussian leaders considered it a gesture of defiance, are understandable.[25] But even the French accepted it with little enthusiasm.[26]

In Austria Beust's appointment to this sensitive position aroused general dissatisfaction and skepticism; in some quarters, it revived hope. Beust himself admitted that he met little sympathy even among those circles that were not positively inimical toward him, and recalled that one colleague had said he had an "unlucky hand."[27] The ministerial conference that considered Beust's appointment expressed apprehension and aversion to Francis Joseph's choice. Staatsminister Count Richard Belcredi believed that the nomination would encounter great opposition in Austria and Hungary. The other cabinet members spoke in the same vein.[28] Beust's new colleagues, both domestic and diplomatic, were skeptical and rather reserved toward him. It wounded their pride that a Protestant and a foreigner had been placed at the head of the Ballhausplatz.[29] They rightly feared that Beust's very nomination would be interpreted as a decision to follow a policy of revenge.[30] Many Austrian newspapers regarded it as a foolish provocation of Prussia and opposed appointment of the "unemployed minister from Saxony."[31]

It is clear from a report of the Bavarian ambassador that the Court party, however, welcomed the designation of Beust: "From him they hope for the rejuvenation that Austria so badly needs; from him they hope for a day of revenge."[32] The clerical branch of the party rejoiced and hoped that Beust would continue to fight against Prussia.[33] Among the members of Austria's diplomatic corps Prince Richard Metternich, ambassador to Paris, and his chargé d'affaires were "very happy" about the appointment.[34]

The Austrian liberal newspapers, above all the *Neue Freie Presse* (established in 1864) which consistently favored Beust, enthusiastically supported the new minister, hoping that he would successfully cope with the empire's much needed internal reorganization.[35] The Hungarian press, on the other hand, received news of Beust's appointment with marked skepticism. The *Pesti Napló* (Pest Journal), which was regarded as an organ of the Deák party, suggested that "his bed will certainly not be made of roses."[36] The paper then wondered "whom the new minister plans to depend on in the face of so many enemies?"[37]

Diószegi was right to point out that the *Pesti Napló* failed to see that the most important force in Austrian politics, the *Verfassungspartei*, supported Beust's nomination. Furthermore, Beust strengthened his power base by pursuing an anticlerical policy and, "with the conclusion of the *Ausgleich* of 1867, he even broadened it precisely with respect to the skeptical Hungarians."[38] But there was a price for both the Austrian and Hungarian liberals' support — peace at any cost.

Beust's past career and his personal feelings, of which he made no secret, gave ample reason to believe that he could shape the monarchy's foreign policy along anti-Prussian lines. That Beust had not changed his ideas is evident from his correspondence in late 1866 and early 1867. "Perhaps we can still pull together in the same cause,"[39] he wrote to his friend Baron Reinhard von Dalwigk zu Lichtenfels, the Hessian minister. A few months later he informed the Austrian ambassador to Berlin that he "would not shrink from any . . . possible consequence" of a French alliance, not "even French aggrandizement in Germany, provided that this were to ensue not as a principal and immediate war aim but as an ancillary result of a battle joined in other areas and for other interests."[40]

Beust sounds rather naïve in the first letter but in the second there is no pretense. Even after his downfall Beust maintained that international conditions had been favorable to his policy: "As long as France and Prussia were opposed to each other on equal terms, and from events the outcome of a possible war could not in the least be foreseen, it would have been downright irresponsible to ignore the advantages of our position and so spoil our chances for a more favorable future."[41]

On the basis of Austria's internal situation, however, the choice of policy was not so clear. The Court party would ally itself unconditionally with any anti-Prussian move, but the Hungarians and Austro-Germans looked for a different course of action.

On entering Austrian service, Beust's primary concern was to reform and strengthen the monarchy's internal structure. He regarded this as a prerequisite for a decisive and effective foreign policy that could restore Austria to its former status among the Great Powers of Europe.[42] Beust believed that only a regenerate Austria would inspire confidence abroad and win the necessary alliances against Prussia.[43] The most important problem was settlement with the Hungarians, which he helped to bring about. But by giving the Hungarians and Austro-Germans an equal voice in the affairs of the monarchy, he undermined his own foreign policy, for neither national group would support a war of revenge against Prussia.[44]

It is indeed a supreme irony of history that the dualistic system, which Beust helped to create with obvious anti-Prussian intentions, facilitated the success of Bismarck's ambitions and the permanence of Prussia's position in Germany, but devoured its own cocreator. Beust was too intelligent not to see the formidable obstacles in his path. After a careful analysis of the internal situation, he informed the cabinet that the imperial government would follow a "policy of peace and reconciliation."[45] It was an impressive demonstration of his realism and mastery of the art of political opportunism. An attempt to recover its German hegemony, Beust believed, "would perhaps cause greater difficulty for the monarchy than Austria's present exclusion."[46] It was, however, in Austria's interest "to prevent the extension of the North German Confederation to South Germany."[47] Circumstances thus dictated a policy of restraint toward the North German Confederation. "Austria must maintain an attitude that would not result in a clash" with the North German Confederation, "for in such an eventuality the impulse of the southern states to join the Northern Federation would be strengthened."[48] Nevertheless, he told the council of ministers, although Austro-French relations were good, he would improve them.[49]

After astutely assessing internal conditions in the empire, Beust made the creation of a South German Confederation, dominated by Austria, the main aim of his policy.[50] This would keep Prussia north of the River Main and would restore Austrian influence in German affairs.[51] Nor would such a policy be at variance with the foreign minister's past views. The status quo that he suggested on the German question was merely a continuation of his old "third force" policy (*Triaspolitik*).[52] Yet already by the time of the Compromise negotiations, as the French ambassador observed, Beust was failing to maintain absolute restraint in German matters.[53] Knowing well that direct action against Prussia was out of the question, Beust planned to realize his aims indirectly through collaboration with France. When the French leaders offered an alliance, he suggested that the east was an area "more favorable for diplomatic action that might lead to a war that would yield significant results."[54] In view of this, it would be an exaggeration to depict Beust as wanting nothing more than the status quo, and an oversimplification to condemn him for seeking revenge. Andrássy had good reason to watch his activities with special vigilance and to make sure that Beust followed his announced policy in international affairs.

Contrary to Beust, Andrássy reflected decidedly anti-Russian, anti-Pan-Slav sentiments, due both to Russia's role in crushing the Hungarian struggle for freedom and independence in 1848/49, and to his awareness of Russia's machinations in Hungary to incite and keep alive Slavic movements.[55] Platzhoff's observation is well made that the Hungarians felt themselves engulfed in the great Slavic sea of Eastern Europe and by the 1860s saw their only hope in an alliance with Germany.[56]

The Hungarians' desire for close cooperation with Germany was personified by Andrássy. In May 1848, in his twelfth report to his constituents in Zemplén County, he warned: "If we can avoid being isolated in the struggle, only then can we be winners, only then shall we not become victims."[57] His solution to the problem seems to have been cooperation with the German national movement. In July of the same year, in the diet's Address to the Throne, which he drafted, he emphasized "our need for close cooperation with the peoples of Greater Germany."[58]

Not twenty years after 1848, Andrássy was aiming to revive the Hungarian alliance with Germany that had been part of the old revolutionary program. But while the Hungarian revolutionaries of 1848 had sought Greater Germany's support for Hungary,[59] Andrássy now wished to have Prussia lead a Lesser Germany against a Greater Germany dominated by Austria[60] and, even more, against the Russian threat.

As prime minister, however, Andrássy could not seek the immediate realization of his views. In view of Prussian agitation within the monarchy and alleged Prussian connections with members of Tisza's Left Center party, he could not fully trust Bismarck's disavowal of Prussian designs to annex Austria's German provinces.[61] Meanwhile, Beust kept Andrássy supplied with exaggerated reports of Prussian moves within the monarchy, no doubt with the aim of disrupting Prussian-Hungarian relations.[62] The Hungarian premier was also suspicious of Bismarck's Russian policy. He feared an eventual coalition between the two powers to divide up the Habsburg dominions.[63]

Andrássy held seemingly contradictory views on the German question. On the one hand, he feared an extension of Prussian power that could result in the annexation of Austria's German provinces to the German empire, and also feared that the Austrian Germans would themselves initiate a union with the *Reich*. This would have destroyed Hungary's defenses against Russian-Pan-Slav encroachment, Andrássy's overriding concern. On the other hand, he regarded further involvement in German affairs as detrimental to the interests of both Hungary and the monarchy. Andrássy therefore demanded that Austria should renounce its ambition to regain preeminence in Germany.

To friends and Prussian diplomats, Andrássy often expressed his fear of Prussian designs on Austria's German provinces. The bitterly anti-Prussian manifestations in Viennese circles and the vigorous, often violent Prussian responses appeared to confirm his fears. The premier made it quite clear that he would do nothing to prevent Prussia from crossing the River Main line[64] and that he had "the greatest interest . . . in maintaining close relations with Prussia."[65]

It appears that Andrássy acted in the hope of exerting a restraining influence on the Prussians. It is also evident that the Hungarian statesman was opposed to revanchist plans against Prussia and even to irritant policies. Speaking of his attitude and activities to the French statesman Adolphe Thiers, Andrássy declared: "For a long time, I watched certain tendencies appearing among us. Those who dreamed of revenge for Prussia's success were numerous. . . . I did not blame them for this feeling, but I fought against it."[66] Bismarck, as always, hastened to reassure Andrássy about his sincerity toward the monarchy and his loyal friendship for the Hungarians.[67] His prompt reactions reveal how highly he valued Andrássy as the most articulate and "powerful opponent" of anti-Prussian policy inside the Dual Monarchy.

Bismarck appeared to have been including the Hungarians in his calculations since the 1850s. From his experiences as Prussia's delegate to the Federal Diet in Frankfurt, Bismarck deduced that Austria had to be excluded from German affairs, either by peaceful means or by force. Of course, he did not mean to destroy the Habsburg Empire. Bismarck aimed only to swing Austria's center of gravity from Germany towards the east, to Hungary.[68] He realized that relocation of Austria's sphere of interest would require basic reorganization of the empire and a vigorous, new, state-creating force to make this process possible. Bismarck appears to have settled on the Hungarians as this new force. On December 10, 1860, he wrote to Adjutant General Leopold von Gerlach that he had advised the Austrian ambassador, Count Alajos Károlyi, that Austria should depend on Hungary.[69]

A few months later, characterizing the desperate state of affairs in Austria to the Prussian foreign minister, Count Alexander von Schleinitz, he wrote:

> If I had the misfortune to be the emperor of Austria, I would move tomorrow to Pest; I would speak Hungarian and ride in a Hussar uniform; I would incorporate everything into Hungary; I myself would also stand before the Hungarian *Landtag* and negotiate with it and in the process tell it the undeniable truth that the Hungarian king-

ship is the Austrian emperor's highest position. The rest are all secondary domains. If things can be saved at all [in Austria], then in my opinion it is possible only by this means.[70]

Convinced that resolution of Austro-Prussian rivalry was "a mathematical impossibility" except through war, Bismarck established contact with Hungarian exiles in France after his appointment as Prussian minister president. To Count Arthur Scherr-Thoss, whom he received on his farewell visit to Paris, he confided:

I want to raise Prussia to the position in Germany due to it as a purely German state. I do not fail to recognize the value of Hungarian help and I know that the Hungarians are not revolutionaries in the ordinary sense. After all, Frederick the Great already conferred with the discontented Hungarian magnates about an alliance. If we win, Hungary will also get its freedom. You can count on that.[71]

What lends significance to his remarks is that he valued "Hungarian help" because the Hungarians were "not revolutionaries in the ordinary sense." He obviously recognized the readiness of the moderate leaders of 1848 and the conservatives for a compromise. To exploit Hungary under their leadership for the reorganization of East Central Europe was in conformity with his conservative principles. He desired no "fresh formations in this area" because such a development "could only be of a permanently revolutionary nature."[72] Hence his reliance on moderate nationalist exiles such as Klapka to prepare a Hungarian insurrection in 1866. Liberal revolutionaries of Louis Kossuth's type were out of the question.

After his meeting with Bismarck and at the latter's request, Scherr-Thoss sent him periodic reports on the Hungarian situation and also kept Andrássy regularly informed of developments pertaining to Hungary. Thus, through Scherr-Thoss, both Andrássy and Bismarck could learn of each other's foreign-policy ideas and this undoubtedly contributed greatly to their eventual meeting of minds.[73]

On December 5, 1862, shortly after the meeting with Scherr-Thoss, Bismarck advised Károlyi that Austria should concede Prussia equality in Germany, move its center of gravity to Hungary and rule it not as an appurtenance but as a vital part of the empire. In return, Austria would have Prussia's unconditional support for its interests in Italy and East Europe. Bismarck accused the Austrians of "inviting catastrophe"[74] should they ignore his advice.

The forcefulness of Bismarck's prediction shows the measure of importance he attached to Austro-Hungarian reconciliation as part of Austria's withdrawal from Germany. Significantly, his warning was accompanied by a concrete proposal, no doubt as an inducement. If Austria were to shift its sphere of interest, Prussia would support its international policies, a prefigurement of Andrássy's ideas that were realized in the Dual Alliance of 1879. As the Klapka episode of 1866 demonstrated, Bismarck's warning simultaneously was an implicit threat.[75] He not only recognized "the value of Hungarian help," but would also use it. Bismarck did not hesitate to use "revolutionary" means to achieve his conservative ends: Prussian hegemony in Germany and a reconstructed Austria in partnership with Hungary. The latter was to serve as a barrier against both Greater Germany and the Russian-Pan-Slav danger in the east, an idea that conveniently paralleled Andrássy's foreign-policy conceptions. Yet despite common interests that dictated collaboration on the German question, Hungarian-Prussian relations oscillated widely between 1867 and 1870. Undoubtedly, this was largely due to Andrássy's lack of confidence, especially noticeable in his attitude toward Prussia during the July crisis of 1870. Only after three years of hesitation, indirect negotiation, and a Franco-German war was the ground cleared for close and sincere cooperation.

In the unsettled and tense state of European affairs following the Austro-Prussian War of 1866, war between France and Prussia was widely foreseen. Andrássy watched with deep anxiety the possibility of such a war, into which Austria, to reverse the verdict of Königgrätz, might be drawn on the side of France against Prussia.[76] As Andrássy most probably calculated, victory or defeat for Austria would equally spell disaster for Hungary. To avoid this, he evolved a logical and effective policy — "to remain strictly neutral in the event of a Franco-Prussian war."[77] Only if Russia intervened would the premier abandon neutrality.

Available sources show beyond doubt that Andrássy's opposition to a revanchist policy aiming at the restoration of Habsburg dominance in Germany was only partly of Hungarian origin. Isacco Artom, Italy's special envoy to Vienna, noted that "Count Andrássy and the Hungarians do not want to see the reestablishment of Austria's lost influence in Germany."[78] Because, as Andrássy pointed out to another Italian diplomat, Count Francesco Curtopassi, "the strengthening of the [monarchy's] German elements would be equal to the destruction of dualism."[79]

Andrássy realized that Hungary's newly attained position within the monarchy depended largely on Austro-Prussian relations. His common sense told him that a struggle between the two powers was unavoidable, a struggle in which Hungary must cooperate with Prussia directly or indirectly to frustrate Austria's return to Germany.

The Prussian minister in Vienna had good reason to report: "Very great sympathy and gratitude exist among all ranks of the [Hungarian] population toward Prussia. . . . We are regarded here as their immediate protectors against any Viennese tendencies to violate [the compromise] in the future."[80] At the beginning of 1869, the Prussian consul, at his first meeting with the premier, observed in the attitude of Andrássy and of most Hungarians something that he called "the 'reflex' of Königgrätz." He attributed it to awareness "that the reestablishment of Hungarian freedom dates from Königgrätz."[81] Associated with it, the consul noted, was "the political calculation . . . that Prussia must retain the position it won in Germany in 1866, even if Austria has to be prevented by Hungary from reverting to its old German policy."[82] Otherwise Andrássy believed that Hungary would not be able to consolidate and safeguard its position of parity in the Dual Monarchy.

Andrássy, in opposing a revanchist policy, was at least as much motivated by imperial as by Hungarian considerations. The monarchy had to discard once and for all its "German impulses." "Now, when we are threatened from the east, retention of German supremacy is next to impossible,"[83] he told Béla Orczy. "Instead of this," he confided to Kállay, "the empire's attention must turn completely to the east."[84] This was the overriding reason for Andrássy's opposition to Austrian *grossdeutsch* dreams: he wanted to concentrate the monarchy's resources in the east rather than the west.

The Prussian consul in Pest reported that "facing east" was regarded by Andrássy "as the prime purpose of his policy . . . Russia is on his mind day and night."[85] The Italian consul general, Luigi Salvini, had a similar impression of Andrássy's attitude. It was "fear of Russia" that seemed to move Andrássy the most, he wrote following a meeting with the premier.[86] Salvini added: "Besides the antipathy for that power [Russia] that has existed here since the war of 1849, Russia is and has always been the obsession, the specter, of Hungary."[87] Thus Russophobia was apparently not restricted to the "Hungarian liberals" or the "Hungarian ruling classes," as suggested by some historians.[88] It was a national phenomenon. But were Andrássy's fears exaggerated? Deák did not think so. On one occasion in 1868, he admonished a deputy who called Andrássy's attitude toward the Eastern Question an "absurd infatuation." Speaking in his usual quiet manner, Deák observed: "Forgive me, my friend, but with all due respect, I think Gyula [Andrássy] sees further than you do."[89]

It is widely held that Andrássy's "turn to the east" was motivated by "blind hatred of Russia" and that his dominating principle was "revanche pour Világos."[90] This interpretation does not hold up under scrutiny. Andrássy was a realist and a moderate, as recognized by prominent historians;[91] hatred and revenge had little place in his diplomacy. But it would be incorrect to claim that he had wholly forgotten Russia's part in the suppression of Hungarian freedom in 1849. His motives, as revealed above, seem to have been fear of Russian aggression. He believed that, as soon as Russia had completed its railroad network and the reorganization of its army, it would attack the monarchy.[92] The threat posed by the secret Russian-Pan-Slav support for the Slav national movements within the monarchy and in the Balkans haunted him with special force. In his view, they jeopardized not only the territorial integrity of Hungary and hence Hungarian domination of the nationalities, but also the very existence of the monarchy.[93] Salvini, whose major interest seems to have been Russia and the Slav national movements, came to much the same conclusion: "Russia, leaning on the Slav population living in Hungary, is disposed to annihilate the Hungarian nationality and walk over its corpse to possess Serbia and ... assure itself of the Danube."[94] The Russian Pan-Slavists' writings no doubt contributed considerably to this pessimistic view.[95] Kann rightly stresses that "this very factor of fear of irredentism backed by a Great Power spurred Austrian foreign policy from the older Andrássy to Berchtold to a kind of preventive dynamism."[96]

The evidence leaves no doubt that the Russian-Pan-Slav problem was the main focus of Andrássy's foreign policy. All other considerations, including the German question, were secondary. "I have always maintained," he told Thiers, "that we were not a German nation, but a European nation placed on the borders of all nationalities." Therefore, "we must not adopt a policy of rancor, but one of equilibrium, ... and intervene only when the interests of Europe absolutely demand it."[97] Here lay another guiding principle of Andrássy's foreign policy, eminently "European" in that it went beyond the pursuit of specifically Hungarian and imperial interests. It aimed at containing the expansionist tendencies of other powers, above all of Tsarist Russia, in the wider interest of European balance. As early as 1850 Andrássy had already voiced his belief that "the existence of Austria can be an advantage to the other powers as a balance to the power of Russia."[98] Twenty years later he expressed the same idea that it was Austria's task "to constitute a bulwark against Russia." As long as it did, "its continuance will be a European necessity."[99] Andrássy, however, like

Metternich, perceived the peril inherent in being merely a "European necessity"; he felt that it would make the monarchy "mute among our nearest neighbors"[100] and dependent on the goodwill of others. To avoid this, "a state must have a mission." "Ours lies in the East . . . where our most important interests are at stake,"[101] he commented in his personal notes. He apparently felt that a sense of mission would command the loyalty of the monarchy's peoples and guarantee its independence in international affairs.

To forestall the Russian-Pan-Slav danger, Andrássy advocated the containment of Russia, preferably by diplomatic means. This involved the maintenance of the status quo in the Balkans and particularly the preservation of Turkey as long as possible.[102] Furthermore, Andrássy believed, the monarchy's foreign policy should aim to prevent the coalition of Russian diplomacy and the Slav national movements, and to disrupt their relations where already established.[103] And Andrássy was precisely the politician "who, by virtue of his Hungarian nationality and European breadth of view, recognized this objective considered to be of vital importance from the monarchy's point of view,"[104] concedes one of Andrássy's severest critics.

Once he became premier of Hungary, it was natural for Andrássy to concentrate his energies on accomplishing this task. He seems to have been willing to win over the South Slavs by concessions.[105] He sought honestly to avoid the appearance of conquest, for he believed that "any growth of territory can only be harmful to the monarchy."[106] He made it quite clear that "we want to make headway in the east by peaceful means, not by war."[107] He hoped in this fashion to establish a definite sphere of influence in the western Balkans to counterbalance any Russian gain in the region.

In any consideration of this policy, two important points cannot be overemphasized: first, the Hungarians' general suspicion and deep distrust, not to mention fear, of Russia; and secondly, Russia's aggressive expansionist policy in the Balkans, where it could count on the support of the fanatical forces of Pan-Slavism.

The war psychology, created by reckless Russian actions and Pan-Slav agitation, seems to have affected Andrássy deeply. Kállay recorded in July 1870: "He does not want war, but it will hardly be avoidable."[108] In one of his dispatches Artom reported: "According to him [Andrássy], Russia is making preparations in great haste and Austria could be forced to forestall them."[109] Two weeks later Andrássy told Artom: "The danger exists in their [the Russians'] secret manipulation of the Slav population of the Danube. . . . There is a peril that Austria must avoid at all cost: that is, dying like a scorpion immersed in excess carbolic." Finally, Andrássy stressed, "in the face of that danger, a strong initiative would become inevitable."[110]

He thus appears to have contemplated a preemptive war, which has advantages from a strictly military point of view, as the 1967 Israeli-Arab war so brilliantly demonstrated. He seems to have been considering the advisability of striking first, before Russian preparations were complete.

Another strategy can also be discerned. According to Kállay, Andrássy "holds a triumphant war necessary for the empire; we cannot wage this war against anyone but Russia and, if we win, we simultaneously break Russian power."[111] Andrássy deemed it necessary "that Russia initiate the war,"[112] Kállay noted. Andrássy then was facing the possibility of a defensive-offensive war. The Russians would launch an invasion of the monarchy, and after exhausting themselves in a fruitless offensive, they would be shattered by a counteroffensive.

Andrássy also mentioned to Kállay that Prince Napoleon, during a recent visit to Pest, had tried to gain his support against the North German Confederation. This he rejected, he went on, but since Napoleon III needed a war, he had advised that together with Austria he should attack Russia.[113] The Prussian consul general reported that the premier considered a conflict with Russia inevitable and that preparations should be made and the opportune moment chosen for it. For the sake of security in the east, the consul general continued, Andrássy desired close cooperation with Germany and was convinced that the latter would not forget its obligations toward the Europeans in the area.[114]

This implies that Andrássy was not thinking in terms of an Austro-Russian war. He knew the monarchy, although a Great Power on the basis of its area and population, did not have the strength because of its multinational character for a war against Tsarist Russia. But he also saw, along Metternichian-Palmerstonian lines, that Austria was an important element in the European balance of power. Indeed, Bismarck valued the Dual Monarchy as a "dam against Pan-Slavism,"[115] France regarded it as a guarantee of French security,[116] and Britain considered it a "bulwark" against Russian expansion.[117] Andrássy hoped to gain the cooperation and support of these powers for mutual aid and security; he wished to check Russia's forward policy by joint European action.

Before condemning Andrássy as an advocate of war,[118] it is well to consider two points. First, his ideas were not connected with any plan of action, nor did he make any serious attempt to translate them into reality. Strategic considerations were oriented to defensive purposes. Speaking to the German ambassador in 1872, Andrássy said: "We have been thrown out of Germany, and that is well; we lost Italy and we became stronger; we do not want to make annexations, but desire peace to defend our vital interests, which are threatened so far as our Slav population is concerned."[119] The second point is that, in accordance with the political principles of his time, Andrássy too considered war as the *ultima ratio*. Austria and Russia, Andrássy once observed, "are immediate neighbors and must live with one another, either on terms of peace or war. A war between the two empires would not be decided by one single campaign but would be inherited by generations to come. . . ; and its end could hardly be other than the total destruction of one of the two states. Before embarking upon such a contest there had to be reasons . . . that made a death struggle inevitable."[120]

The defensive tone of Andrássy's prognosis of relations with Russia is in sharp contrast to the "warlike Andrássy" of his critics. In reality, his policies were always pacific and within constitutional limits. His sometimes aggressive tone suggests fear rather than intent, for, as has been seen, he was aware that the advantages even a successful war could bring the monarchy were not very tangible and that the dangers involved in resorting to armed conflict were almost overwhelming.

III

Austria's Emergence from Isolation

During October of 1866 the rumors of Beust's nomination to the Ballhausplatz increased Andrássy's disquiet about the uncertain future of Hungary and the empire. Expressing his apprehension, Andrássy told Empress Elizabeth: "One can expect no good from this man."[1] His main reason for thinking so was the Saxon diplomat's virulently anti-Prussian attitude. Andrássy feared that Beust would attempt an accommodation with France on German affairs. After Beust assumed his duties, Andrássy watched his activities closely, and within a short period of time his suspicions and distrust were confirmed.

Beust, while presiding over the constitutional reconstruction of Austria,[2] did not neglect foreign affairs — and foreign affairs for him meant the creation of an anti-Prussian alignment. His thinking seemed logical, for both Austria and France were of necessity on the defensive against the growing power of Prussia. Prussia's victory over Austria had changed the situation in Europe to France's disadvantage,[3] and Napoleon III aimed to redress it. In accordance with the concept of balance of power, he demanded territorial "compensations" from Bismarck to offset Prussia's gains.[4] Although his attitude was friendly toward Vienna, at this stage of the game Napoleon kept his distance from defeated Austria.

Scarcely had Beust assumed office than, encouraged by the French ambassador, the Duke of Gramont, he approached Paris to help Austria recover its Great Power position.[5] Moreover, faced at once with the revival of the "Eastern Question," Beust also sought Austro-French cooperation in the east.[6] Citing internal difficulties, Foreign Minister Moustier declined to act on Beust's proposals.[7] Beust's hopes were raised anew, however, when, at the signing of new Austro-French maritime and commercial treaties, Gramont expressed his belief that they would strengthen already existing bonds and bring about a rapprochement between the two countries.[8] In his reply, unexpectedly exuberant and bold, Beust told the astonished ambassador that he wished for an Austro-French understanding on as wide a basis as possible.[9] Embarrassed by the "friendship [Beust] had extended with outstretched arms," Gramont only repeated his earlier statements.[10] It appears that Gramont had already gone further in expressing his pro-Austrian feelings than his government was ready for. The time was not ripe for a positive response from France.[11]

Napoleon, never an austrophile,[12] disliked the idea of an alliance that would appear to contradict all his previous policies as a champion of nationality. He had been against alliance with Austria before the war and was no more eager now that Austria was in a state of defeat.[13] Instead he turned to Prussia directly, offering an alliance in return for Prussian consent to the French annexation of Luxemburg and Belgium.[14] As negotiations with Prussia drifted toward deadlock, Napoleon attempted to bring about a Franco-Russian entente on a basis of cooperation and understanding in the Near East.[15] If successful, France would gain an ally against Prussia in the west.

Disappointed, Beust complained bitterly that the "Paris terrain, like quicksand where no sure step is possible and the prints of steps made disappear immediately, presents the greatest difficulties."[16] Press reports of these exchanges revealed the direction of Beust's policy to the public, and especially to Andrássy, who with Deák was in the midst of negotiating the settlement with the Austrian government.

France would deal only with a regenerated Austria, for, as Prince Jerome Napoleon stated bluntly, "On ne s'allie pas avec un cadavre."[17] Napoleon advised Beust to understand that as a first step Austria had to institute basic reforms in the army and the administration, and, above all, must conciliate Hungary.[18] Moreover, the emperor stressed, Austria should give up its rivalry with Prussia and work out some kind of plan with regard to the east.[19]

The French snub to Beust made success in reaching agreement with Hungary all the more important. On December 20, 1866, he made a sudden visit to Budapest to sound out Deák and Andrássy about the possibility of an early settlement.[20] Andrássy, however, saw through him. Shortly before Beust's visit, he received a surprising and at the same time revealing letter from Paris, written anonymously. It was obvious to Andrássy that the sender was Prince Jerome Napoleon, a friend from his days in exile. The prince's pretext for writing was to impart the information that Andrássy would receive an eminent post in the next Hungarian government. He reminded Andrássy: "As far as France is concerned, an alliance with Austria could be worthwhile only if, by satisfying its peoples, Austria could rely on their support and thus be capable of meeting foreign commitments. In this hope France has so far refrained from concluding alliances."[21]

Discerning an intimate connection between Prince Jerome's remarks and the motives of the visiting Austrian minister, Andrássy wrote of Beust: "If nobody helps, he will lose this monarchy just as he lost that other country [Saxony]."[22] To prevent foreign political developments contrary to the interests of Hungary and the monarchy, Andrássy redoubled his efforts to conclude the compromise. This explains why Andrássy "was in a hurry," not because he "wanted to display his diplomatic talents to Europe," as one historian so absurdly asserted.[23]

After failing to achieve his aims in the west, Beust turned his attention to the east. He dreamed of restoring Austria's prestige and diplomatic position in the Balkans.[24] This was a policy that could find French support. But the situation in the east was unstable. In the summer of 1866, the Cretan revolt once again reminded European statesmen that the "Eastern Question" was by no means a dead letter.[25] It produced angry ripples in Greece and found uneasy echoes in the Balkans, where the Serbs were working steadily for an alliance of the Balkan states against Turkey.[26] Collapse of the Ottoman Empire seemed quite possible.

In view of the growing Pan-Slav sentiment at home, the Russian government could no longer ignore affairs in Turkey. To avert a general conflict that Russia could ill afford, Gorchakov proposed an inquiry into the Cretan affair by the European powers.[27] Abandoning earlier Austrian policy of supporting the Turks, Vienna too became concerned with the fate of the Balkan Christians.[28] This new policy was given clear expression under Beust's guidance. With the revival of an active Balkan policy on Austria's part, the possibility of renewing cooperation with Russia came again into question.[29] Finding Austria favorably disposed toward the Cretans, Gorchakov could not conceal his pleasure at the change in Vienna's attitude.[30] Beust's initiative seemed realistic, for it appeared to correspond to the foreign political ambitions of the Court party which desired an Austro-Russian understanding in the Balkans. Especially in conservative military and aristocratic circles there was strong sentiment in favor of reestablishing cordial relations with St. Petersburg.[31] Diószegi's research has revealed reciprocal feelings among conservative forces in Russia.[32] More farsighted than his Russian counterpart, Beust felt the new Austrian policy might equally inaugurate a period of sharp rivalry between the two powers.[33] However, if an agreement could be reached between them on a common policy in the Balkans, which Bismarck had always favored, conflict could be avoided.

In Vienna preservation of the Ottoman Empire as it then existed had been a major Habsburg interest that enjoyed British and French support. This policy was, however, inherently weak because, it now appears, Beust regarded it as provisional in nature.[34] The Austrian foreign minister made no secret of his own views. He could agree to some Russian gains in the Balkans if, in exchange, St. Petersburg would recognize Vienna's special interest in Bosnia and Herzegovina.[35] But for the time being, Beust wished to avoid a general conflict and the possible partition of the Ottoman Empire until Austria had recovered from its disastrous war with Prussia. To prevent unilateral action by Russia and to secure its cooperation in settling the "Eastern Question" jointly with the other powers, Beust suggested rescinding the clauses of the Paris Treaty of 1856 neutralizing the Black Sea.[36]

The Austrian proposal met with firm opposition both in Paris[37] and London.[38] Napoleon III wanted Russia's backing against Prussia in the west without sacrificing the integrity of Turkey. In principle, he would have preferred a triple entente of France, Russia and Austria,[39] but Beust was unable to offer Napoleon any real inducement to renounce the gains of 1856. Beust suggested Egypt. While Napoleon was not averse to the idea, he thought it hopeless: "Unfortunately England is always in my way."[40] With that he dismissed Beust's idea.

The Austrian foreign minister was not the only one to make the French an offer. Trying to turn the "Eastern Question" to good account, Bismarck hit on the idea that France should be made "contented and pacific" by concessions in the east.[41] He therefore offered to support the French in that area,[42] but Paris would consider compensation only in the west.[43]

To make things worse, after receiving the French rejection of his proposal, Beust unwisely informed Gorchakov of his action, urging him at the same time to back a conference on the eastern problem.[44] The Russian chancellor, intent on his own private negotiations with Paris, resented the meddling of the "old rope-dancer," whom he believed to be on close terms with Napoleon. In particular, Gorchakov deplored the inopportune mention of the Black Sea clauses.[45] Beust's ambitious plan fell flat. He was forced to recognize that agreement between Austria and Russia was unlikely.

In addition, Beust's domestic political situation did not conduce to close relations with Russia. The Austro-German and especially the Hungarian liberals, soon to take power, were hostile to an entente with Russia.[46] Andrássy's prime concern was to preserve "the integrity of the Turkish Empire."[47] He had explained his reasons in remarks in the ministerial conference of January 29, 1875: "Turkey is almost a providential utility to Austria. Its existence is essential to our well-understood interests. It preserves the status quo among the small states and hinders their aspirations to our advantage. Were there no Turkey, then all these heavy obligations would fall on us."[48] Andrássy confided to Kállay his intentions "to offer active assistance to the Turks in the event of a Russian war."[49] Beust, on the other hand, was ready to compromise on the issue. Alarmed by Andrássy's attitude, he remarked: "Austria and Russia came to a secret understanding before the Crimean War that, if Turkey should collapse, the two powers would divide the remains between themselves, and this pact would now be even more advantageous for Austria than a Turkish alliance."[50] But Andrássy, Kállay noted, "explained to him firmly and effectively the perils of Russian friendship."[51]

Beust's endeavors, as Diószegi pointed out, for complex external and internal reasons could not succeed.[52] Deepening suspicion, aggravated partly by Russian-supported Pan-Slav agitation inside the Dual Monarchy and partly by Austria's liberal policy in Polish Galicia,[53] typified relations between the two states.

The situation between Paris and Vienna changed considerably after Beust's overture had been rejected. In face of the aggressive French demands, Bismarck demonstrated his extraordinary superiority in all areas of the great chessboard of diplomacy and succeeded in warning Napoleon off German territory.[54] Foiled in his bid for compensation from Bismarck, hard-pressed by rising public resentment in France against what appeared to be a complete failure of his foreign policy,[55] Napoleon was forced to reconsider his attitude toward Austria. Already in early January of 1867, as negotiations with Prussia were reaching deadlock, he secretly approached Vienna.[56] Then in February Napoleon declared that he wanted "Austria to regain its former position in Germany" and wished that Beust's "intentions should be realized."[57]

Fresh from the triumph of concluding the Compromise with the Hungarians on February 17, 1867, the facile Austrian foreign minister felt free to make the preparations necessary to realize his southern German scheme.[58] As part of his project, it now became possible again to encourage French approaches and give them serious consideration.

An active anti-Prussian course was out of the question, especially after the dramatic disclosure on March 19, 1867, of the defensive and offensive alliances between Prussia and the German states south of the River Main.[59] Although Beust regarded these agreements as in violation of the Treaty of Prague and a danger to South German independence, he only lamented sadly that there was nothing Austria could do.[60] Above and beyond all this, divisions within the government of the Dual Monarchy advised restraint.

One of the most important developments following conclusion of the Compromise was Andrássy's advent as premier of Hungary. His irresistible rise was to doom Beust's western-oriented foreign policy that had been set so dangerously close to a collision course. After his appointment as premier, Andrássy wasted little time in claiming a full voice in the formulation and direction of the monarchy's foreign policy. "It is a significant development," wrote Lónyay of the Council of Ministers for Common Affairs of March 28, 1867, "that Andrássy has begun to exercise his influence on foreign policy."[61] The premier hastened to point out to Beust, and quite often to foreign diplomats,[62] that from this time on Austria must consult the wishes of Hungary in foreign-policy matters.

Andrássy's influence on the policies of Austria grew increasingly important and, as Beust was anxiously aware, he had no desire to contribute to putting a possible check on Prussia. In view of the very tense atmosphere in European diplomacy, Beust's activities deeply troubled the Hungarian leaders. Lónyay reminded the foreign minister that an anti-Prussian policy was not in line with Hungary's interests. "I had a discussion with Beust about foreign affairs," Lónyay wrote. "I asked him to stay clear of war as much as possible." Beust, he added, "is leaning toward a French alliance."[63] If Lónyay's remarks surprised the foreign minister, then Andrássy's statement a few days later must have bowled him over. On March 28, Andrássy bluntly recommended in the common ministerial council that "Austria not join closely with Napoleon, but work for a Prussian alliance."[64] Familiar with Bismarck's view of the monarchy, Andrássy preferred friendship with Prussia, so that it would not attempt to annex the Austro-German provinces and leave the Hungarians alone among their hostile Slav neighbors. Nevertheless, Andrássy still hesitated now and then, reacting with suspicion to Bismarck's policy of friendship with Russia.[65] Though this did not influence the Hungarian premier's efforts for neutrality during this period of deepening Franco-Prussian conflict, it did affect his attitude toward Prussia.

As for the Austro-German liberals, Karl Giskra, in an exchange of thoughts with Julius Fröbel, the former revolutionary radical, declared categorically that Austria "will not start a war on account of the southern German states' entry into the North German Confederation."[66] After all, dearest to the heart of the Austro-German liberals was the unification of Germany and this was being achieved by Bismarck. Beust, in fact, was forced to recognize that his foreign policy must be in harmony with the interests of both the Hungarians and the Austro-Germans.

Beust was still brooding over the setbacks he had suffered when the Luxemburg crisis exploded at the very beginning of April over the grand duchy's proposed sale to France.[67] It was to have been the culmination of Napoleon's attempts to secure compensation. When the plan was prematurely disclosed through Bismarck, Napoleon was forced to back down. France suffered a new humiliation and for some time war seemed imminent.

The possibility of armed hostilities prompted Andrássy to keep an anxious watch over the course of events, but he refused to be drawn directly into what he considered a "purely German concern." When the crisis arose, he came out for Austria's strict neutrality.[68] Andrássy knew that the monarchy could not afford involvement in war, regardless of why and how it started. It was an open secret that Austria's economy was in a dreadful state. It had been bad before the Austro-Prussian War of 1866 and it became worse as a result of it. Even before the war, on February 20, 1866, Andrássy had noted: "The economic condition of the empire . . . is in such a bad state that it may require nothing so much as the beneficial influence of peace."[69] The premier felt Austria needed a long interval of tranquility to be able to put its chaotic finances in order, to rebuild its demoralized army, and to resolve internal problems resulting from the monarchy's constitutional reorganization. Moreover, only peace would permit Hungary to consolidate its position within the monarchy. Foreign observers, too, commented that "the Hungarians do not wish for a war that would be waged to recover Austria's German supremacy, because they know they would be reduced to a dependent position if the Austrian Emperor were to regain his power in Germany."[70] With this in mind Andrássy made it perfectly clear to Gramont that "Austria-Hungary needs peace to a high degree, so the maintenance of neutrality is of the utmost importance."[71]

In view of the Hungarians' antiwar attitude and the hostile stance of the Austro-Germans, as well as Austria's military and economic impotence, Beust dared not try to use the occasion to stem the Prussian tide. He left it to Bismarck to resolve the conflicts arising from the dissolution of the Germanic Confederation.[72] Yet Beust refused to commit himself to neutrality, as Andrássy demanded, and insisted on a "free hand in policy,"[73] no doubt to improve his maneuvering position. Since a conflict between Prussia and France seemed to present no benefit to Austria, still smarting from its recent defeat, Beust offered to mediate in the dispute.[74] The Austrian initiative was immediately supported by Gorchakov. The Russian statesman was exceedingly jealous of Bismarck and detested his constant manipulation of public opinion as well as his suggestion of an Austro-Russian-German understanding guaranteeing Austria's Turkish frontiers, which would deprive Russia of its influence in the Balkans.[75]

Uncertain of Vienna's intentions, both Prussia and France sought to strengthen their positions by trying to conclude an alliance with Austria.

On April 12, as the crisis was coming to a head, Bismarck, grateful for Beust's offer of mediation, stressed to Wimpffen, the Austrian ambassador in Berlin, the necessity of an alliance between Austria and the German states.[76] Bismarck also used Bavaria's good offices in Vienna to find out what support he could expect from Austria in the event of war with France. Count Tauffkirchen was commissioned by Prince Hohenlohe, the Bavarian minister president, to win Bismarck's approval for an Austro-Prussian alliance, which would then have been presented in Vienna. When the count approached the German chancellor on April 13, the latter welcomed the idea and in the name of Prussia and Bavaria offered Austria an alliance. He agreed, moreover, to guarantee the integrity of Austria's territories against Turkey, Russia and Italy.[77]

It emerges clearly from his instructions to Werther that Bismarck was thinking in terms of a triple entente of Austria, Prussia and Russia.[78] Beust summarily rejected the proposal, which contained no specific guarantee of Austrian concessions in Germany. He replied indignantly that Bismarck could not expect him to be satisfied "with a specially bound copy of the Treaty of Prague on parchment."[79] To Wimpffen he justified the rejection of Bismarck's offer quite realistically by stressing that acceptance of the Prussian proposal would arouse the wrath of France. If it resulted in a war and an Austro-Prussian victory over France, it would still only confirm the monarchy's status quo after its recent defeat.[80] It is not at all surprising that Beust's action was accepted by liberals and conservatives alike, though for different reasons. Beust himself noted: "When this telegram [to Wimpffen] appeared in the first *Red Book* in 1869, it met with the unanimous approval of the Viennese press and, I also remember, a verbal but fully approbatory statement by Andrássy."[81]

Beust's assertion is quite believable. Andrássy wanted no part of an *entente à trois* that would include Russia, Hungary's archenemy. What Andrássy desired was a dual alliance directed against Russia.[82] The anti-Russian sentiment that Andrássy reflected was well expressed by the organ of the Deák party: "In our opinion he who does not regard Russia as the main enemy of Hungary — and who does not see in the natural opponents of the Russians the natural allies of Hungary — does not deserve to be called a Hungarian politician."[83] Only if Berlin were to renounce its traditional friendship for Russia would the Hungarian liberals ally themselves with Prussia.[84]

France also tried for an alliance with Austria, though only when the crisis became acute. Most probably the French proffer of an alliance to Austria was intended primarily to counteract Bismarck's advances. On April 23, the Duke of Gramont called on Beust with a sweeping proposal for an offensive and defensive alliance by which France would gain the left bank of the Rhine while Austria acquired Silesia and a free hand in south Germany.[85] To underline the significance of his instructions, Gramont insisted that France was well prepared and needed help from no one.[86]

Beust immediately rejected this "somewhat adventuresome plan," arguing that it did not correspond to the wishes of the monarchy's public. First he referred to the opposition of the Hungarians, who had been quite unhappy about France's attitude over the past few years and so could not be expected to embrace the French cause. The Slavs similarly would be opposed to a French alliance because it would lead to a break between Austria and Russia. Finally, Beust stressed, the hostility of ten million Germans in Austria made a direct alliance against Germany impossible.[87] Beust made no secret of his preferences. He would tolerate French ambitions in Germany only if they arose from a war "in other areas and for other interests."[88]

Beust's analysis of public opinion showed that he was a prisoner of it. As for Gramont, it appears that at this stage he had still failed to see Andrássy as a major force in the affairs of the monarchy.[89] Otherwise, he would not have ignored the premier's rejection of his overture in early April, when he had asked for Andrássy's support for an Austro-French alliance.[90]

It is true that the principal object of both Andrássy and Beust was to restore the monarchy's prestige and maintain its Great Power position. They differed, however, on what Austria's ultimate foreign-policy orientation should be. Beust's policy of a "free hand," bent on an anti-Prussian and pro-French course, was incompatible with Andrássy's policy of "compelling direction" toward the east.

The end of the Luxemburg crisis dispelled the obvious clouds of war. Andrássy could now turn his driving energies undividedly to building a modern Hungary and fortifying its position within the monarchy to be able to prevent developments contrary to the interests of both.[91] The calm that succeeded the intense excitement of April did not deceive the Hungarian premier. He continued to keep a sharp eye on the international scene, for the recent crisis had fixed his attention on the unresolved problem at the heart of Europe. He had to face the prospect of a Franco-Prussian war and the problem of possible Austrian involvement. More than anything else, what preyed on his mind was Beust's susceptibility to the machinations of the Court party, and especially to French pressure. Anxious to prevent unpleasantness, Andrássy took a hard line with the foreign minister to force implementation of his policy of "peace and neutrality" and avoid entangling commitments in Paris. Andrássy held firm to this position, particularly during Napoleon's visit to Francis Joseph in Salzburg in the middle of August.[92]

The Luxemburg crisis and France's drift away from Russia, whose support had brought France no gains in the west, underlined Napoleon's desperate need for support against Prussia. Under such circumstances the most natural ally appeared to be Austria, and this was one reason the two emperors met from August 18 to 22, 1867. Napoleon also wished to express his sympathies to Francis Joseph over the execution of his brother, Archduke Maximilian, in Mexico.[93] Another reason besides these was that Beust had advised Francis Joseph not to go to Paris except to return a visit.[94]

Andrássy was not pleased at the news of the forthcoming meeting. "As I read from the papers today, Napoleon is coming to Salzburg; it is slightly better than Vienna, but there is not much difference. I regret that it is going to happen,"[95] he wrote his wife.

The French emperor was accompanied to Salzburg by Empress Eugenie, major figures like General Fleury and the Duke of Gramont, and the entire staff of the French embassy in Vienna. Francis Joseph brought with him Empress Elizabeth, Beust, Andrássy, and Count Taaffe, the vice premier of Cisleithania.[96] As Beust and Andrássy had anticipated, the French brought up the question of an alliance. Gramont presented the draft of a treaty to compel Prussia to comply with the Treaty of Prague. It was suggested that at the end of a victorious war with Prussia, Austria would have a free hand in most of southern Germany while France would take the left bank of the Rhine.[97] Realizing that he had no adequate support in the monarchy for such direct action, Beust was forced to shift his ground. The mood of the public, both in Austria[98] and Hungary,[99] was overwhelmingly against collusion with France for war against Prussia. Andrássy recognized this as an especially propitious opportunity to make his views clear to the French. Aware of Hungarian public opinion, Andrássy told Napoleon that, "in the event of a Franco-Austrian alliance, and war resulting from it, [he was] not to count on the Hungarians." For good measure, he added: "The Hungarians are the most egotistic nation in the world, and they want above all to retain the greatest possible independence and freedom."[100]

Andrássy's statement corresponded with the views of the ruling Deák party. Menyhért Lónyay, one of the party's most powerful members, wrote to him at the time of the Salzburg meeting: "I hope you have participated in achieving good things and did not commit the empire's future to one-sided compacts."[101] The party newspaper, *Pesti Napló,* stated peremptorily: "In German affairs there can be no community of interest between Austria and France."[102]

In principle, Andrássy was well disposed toward a cordial political liaison with France, but only in eastern affairs, not the Rhenish problem.[103] Anxious to preserve the balance of power in Europe, which he believed to serve Austria's best interests, he rejected any idea of joining France against Prussia or vice versa.[104] He wished to be on friendly terms with both.

As for Beust, the memorandum he drew up for Francis Joseph prior to the meeting with Napoleon showed the foreign minister had a realistic understanding of prevailing sentiments in the monarchy and of what Austria could and should do.[105] Not surprisingly, he turned down Gramont's proposal and submitted a brief draft of his own, out of which came an agreement that in particular laid down a common policy toward the east. The British, too, were invited to subscribe to it as a basis for closer relations with Vienna and Paris. In Germany France and Austria were to adhere to the provisions of the Peace of Prague and impress on the southern states the necessity for reserve toward the Northern German Confederation. Both Austria and France would avoid any interference in German affairs that might provoke a nationalist reaction.[106] Although Britain refused to join them, Austria and France in the fall of 1867 began a period of cooperation in Turkish affairs.[107]

The negotiations stopped short of a formal alliance, to which Andrássy's opposition probably contributed most significantly.[108] Although nothing very concrete resulted from the emperors' meeting, it signaled Austria's emergence from isolation. Whatever motives Beust may have had, the result was a tribute to his political skill. The first steps had been taken toward a closer understanding between the two powers.

The Salzburg conference predictably triggered a round of guessing and exaggerated rumors throughout Europe.[109] Napoleon's failure to visit the king of Prussia on his way back to Paris caused uneasiness that found expression in the German press, no doubt under Bismarck's prompting.[110] Privately the German chancellor was sardonic rather than apprehensive, dismissing the meeting as "politically of no consequence,"[111] but publicly he suggested that the aim had been a south German confederation under Austro-French tutelage.[112]

The conference and especially Bismarck's reaction to it deepened the fear of a Franco-Prussian war both in the Austrian[113] and the Hungarian[114] halves of the Dual Monarchy. Andrássy realized that Hungary's position within the monarchy depended to a large measure on Austro-Prussian relations, and that in the struggle over them the Hungarians would have to be on Prussia's side, even if not overtly. He saw that the Hungarians would achieve their foreign-political ambitions only if they gained a decisive say in common governmental decisions.[115] Lónyay, who shared Andrássy's views, urged him "to talk His Majesty into not giving Beust unlimited power."[116] With this Andrássy could not have agreed more. He acted without delay. After meeting the monarch, the premier confided to Lónyay that "His Majesty received him with great cordiality and acquiesced in Beust's acting in concert with Andrássy."[117] Andrássy thus advanced to a new position of strength in order to secure Hungary's interests.

Against this background, Beust felt it necessary to give private and public assurances, especially to Bismarck, about Vienna's peaceful intentions.[118] Paris also hastened to disclaim any ill intentions toward Prussia.[119] Bismarck responded positively to these explanations, though he served notice that "German national sentiment" would not tolerate the "guardianship of foreign intervention."[120] The furor slowly subsided.

The North German federal chancellor could easily afford to make an immediate protestation of goodwill and allow animosity to subside. He was in a stronger position than his opposite number in the Dual Monarchy. Bismarck knew that through common interests and intentions Andrássy was on his side. He likewise knew that among the Austro-German liberals he had sympathizers who would foil Beust's anti-Prussian plans.

On October 5, Wimpffen, the Austrian ambassador in Berlin, reported that Bismarck attached great importance to satisfactory relations between the two countries. He viewed the policy of the Dual Monarchy with deep satisfaction and recognized that Vienna intended to guide relations with Berlin in the interest of peace. In particular, Wimpffen said, Bismarck had absolute faith in Beust (*sic!*).[121] Beust received Bismarck's expressions of goodwill with considerable skepticism. He was deeply concerned over the possibility of secret dealings between the Hungarians and the Prussians. He therefore complained sharply to the confederation's legate about the alleged Prussian payment of subventions to members of the Hungarian Radical party. There were indications that "Hungary's attitude is still being taken into Prussian political calculations," Beust claimed.[122]

Bismarck answered Beust's charges in characteristic manner. Through Minister Werther he assured the Austrian foreign minister that there was no possibility for large sums of money to be passed behind the public's back, so the accusations were baseless. As for the Hungarians, only Vienna's aggressive anti-Prussian policy could force him to look at them differently from before.[123]

Apparently anxious to allay Beust's suspicion, the Prussian statesman went deeper into the matter in a reassuring statement to the Austrian ambassador. Bismarck told Wimpffen categorically that allegations of illicit Hungarian-Prussian connections were without foundation. He conceded, however, that the public relations office of the Prussian government, which had correspondents in Hungary, could have given rise to speculations. He wanted the reconstruction and consolidation of Austria to proceed undisturbed, he said, and wished success to the Compromise, for in his opinion Austria and Germany must sooner or later become allies. "We want nothing from Austria, we are satisfied," he continued, adding with a slight edge: "Connections with opposition parties in Hungary could only have significance and value for us if there existed an Austro-French alliance of aggressive nature against us." Returning to the allegations of Prussian subsidies in Hungary, he repeated his denial emphatically and remarked: "I am not lying. As a rule I am used to lying only in cases of extreme necessity [*sic!*]."[124]

The real truth in this controversy is hard to discover. It is a fact that Beust suspected Bismarck of being in touch with the Hungarians. He often voiced his fear, perhaps exaggeratedly, to separate Andrássy from Bismarck or to deflect attention from his own constant intriguing with Napoleon III, but neither then nor later could he ever substantiate his uneasy feelings.[125] In any event, Beust shrewdly used such tactics whenever he was forced to defend his anti-Prussian policies to Andrássy and the other Hungarian leaders or to try to win them over to his support.[126] Beust failed to change Andrássy's mind, but his constant references to the bogey of Prussian subversion periodically caused the Hungarian premier to vacillate,[127] though Andrássy never wavered on his position of neutrality.

Francis Joseph's return visit to Paris from October 23 to November 4, 1867, in the company of Empress Elisabeth, Beust, Andrássy and a sizable entourage, strengthened the cordiality between Vienna and Paris, both on state[128] and personal[129] levels. Beust denied categorically that there were any political negotiations in Paris,[130] but the informal talks he and the emperor had with the French leaders dealt with political issues, clearing the way for an Austro-French entente. That the conversations went beyond innocent exchanges of views is evident from Francis Joseph's remark to the French General Auguste-Alexandre Ducrot on his way back to Vienna: "I hope that one day we shall march together."[131]

The main discussions centered on the situation in Italy, where Garibaldi's invasion of the Papal States had provoked a new crisis, and the "Eastern Question" in view of the continuing Cretan uprising.[132] In the end Beust won Napoleon's promise to coordinate his eastern policy with that of Austria but without a formal alliance.[133] To Andrássy's intense satisfaction, Beust stayed within bounds. It is not that the premier failed to grasp the significance of the visit. On the contrary, he attached great importance to the meetings of the two monarchs for he hoped that they would be in the interests of peace. "It would be useful," he wrote his wife, "if the rapprochement between the two states became visible, but without provoking war."[134] Andrássy seems to have interpreted the outcome of the meetings as a victory for peaceful solutions in the east and as a sign of French willingness to support Austria in blocking Russian expansion in the Balkans. This would explain what Andrássy meant by his remarks to General Ducrot: "I cannot visualize a question that could lead to the least divergence in our views or in our common action."[135] But Andrássy could not be drawn into an anti-Prussian alignment.

Letters of the Hungarian statesman, written during the Paris visit, reveal deep-seated suspicions of Napoleon's policy.[136] Although Andrássy knew Napoleon III as an exile and was entertained at his court often, no trace of trust or admiration for the pathetic figure of the French emperor can be found. In January 1852 Andrássy had witnessed the overwhelming vote in favor of Napoleon's referendum that resulted in the establishment of the Second Empire. Under its impact the young liberal had exclaimed: "The French nation has accepted slavery; it depends on the will of an adventuring tyrant."[137] There is no indication that he changed his opinion of Napoleon in the years that followed. Rather, his distrust of the French emperor deepened, a fact that became only too evident in the tense days of July 1870.[138]

As for Beust, his success, limited by necessity to Austro-French cooperation in the east, was the Russian chancellor's failure. It was already clear at the time of Tsar Alexander II's visit to Paris, during which Napoleon and his ministers avoided all serious political discussions with their Russian counterparts, that Gorchakov's hopes to gain French support for his Turkish policy were in vain.[139] The visible Austro-French cooperation in the Ottoman Empire in the fall of 1867 underlined the failure of Russian diplomacy.[140] After the breakdown of Franco-Russian exchanges, to avoid isolation, St. Petersburg had no alternative but to swing back to its old ally, Prussia.

Andrássy and the Danger of a Franco-German War

The year 1868 was little more than a time of armed neutrality for Europe.[1] All eyes were turned on the two rivals, France and Prussia, whose repeated asseverations of peace only increased forebodings of war.

The first demarche came from Vienna in January. Through Count Vitzthum, Beust suggested a triple alliance of France, Great Britain and Austria for the purpose of solving the Cretan problem, by force if necessary.[2] The Austrians' bellicosity created uneasiness in Paris[3] and as a result the French evaded the Austrian proposal. Instead Napoleon proposed a conference of all powers, including Prussia, to deal with eastern affairs.[4] Vitzthum's approach to London was even less successful. The British foreign secretary, Lord Stanley, listened with "much interest" but would not abandon his policy of nonintervention.[5]

It is beyond doubt that Napoleon's initiative was influenced by Bismarck's gestures toward better relations with France.[6] Believing that Prussia might support France in the Near East, Paris responded positively.[7] Bismarck, in fact, had no desire to commit himself to any kind of coalition unless it suited Prussia's needs. His moves toward Paris were intended to thwart Vitzthum's mission, and in this he succeeded.

A by-product of Bismarck's maneuver was speculation about a Prussian rapprochement with Austria and France which alarmed St. Petersburg.[8] Bismarck at once flatly denied all the rumors.[9] Anticipating war in the spring, Alexander II dared not be without a reliable ally. In early February the tsar offered to keep Austria at bay by deploying Russian forces along the Austrian border, and expected Prussia to do likewise in case of war in the Balkans.[10] But Bismarck had no more intention of binding Prussia to Russia than to France and responded noncommittally to the proposal.[11]

In March Alexander tried again by repeating more explicitly that he was ready to keep Vienna in check should Prussia become embroiled with either Austria or France. Russia would station an army of 100,000 men on Austria's frontier if Prussia would do the same in the event of war in the east.[12] Bismarck again temporized. "Of course neither power could afford to allow the destruction of the other," he assured the tsar.[13] In the event of an Austro-Russian war he was prepared to keep France in check rather than Austria, just as Russia would ensure Austria's neutrality in case of war between Prussia and France.[14] Although no formal alliance resulted, both Alexander II and Gorchakov expressed satisfaction with Bismarck's reply[15] and with the personal friendship of the tsar and William I.[16] Thus Bismarck cut the Gordian knot and separated the eastern and western questions. With the Prussian-Russian entente he created a new constellation that was to act as one of the most powerful deterrents to Beust's effort to solve the German question by involving all four powers in a war over the "Eastern Question."

Meanwhile Andrássy received bits and pieces of information about Beust's feverish activities, information that rounded out what he already knew or suspected. The foreign minister's disregard of Hungarian sentiments on foreign-policy matters widened the gap between the monarchy's two most outstanding statesmen. What made the matter worse was that Beust's conduct had aroused the opposition in the Hungarian parliament.

Andrássy and the leadership of Tisza's Left Center party, although in disagreement about virtually everything else, were united on questions of foreign policy.[17] The spokesmen of the party, however, were often severely critical of the premier's alleged failure to represent the foreign-policy views of the Hungarian parliament with sufficient vigor and determination in the councils of the monarchy. The premier, while aware of what Beust was up to, felt it necessary to defend the monarchy's foreign policy in the interest of internal peace and unity, but at the same time also to adumbrate his own views on it to warn Beust and make Hungary's position known to friends and foes alike.

Only the previous December, much concerned over the foreign minister's actions and the adverse international reaction, the Left Center had considered it its patriotic duty to mount an offensive and bring the issue into the open to prevent unpleasant surprises. On December 17, during debate of Austria's national debt, an attack was interjected by one of the party's most colorful deputies, Mór Jókai, of 1848 fame and a writer of international repute. He sharply criticized the foreign ministry's "provocative policy" and interference in the internal affairs of other states, alluding obviously to Beust's machinations in Germany. Then, with a sudden change of tack, he fired an indirect salvo at Andrássy. "It is distressing," Jókai protested, "that parliament has no say in Austria's foreign policy either here in Pest or up in Vienna, so it might well ask: 'Sick man of Europe, where are you rushing to?'"[18]

Stung by this, Andrássy answered the next day. The premier showed his usual self-assurance as he rose to speak. His first care was to answer remarks on the national debt.[19] Then, lashing at Jókai's statements on Austria's foreign policy, he ridiculed his argument and asserted forcefully that "the monarchy does not want anything but peace at home and abroad."[20] For the moment Andrássy's firmness deterred Jókai from pressing the issue further.

During the early months of 1868 Beust continued to play with fire. The restless foreign minister evidently relished the opportunity for action that an early formalization of an Austro-French entente would open up in the east. Beust's apparent disregard of the Hungarians' feelings on the issue, however, provoked the Left Center anew, further increasing Andrássy's difficulties in parliament. In the course of a debate on the military budget Tisza's chief lieutenant, Deputy Kálmán Ghiczy, questioned the peaceful intentions of the Ballhausplatz. "If the monarchy sincerely wants peace, there will be peace. . . . The moment we take an understanding look at its recent transformation, Germany will have no reason to undermine us," he observed. Italy and Turkey posed no danger to the monarchy's security, "so we have only Russia to fear."[21] To forestall lengthy debate on the issue, Andrássy answered immediately.

He curtly brushed aside Ghiczy's insinuation that his government had failed to make its influence felt at the foreign ministry. Then in a conciliatory tone, he agreed with Ghiczy that, to preserve peace, "goodwill toward the German governments, including Prussia, without any ulterior motive" was imperative.[22] It was an unassailable position that found approval among a majority of the deputies. Andrássy had achieved his purpose and averted a crisis.

At this point, spurred by Beust's double-game and by parliamentary pressure, Andrássy took steps to enhance his influence over the foreign minister's activities and thus over the foreign policy of the monarchy. In early March, the premier arranged to have one of his confidants, Baron Béla Orczy, appointed a department head at the foreign ministry, his duty being to press Andrássy's views against Beust. This appointment no doubt clipped Beust's hitherto virtually unrestrained wings.[23] Emperor Francis Joseph acceded to Andrássy's request that

Orczy should continually keep the Hungarian premier informed on all matters of foreign policy.[24]

At the same time Andrássy prevailed on Beust to accept the appointment of another trusted friend, Béni Kállay, as consul general in Belgrade, capital of Serbia.[25] Belgrade, a center of Russian-Pan-Slav agitation, was regarded by Andrássy as the most sensitive diplomatic post with respect to the monarchy's South Slav nationalities.[26] It was Kállay's duty among others to prepare the ground for Serbia's removal from Russian influence, and to learn the real motives behind Beust's Balkan policy.[27] Furthermore, Kállay was charged with keeping a sharp eye on the activities of the military members of the Court party in the frontier region.[28] Evidence of their continuing agitation among the area's inhabitants had been causing considerable anxiety in Budapest. Reactionary circles in Vienna apparently still considered the Military Frontier District Hungary's potential Vendée.

The views Andrássy expounded in parliament and these two appointments testified both to his profound antagonism for any anti-German policy and to the grave importance he attached to the Russian menace in the east. Andrássy's growing authority in the councils of the monarchy did not escape the attention of foreign powers.[29]

In late March, obviously reacting to Andrássy's rising power, Napoleon III commented pointedly to an Austrian diplomat on the undue growth of Hungarian power in the monarchy.[30] Some days later both the French emperor and empress expressed much anxiety about the strength of the Hungarians and the Austro-German liberals. The imperial couple also made clear their dismay that, while the French armed forces were reaching the point of full readiness "for any eventuality," the Austrian army had trimmed its ranks.[31] French concern over Austria's military strength showed that Paris looked to the monarchy for an offensive combination.

Beust lost no time in reassuring Napoleon that Austria's reduced but rearmed army remained strong. He also assured him that the power of the Hungarians as well as the Austro-German liberals was a myth. Then he drew Napoleon's attention to the impressive victory of the South German particularists in the March 1868 elections for the *Zollparliament*.[32] Beust's assurances seem to have convinced Napoleon that the foreign minister was in full control of the monarchy's affairs,[33] but he was skeptical about South Germany. He felt that it was still within the realm of possibility that Bismarck might effect German unification through the Customs Union. Prince Napoleon, who visited Berlin in mid-March, returned with the depressing conviction that

German unity could no longer be arrested. Reports of the French ambassador in Berlin offered the same opinion.[34]

It was under this pressure that Napoleon decided to resume the Salzburg policy of trying to win a pledge of Austrian help should Prussia attempt to absorb the South German states. On April 7, 1868, Napoleon asked Prince Metternich what Vienna intended to do if the South Germans "threw themselves into Prussia's arms," if Prussia violated the Treaty of Prague, or if the Rumanian principalities proclaimed their independence. He also wondered whether a new attempt should be made to bring England into the Austro-French entente. Napoleon suggested that Vienna should initiate "preventive diplomatic action or protest" to avoid arousing German national sentiment. Naturally, France would support Austria "in the second line."[35]

In his reply, Beust discounted the eventuality of the South Germans voluntarily taking Prussia's side and paid tribute to his own prudence in contributing to the rise of their resistance. Bismarck, he believed, was unlikely to compromise Prussia by an "act of desperation." The question of the principalities, Beust stressed, was more important as a "basis for our entente." As for Britain, while expressing his support for Paris, he left it to Napoleon's wisdom to decide whether it was the right moment to resume negotiations with that country.[36] Satisfied with Beust's reply, Napoleon thought it useful to continue their exchange of thoughts.[37]

A few weeks later, Beust suggested that French support in the Danubian Principalities might influence public opinion in the monarchy in favor of an Austro-French entente.[38] It was obvious that, by pressing for closer cooperation in the east, he was primarily thinking of making the Hungarians more receptive to the idea of an Austro-French alliance. They would also support the army reorganization program.[39] Therefore, he stressed, relations with the Hungarians must be prudently fostered.[40]

The treaty-bargaining gained momentum in May when Francis Joseph, no doubt on Beust's advice, "initiated" Count Vitzthum, the newly designated minister to Brussels, into the confidential negotiations and placed the diplomat's "leisure" at Napoleon III's disposal.[41] Most probably Beust procured Vitzthum's appointment to the Belgian capital so that he could be sent to Paris without arousing wild speculations as often as the foreign minister deemed necessary.[42]

Orczy, of course, informed Andrássy of the new development. The Hungarian premier's brooding uneasiness over Beust's activities, which included covert kindling of passions in the North German Confederation and South Germany, to which Bismarck reacted in like manner,[43] was heightened by Vitzthum's mission. Andrássy considered it a needless provocation. This confidant of Beust, who appeared to have no scruples of conscience, inspired intense antagonism and distrust in Andrássy.[44] Although Beust's latest moves warranted strong reaction by Andrássy, the premier out of caution and his natural tendency to hesitate held back in anticipation, no doubt, of Bismarck's countermeasures.[45]

Instead of making his opposition felt in the strongest possible fashion, Andrássy decided to bide his time. To Orczy he made his indignation clear: "It is not for us to make a pretext for setting France and Prussia at odds. By the Peace of Prague it is no concern of ours how Prussia carries out the operation of unification. . . . We should not intervene in this."[46] It would be a few months before Andrássy adopted different tactics with Beust. His present strategy was evident from his concluding remarks to Orczy: "If we could talk with Bismarck frankly, we should be telling him that we do not waste our time on the process of German unity, but we object strongly to his meddling in our affairs."[47] It is obvious that Andrássy was waiting for the most opportune moment to strike against Beust before Austria and Prussia came to blows.

Alive to the domestic limitations on his German policy, Beust directed Vitzthum to employ prudence in his talks with the French.[48] Growing impatient with Vienna's hesitancy, the French emperor on July 3 expressed his regret to Metternich that Austria and France had not yet reached an understanding with a "determined objective." Napoleon made clear his concern about two factors that might still prevent a formal alliance — Hungarian opposition and South Germany.[49] Heartened by the assurances Metternich gave him in reply, Napoleon on July 20 asked the ambassador explicitly whether an Austro-French "active alliance" with a "common, specific end" were possible for the sole purpose of reestablishing Austria's dominance in Germany. If not, would Austria consider a "passive alliance" in support of an international congress to guarantee the present status quo in Europe.[50]

Once more Beust temporized by pointing out that an offensive alliance with a foreign power would serve only to alienate the Germans from Austria and enhance Prussia's prestige all over Germany.[51] Beust preferred to make a diplomatic issue out of general disarmament.[52] He correctly calculated that Bismarck, busy organizing the military system of the North German Confederation along Prussian lines, would certainly reject any limitation on armament. The issue could lead to a diplomatic victory, and in case of war, moral responsibility would rest with Prussia.[53]

Napoleon agreed to consider Beust's counterproposal, though he feared that disarmament could make him fall into a Prussian trap,[54] and as always he questioned the reliability of the Hungarians.[55] He urged Vienna first to pass the army act because, "before talking about disarmament, one must be armed and you are not."[56] Meanwhile he commissioned his minister of state, Eugène Rouher, to draw up an aide-mémoire on the subject in utmost secrecy.

The Rouher plan of September 24 proposed a ten-year period of "effective and serious disarmament," which would benefit France and work to Prussia's disadvantage.[57] Paris solicited British support for the plan but in mid-October Lord Clarendon, the prospective British foreign secretary, told Napoleon that the disarmament scheme "would only serve to make war more inevitable."[58] Clarendon's opposition was unqualified, so the matter of disarmament was dropped.

After the failure of his disarmament proposal Beust worked out a new basis for an understanding with France. He chose the "Eastern Question" for this purpose. After some hesitation Napoleon accepted it as a point of departure.[59]

Meanwhile, as the year wore on, Austro-Prussian relations deteriorated steadily. Through much of 1868 the rivalry between Beust and Bismarck led to a number of incidents. Andrássy viewed the worsening relations between the two states with much concern. Beust seemed to let no opportunity slip to irritate Bismarck. His open support for King George of Hanover, and the publication of documents relating to the war of 1866 and the Tauffkirchen mission in the first *Red Book* (February 1868) occasioned angry press polemics.[60] Beust's speech at the German Hunters' Festival in Vienna (July 26–August 2), in which he emphasized "Austria's sympathy with Germany,"[61] only added fuel to the flames.

It was foolish of Beust, whose participation in the festival and speech showed a grotesque disregard for practical realities. The *Pesti Napló,* obviously with Andrássy's encouragement, denounced Beust for meddling in German affairs and reminded him in the same breath that ventures contrary to Hungary's interests "will be energetically and firmly thwarted."[62] Beust realized that his *faux pas* had compromised him in Andrássy's eyes — the last thing he wanted. Beust needed the premier's support, not his hostility. Realizing the full implications of what he had done,[63] Beust hurriedly wrote Andrássy a letter to explain away his conduct. Characteristically, he took refuge in the equivocation that came naturally to him. He disclaimed all chicanery or artful stratagems, and protested his goodwill and friendship for Andrássy.[64] His intention was to induce Andrássy to disavow the Hungarian offensive, but Andrássy refused to do so. A truce was called but the damage had been done. Beust could not hide from the outside world the deepening rift between himself and Andrássy.[65] It had yet to be seen whether taking him down this small peg would chasten him, but Andrássy was too much of a realist to pin his hopes high.

A few weeks later, depressing intelligence about a disarmament memorandum of Beust and Vitzthum showed the Hungarian premier the Austrian chancellor had not changed his policy.[66] Andrássy tried again to reason with Beust but to no avail. In mid-October Andrássy complained acidly to Kállay: "Unfortunately, Beust has begun to flirt with France again and is saying that the South Germans cannot be completely abandoned yet."[67] He added emphatically: "We must dissuade him from this course and secure ourselves in the east."[68] He also felt it necessary to allay Prussian suspicions: "In the event of a Franco-Prussian war there is only one safe course to follow, to remain totally neutral, because then the Prussians could be persuaded to stop the agitation they are stirring up in some parts of Rumania, Bohemia and Hungary."[69] Speaking to Orczy at the end of October, he reiterated his position: "We must declare openly that we want full neutrality. If we preserve peace by this means, so much the better; we need tranquility to put our own house in order and at least we are a threat to no one."[70] At the same time he made it clear that in the event of a Franco-Prussian war he would do the utmost to prevent the intervention of a third power, referring primarily to Russia. "This way we also give proof of our goodwill toward France."[71] His reasons were excellent, and closely bound with the consolidation of the Hungarians' position in the monarchy, ·and the latter's recovery and security, which he felt threatenened from the east. It was obvious that Andrássy was looking to come to new terms with Beust but for the moment his attention was distracted by urgent matters elsewhere.

As the winter approached, the Cretan embers flared up again and the ferment in the Danubian Principalities attained such proportions that it threatened to lead to a European conflagration. A nationalist ministry in Bucharest under Ion Brătianu mounted an irredentist campaign against Hungary,[72] no doubt with the tacit approval of Prussia and Russia.[73] The Rumanian agitation caused great concern in Hungary. Feelings ran high on both sides, and the heated polemics between the Hungarian and Rumanian press that had been going on since the previous summer only swelled the tide.[74] Reports of Rumanian rearmament with Prussian arms[75] and of troop concentrations on Hungary's Transylvanian border[76] added fuel to the fire.

The Hungarian government took the situation very seriously. Andrássy demanded positive but conciliatory diplomatic action.[77] Beust, while ostensibly in accord with Andrássy, in reality exploited the situation ruthlessly. It is fair to point out that Beust too recognized the danger of Austria's position in the east,[78] but the fact remains that his primary interest, due to understandable emotional factors, was to solve the German problem. In the Rumanian crisis he saw a superb opportunity to realize an Austro-French entente and to involve Prussia in a conflict over eastern issues.[79]

Beust therefore instructed Metternich to advise Napoleon that an alliance directed toward the east admitted a more desirable *casus belli* against Prussia than the Rhine, for it "might develop into a war that would yield significant results."[80] For good measure he noted that in this area Hungary's support was assured, and if war broke out in the Balkans, Britain would probably support the allies. Prussia would then have to choose between abandoning its ally Russia and intervening at the cost of losing the support of German public opinion. Beust also suggested drawing Italy into the alliance scheme,[81] but while the idea of Italy's participation was favorably received, the eastern theater did not suit the French. It would result in "fragmentation of the French forces,"[82] declared Rouher. Napoleon wanted a treaty on the Rhine, while Vienna was shy of involvement in the west.[83] Nevertheless, negotiations including Italy were started on the lines proposed by Beust.

Beust, of course, knew he had to watch his step not to antagonize Andrássy further. Apparently to placate the Hungarian premier and blind him at the same time to his real motives, Beust made a number of remonstrations in Bucharest.[84] Simultaneously he moved to increase the apprehension of the Hungarian and Austro-German liberal leaders by exaggerating the extent of Prussian and Russian involvement in Rumania.[85] The Austrian press was inspired to mount a vicious campaign against Prussia, accusing it of turning Rumania into an "arsenal of arms" and so posing a threat to Austria-Hungary.[86] Beust's speeches and remarks to diplomats harped on the same theme.[87] For even greater effect he made use of the *Red Book*. In the November edition he published a series of highly colored reports by Austrian diplomatic agents to show that the situation in Rumania was really explosive.[88]

There can be no shadow of doubt that, by denouncing Prussia and Russia for disturbing European peace, Beust aimed both to detach Andrássy from his Prussian bias and to win him over to his own policy.[89] Apparently Beust thought that, since Andrássy's worst anxieties were over the east, he could lure him into supporting an Austro-French alliance if it was confined to that region. Furthermore, he hoped to arouse anti-Prussian sentiments in Austria and the South German states.

But Andrássy, whose distrust of Beust was by this time ineradicable, was not taken in. The evident closeness between Vienna and Paris, as well as the contradictory policy of rather mild remonstrations in Bucharest and the furious public campaign against Prussia, lent color to Andrássy's suspicions.[90]

It is not that he believed Bismarck to be innocent. On the contrary, Andrássy was convinced that along with the Russians he was deeply involved in the Rumanian affair. But with statesmanly acumen he understood that Bismarck was using Rumania mainly as a counterweight to Beust's policy. Yet the Rumanian irredenta was a threat to Hungary for which Andrássy held Bismarck accountable.[91]

Bismarck's famous saying that the Balkans "were not worth the bones of a single Pomeranian grenadier" did not mean that Prussia had no interest in the area.[92] At this stage of the diplomatic game Rumania played a special role in Bismarck's energetic struggle against Austria.[93] The South Slavs, especially the Serbians, were also included in his calculations.[94] It was not, of course, his intention to accelerate the national movements in the Balkans but to manipulate them in Prussia's interest.[95] Unhappily, the intransigence of the Rumanian national movement toward Hungary had almost spoiled everything. Berlin became quite uneasy about the possibility of alienating the Hungarians.

To prevent this, Thile suggested to Bismarck on November 4 that "perhaps it would be advisable to send a note to Bucharest to call off" the press polemics with Hungary's newspapers.[96] On November 10, worried by new reports of Rumanian agitation in Transylvania, Thile inquired of Bismarck whether for the Hungarians' sake it would be wise to warn Bucharest off these activities.[97] With Bismarck's approval, a notice was sent on November 14 to Prince Charles through the Prussian ambassador to have him end nationalist agitation in Transylvania "because the Hungarians are our friends and, if the Rumanian papers (the 'Étoile d'Orient' etc.) continue to stir up the Transylvanian Rumanians, they will inevitably be driven into a hostile camp." The note stressed in particular that "serious danger threatens Rumania only on Austria's part because it is its natural interest to expand in that direction. Thus it is even more indispensable for you not to irritate Hungary."[98]

This noteworthy differentiation between Austria and Hungary was not only a strong indication of deepening antagonism between Bismarck and Beust but also a patent demonstration of Prussia's appreciation of, and interest in, Hungary.

Andrássy, who was evidently aware of Berlin's growing irritation with Brătianu's dangerous pretensions, thought it opportune to try to force Bismarck to reveal his true intentions. Through the good offices of Marquis Gioacchino Pepoli, the Italian ambassador in Vienna, he declared "that Hungary is in complete sympathy with Prussia's national policy . . . and will not impede the pursuit of its aims in Germany." To this Andrássy added the warning: "If Prussia supports anti-Hungarian efforts in the Danubian Principalities, then the Hungarian government will have to look for necessary support in Vienna and Paris."[99] At the same time Andrássy adopted a conciliatory attitude towards Rumania. He had Marquis Pepoli, Charles's uncle by marriage, write to the prince urging him to respond in kind because Hungary and Rumania had to depend on each other in face of Russia's advances.[100]

Bismarck's alternative was now Bucharest or Pest. He chose the latter. Bismarck realized that in the last resort the Hungarians would be a more effective force in neutralizing Austria than Rumania. He also realized that cooperation with Rumania offered him nothing but liabilities: it would turn German sentiment against him and force the Hungarians into his enemies' arms. Worse yet, the agitation for a Greater Rumania that had already brought Prussia into conflict with the Great Powers entailed a grave risk of war — the last thing Bismarck wanted.

Reacting to the situation, Bismarck initiated another vigorous press offensive against Beust with an article in the *Norddeutsche Allgemeine Zeitung.* This shrewdly calculated article treated France very amiably but took Vienna severely to task. Blame for the Rumanian complications was placed on anti-Hungarian commentaries in the Austrian newspapers. The article also contained a sharp warning to Rumania, accusing it of endangering peace.[101] A day later, on November 22, in a strongly worded telegram, Bismarck saw to it that Prince Charles silenced his troublesome ministers,[102] thus cutting the ground from under Beust. It now appears, contrary to the assertions of some historians,[103] that in the end not Beust but Andrássy and Bismarck emerged the victors.

Andrássy's well-timed intervention was no doubt one of the major factors behind Bismarck's change of heart to the advantage of Hungary. By abandoning the Rumanians, Bismarck defused the crisis and made it possible for Andrássy to maintain his neutral posture. At the same time Bismarck spared himself the necessity of having to take sides in a possible conflict between Austria and Russia.

In addition, Bismarck once more outwitted Beust in the Balkans by promoting an international conference that compelled the Greeks to drop their support of the Cretans. Without the aid of Greece their revolt fizzled out.[104] Beust's hopes for settling the German question in the east also vanished.

The most serious turn in Austro-Prussian relations had still to come. Beust's latest *Red Book,* appearing on November 21, did much to poison the atmosphere.[105] Bismarck and Thile could not conceal their anger and resentment at this new and uncalled-for provocation.[106] As a result, Bismarck's press offensive against Beust grew in intensity and the latter responded with equal vehemence.[107]

This unfortunate development accentuated the discord between Andrássy and Beust, and a new incident in December led to an open breach.[108] It was the result of two articles published in the *Pesti Napló* that declared that Hungary, like Austria, would regard Prussia's crossing the River Main as a *casus belli.*[109] Since Bishop Danielik, the author of the articles, had been a member of the Deák Party, and the paper was considered its organ, they created an international sensation.

Beust and his circle in the foreign office were elated. It seemed to them that here was a hint of change in the attitude of the Hungarian leadership toward the German question. Press releases advised foreign correspondents and the local press to treat the Main line issue as the *Pesto Napló* had done.[110] It goes without saying that the French ambassador happily transmitted the "good news" to Paris.[111]

But Danielik's articles did not represent the views of Andrássy or the majority of the Deák party. István Tisza blamed the small right-wing faction of the Deák party, comprised of aristocratic Old Conservatives, who were close in sentiment to the Court party.[112] Beust himself appears to have maintained close contact with this group.[113] In a sober and realistic report Marquis C. Castellane, the French consul general in Pest, warned Paris it would be a mistake to take the articles in the *Pesti Napló* as an expression of the dominant views of the Deák party.[114] Stationed in the Hungarian capital, Castellane was in a better position to judge Hungarian domestic politics than Gramont, who took delight in criticizing the consul general's opinions.[115] Only a few days earlier Andrássy, who had a cordial relationship with Castellane, had made it clear to him that France should expect no military aid from the monarchy.[116]

Andrássy was not to be swayed from his original position. On his insistence the Deák party disavowed Danielik's articles. A notice was published in the *Pesti Napló* to the effect that the articles were a private opinion. This created much consternation and confusion in the foreign office.[117] Beust complained with chagrin to Orczy that he had been made a laughing stock, for the denial in the *Pesti Napló* amounted to saying that he himself had inspired the articles. He asked Orczy to plead with Andrássy to tone down his disavowal.[118]

In his reply to Orczy, Andrássy, alluding to principles involved, said the forthcoming parliamentary elections made the denial necessary. He stressed that an issue such as the Main line could become a dangerous weapon in the hands of the opposition, especially since Beust himself had expressed views in the delegations diametrically counter to Danielik's articles.[119] Andrássy's answer failed to soothe the chancellor's ruffled feelings. He urged Orczy to press Andrássy again to make some sort of gesture in his behalf.[120] The Viennese press complicated the situation by treating the whole controversy mockingly, suggesting that in reality Andrássy was already foreign minister.[121]

Andrássy now saw fit to make an effort to shed a softer light on his disagreement with Beust. He commissioned his friend Miksa Falk, a distinguished journalist, to restate the Hungarian position.[122] Falk's noteworthy article, appearing in the *Pester Lloyd* on Christmas Eve, was couched in firm terms and was an eloquent reflection of Andrássy's views. It emphasized that the Main line was not an obsession of Andrássy and that he was by no means fired with bellicose spirit. The writer argued that Austria could not make war without Hungary's rich resources and that Andrássy could not consent to war on any issue save one that threatened the integrity of the monarchy. For good measure he added: "Beust is an intelligent statesman; *he certainly wants only what he can have; and he can have only what Hungary wants* [italics supplied]. Hence there exist no such differences as to prompt us to break with Beust's policy."[123]

Falk also lashed out against Bismarck. His Rumanian decision had lessened but not eliminated Hungarian bitterness and suspicion toward Prussia.[124] Bismarck's press war with Beust seemed to many to be directed against the integrity of the monarchy.[125] Falk warned him peremptorily not to lay hands on Hungary. Austria and Hungary, he went on, closely united would repel any hostile action on Prussia's part.[126] Bismarck's reaction was to express his sincerity and loyalty towards the Hungarians. Instead of a tirade, a flood of exceedingly cordial reassurances were his answer at all levels of communication.[127]

In Beust's case, contrary to Andrássy's expectations, the situation was not taking the turn he had hoped for. The chancellor was in a panic. He spoke bitterly to Orczy against the Hungarians who made his "position untenable."[128] The ugly tone of the Austrian press, accusing Andrássy of interference in foreign affairs,[129] made matters worse.

At Orczy's request, Andrássy came to Vienna at the end of December. To Orczy, who welcomed him on his arrival on December 30, Andrássy expressed irritation at the suggestion that Beust should be given some satisfaction. He criticized the chancellor "whose German policy is inciting all the powers against us." It was natural, Andrássy continued, for Prussia to resent Beust's agitation in southern Germany, where the monarchy, unable to defend itself against Prussia, would be forced to retreat ignominiously. Quite excited, he concluded: "I shall resign rather than let myself be involved in such a shameful defeat."[130] Andrássy's anger seemed to suggest that he suspected Beust to have inspired Danielik's articles.[131] Yet no such proof has ever been discovered. For fear of losing his temper, Andrássy refused to visit Beust first.[132]

Avoiding the chancellor, he went straight to Francis Joseph. There he restated his views in detail and explained the dangers inherent in Beust's policy. He emphasized again the necessity of Austrian neutrality in case of a Franco-Prussian showdown. Andrássy argued impressively for an eastern-oriented foreign policy. According to Orczy, his clever reasoning and sincerity brought Francis Joseph round to his way of thinking.[133] Following this meeting, Andrássy had an exchange of ideas with Beust in which they reached an understanding on a mutually acceptable policy.[134] Andrássy was equally anxious to convince the French ambassador that, if France wanted allies, it would have to look elsewhere. He told Gramont bluntly: "Do not believe half-words and half-promises, because whoever utters them in your presence is lying."[135] There was no doubt about the Hungarians' peaceful intentions, Gramont reported to Paris. "Hungary's program is 'peace at any price,' and when Hungary wants peace at any price, it is evident that Austria cannot want war."[136] Marquis Castellane's speculation the previous October that "Count Andrássy's growing authority in His Majesty's councils might soon perhaps force the chancellor of the monarchy to reckon with his colleague"[137] had become a reality. Andrássy was now the most powerful political figure in the Dual Monarchy.

Of no less concern to Andrássy was the deterioration of Austro-Prussian relations, which by the end of 1868 had become critical. The mutual recriminations of Beust and Bismarck in the press gave the Hungarian leadership the impression that Bismarck's attacks on Beust were also directed against the integrity of the monarchy. To stave off the threat, besides his steps to awe Beust into keeping Austria unentangled and to dispel any French illusions about an alliance, Andrássy also made his misgivings known to Berlin through several channels. His purpose was to take the steam out of Bismarck's offensive.

Andrássy made his first contact through an old friend, Count Scherr-Thoss, who was about to leave for Berlin on a business trip at the end of December. He entrusted Scherr-Thoss with the task of speaking with "important persons" during his stay in Berlin about his fears that the press war against Beust and Prussian agitation in Hungary might have "bad consequences" for Hungarian-Prussian relations. Scherr-Thoss was to point out that, as long as Andrássy was premier, Hungary "would do nothing to prevent Prussia from crossing the Main line." He was also to emphasize that any attempt to sow discord between the dynasty and the Hungarians would be resisted. Bismarck received Scherr-Thoss on January 2, 1869, and after listening to him, declared that not only had he not sent agents provocateurs to Hungary but he had even threatened the Rumanian government that, if it did not end its anti-Hungarian agitation within two weeks, he would be forced to recall his legate. Bismarck then revealed the mystery of the alleged "Prussian agitators" in Hungary.[138]

Bismarck followed this up with an assurance that Prussia had no interest in stirring up dissension between Hungary and Austria. Prussia, he went on, wanted the Austro-Hungarian monarchy powerful, so that they might in future enter into an intimate relationship. Austria-Hungary was of great value to Prussia, he stressed, but such feelings were not yet understood in Austria, as evidenced by the anti-Prussian intrigues of Beust and Metternich. Sooner or later there would be war with France, he averred, in which Prussia would be victorious. Perhaps after that the Germans and French would learn to be good neighbors. By an interesting coincidence, Bismarck, like Andrássy, expressed the conviction that the real future enemy of "civilized Europe" would be Russia, which only a European coalition could withstand. When Bismarck returned again to the problem of Viennese machinations against Prussia, Scherr-Thoss assured him anxiously, "Andrássy will use all his influence to put an end to these intrigues." He coupled this remark with a plea that "Bismarck should stop the 'war of pens'." After due reflection, Bismarck agreed to do so.[139] Sure enough, a few days later Bismarck unilaterally halted his press attacks.[140]

Meanwhile, Andrássy used the opportunity offered by a conversation with Werther on January 6 to express his apprehension about alleged Prussian connections with the opposition in Hungary. Distressed by the strained relations between Vienna and Berlin, Werther was the last person to play down the gravity of the situation.[141] Nevertheless, within a week Werther sought out the premier with assurances from his government to "dispel the suspicions" of Andrássy.[142]

Additional pressure was brought on Berlin through the premier's protégé Kállay. In mid-January Kállay visited Dr. Rosen, the Prussian consul general in Belgrade, and during their conversation Kállay asked whether Rosen thought the attacks of the semiofficial Prussian press were directed against the integrity of the monarchy. Kállay emphasized, evidently with the intention that it should come to Bismarck's ears, that "the integrity of the monarchy is of vital importance for Hungary." It had been questioned, he went on, whether the attacks on Beust were aimed at the monarchy's existence. "Hungary has a great deal of sympathy for Prussia, but in this case," Kállay warned, "the duty of self-preservation would force it to take the field heart and soul against Prussia."[143]

Rosen reported the conversation to Bismarck, who, significantly, responded at once that Prussia nurtured no hostile thoughts against the integrity of the Austro-Hungarian monarchy. The press campaign was being used only to curb Beust's provocations.[144] After Rosen had communicated to him the substance of Bismarck's message, Kállay assured him in acknowledgment that under no circumstances would Hungary aid an attack on Germany and, in the event of a Franco-Prussian war, it would remain strictly neutral.[145]

Bismarck's repeated demonstrations of support for the dualist system and expressions of friendship for the Hungarians enabled Andrássy and his circle to understand better the ulterior motives for the chancellor's attacks on Beust. At the same time they strengthened the position of the Hungarian leadership on Beust's foreign policy. Without detracting from the sincerity of Bismarck's sentiments toward the Hungarians, his continuous support of them turned out to be one of his most successful short-term investments. The Hungarians paid him the dividend of denying Austria the chance to take the field on France's side against Prussia during the fateful summer of 1870. Beust tried without surcease to sway the Hungarians from their Prussian orientation,[146] but his failure to restore his credibility with Andrássy rendered these efforts futile.

It soon became clear that Beust was acceding to Andrássy's demands only in appearance. Despite the agreement he had reached with Andrássy at the beginning of the year, Beust continued a steady exchange of diplomatic confidences between Vienna and Paris. Italy also joined the discussions.

Rouher's note of December 30 served as the point of departure for the negotiations. By its terms the French accepted the east as an area for an Austro-French entente on condition that the aid and assent of Italy should be secured.[147] To cover up his tracks, Beust insisted on the utmost secrecy and urged a detailed agreement so that at the crucial moment an exchange of telegrams would suffice to turn the understanding into an alliance.[148] Out of this emerged a French treaty project on March 1, 1869. The draft provided that in case of an Austro-Russian war France would deploy an observer corps along the Rhine and would come to Austria's aid if Prussia joined Russia. The quid pro quo was that in the event of a Franco-Prussian war Austria would mobilize and would enter the war if Russia intervened on Prussia's side. In either case, Italy would furnish a contingent of 200,000 men in return for specified concessions.[149]

This proposal was essentially acceptable to the Austrians. It "binds us very little and strangles Emperor Napoleon,"[150] Metternich wrote with evident pleasure. In repeated exchanges of notes certain stipulations of the treaty project were modified. In none of the preliminary drafts, however, were the participants' full intentions revealed. Beust, more careful than ever before, continually reminded Metternich to include nothing in the records that would upset the "sensibilities" of the Hungarians and the "sentimentality" of the Austro-Germans.[151]

Beust realized that before proceeding further he would have to obtain Andrássy's assent, and an unexpected development seemed to give him his chance. In early March 1869 both Beust and Andrássy joined the monarch on a visit to Agram (Zagreb), the capital of Croatia. Andrássy used the occasion to approach Francis Joseph on the complete abolition of the military frontiers which he regarded as "an everpresent tool with which the reactionary circles in Vienna may undo Hungary's new status the first opportunity they get."[152] Supported by Beust and the military, Francis Joseph refused to discuss the issue for the time being.[153] Beust, however, in need of both Hungarian and military support for his policy, changed his position within days and took a neutral stand.[154] On March 11 he tried to persuade Andrássy to approve the French project, but the premier vetoed such a treaty.[155] According to Orczy, Andrássy would side with France only if Prussia and Russia entered into an alliance.[156]

Undeterred by this setback, Beust continued his efforts to find a workable solution in the hope he could still make a deal with Andrássy. He would yield to Andrássy on eastern issues only in return for the premier's support in the west.[157] But Andrássy was unmoved. "Andrássy wants to avoid a French alliance," Kállay noted, "and concentrate the monarchy's energies wholly in the east."[158] Not even flattering messages from Napoleon on the need to agree on common policy could change Andrássy's mind.[159]

Finally, after tortuous negotiations, the representatives of the three parties produced a draft treaty on May 10, 1869. In it the three governments bound themselves merely to pursue a common policy and in the event of a European war to conclude an offensive and defensive alliance, the conditions to be settled at that time.[160] A final arrangement could not be concluded, however. Italy demanded the withdrawal of French troops from Rome, whereupon the alliance lost its attraction for Napoleon and he broke off negotiations. Because of domestic difficulties, clerical support was apparently more important to Napoleon than any diplomatic alignment. In the end the three sovereigns contented themselves with an exchange of assurances that amounted to a "moral" alliance. Only Napoleon promised armed assistance to Francis Joseph if Austria-Hungary were attacked.[161] Thus the projected Triple Alliance against Prussia and Russia came to little.[162]

As an epilogue, diplomatic communications between Vienna and Paris continued and military missions were exchanged to give some effect to the "moral" alliance of Francis Joseph and Napoleon. In February 1870 Archduke Albrecht visited Paris with a plan that envisaged a joint military operation by the allies against Prussia. The allies would invade South Germany, each with an army of 100,000 men. The main allied striking forces would be concentrated behind this screen, strengthened with South German troops. The decisive battles would be fought in the vicinity of Leipzig and peace terms would be forced on Prussia in Berlin.[163]

In June General Lebrun paid a return visit to Vienna with a French plan, which called for a simultaneous declaration of war by Austria, Italy and France.[164] Francis Joseph made it clear that the simultaneity envisioned in the French plan was politically and militarily impossible. He added, however: "If Emperor Napoleon . . . entered South Germany not as an enemy but as a liberator, I should be forced to make common cause with him."[165] Neither Francis Joseph nor Beust could go against Hungarian and Austro-German opinion inside the monarchy. Thus nothing was settled and when the Franco-German War broke out in July 1870 France and the monarchy were not in alliance.

The Hohenzollern Candidacy

By the summer of 1870 both France and Prussia were ready for a decisive trial of strength. The conflict was precipitated by French mishandling of the candidacy of Prince Leopold of Hohenzollern-Sigmaringen for the Spanish throne.[1] On the eve of the crisis Europe had the appearance of tranquility,[2] but the calm was to vanish in a flash.

On July 3, the fourth anniversary of Königgrätz, the news of Leopold's acceptance of the Spanish crown was all over the French capital.[3] In Paris government and public were both surprised and shocked. Three days later Gramont, since May the French foreign minister, read a declaration to the Chamber of Deputies that France would not permit a foreign prince on the throne of Charles V and would "know how to discharge ... [its] duty without faltering or weakness."[4] It seemed to foreshadow military action by France unless the candidacy was withdrawn.[5] Although Prince Leopold's father, Karl Anton, renounced the throne in his son's behalf,[6] the French insisted that King William I of Prussia should issue a statement renouncing the candidacy of his house for all time. In the talks that followed the famous interview at Ems on July 13, both Napoleon III and Bismarck showed themselves willing to allow the power struggle between France and the North German Confederation to be settled on the battlefield.

As the crisis unfolded, there was little opportunity for the Dual Monarchy to offer anything but largely empty diplomatic gestures. Surprised by the fast pace of events and paralyzed by internal dissension, the monarchy was relegated to being little more than a mere bystander. Yet Austria and the other great powers, Britain, Italy and Russia, were far from inactive. They all had something to say, all made some efforts to cure or if possible exploit the deteriorating situation — and they were all too late.

Although news of the Hohenzollern candidacy surprised Pest and Vienna, there was at first some hesitation in government circles and the press of both halves of the monarchy to take the affair seriously. At least not until the details of Gramont's "very stiff declaration" of July 6 were received.

Andrássy was conscious of the general state of tension prevailing in Europe and realistic enough to appreciate its dangers, but initially he betrayed no outward nervousness. His attention was ostensibly focused mainly on the parliamentary debate over a proposed law to reorganize local government.[7] It is evident, however, that behind his appearance of calm resolution there was a great deal of anxiety and uncertainty.[8]

Beust's attitude was no different. The "explosion of the Spanish bomb" did not at first alarm him and on July 5 he still saw no reason why he should not leave for his usual summer vacation the next day.[9] Beust could not, however, hide his uneasiness about the unexpected development. In a telegram to Metternich the same day, Beust expressed his regret over the Spanish affair and instructed the ambassador to keep him fully informed.[10] A day later he assured the Prussian ambassador that his government would remain neutral in any eventual conflict,[11] though the assurance was meaningless, for, following a meeting with General von Schweinitz, he sent another telegram to Metternich that "news of our proposed neutrality in the press is totally false."[12] Then at the request of Paris he agreed to assist France to reach a peaceful diplomatic victory by directing warnings to Berlin and Madrid to abandon the candidacy.[13] In response to an inquiry by Napoleon whether Francis Joseph could be counted on, the Austrian chancellor replied cautiously: "We are first loyal to engagements consecrated by imperial letters, which excludes any entente with Prussia. We are also loyal to our policy of intimacy and friendship toward France." Then he added pointedly: "We are trying to avoid anything that jeopardizes peace. Our attitude will be governed subsequently by the way things develop."[14]

The press reflected the calm of the monarchy's leading statesmen. *Hon* (Fatherland), the organ of Tisza's Left-Center party, mentioned the effect of the Hohenzollern dispute on the Viennese stock exchange but made no comment on the gravity of the situation.[15] The incident had been blown out of proportion, the *Pesti Napló* insisted, and it ventured the optimistic opinion that it would be forgotten within a few weeks.[16] For the *Neue Freie Presse,* Vienna's leading paper, it appeared to be a childish affair that would not seriously imperil European peace.[17]

By July 9 the chancellor of the Dual Monarchy was thoroughly alarmed by Gramont's bellicose declaration of July 6 in the Chamber of Deputies. Beust's situation became unhappy in the extreme. All indications were that Paris was fully determined to force a military decision of the issue.[18] Worse yet, the French seemed equally resolved to drag Austria into the struggle. Paris was apparently under the illusion that it would receive all-out aid from Austria. Gramont informed the council of ministers that Austria had promised to station an observer corps on its frontiers with Prussia.[19] At the same time, well aware of Vienna's anxiety about its eastern flank, Napoleon and Gramont tried to reassure Austria that it should not worry about Russia.[20]

Gramont's continued optimism about Austrian policy was no doubt due partly to the impressions he had formed during his nine years' embassy in Vienna. Partly it was fed by the reports of the French chargé d'affaires, the Marquis de Cazaux, who was temporarily in charge until the arrival of Prince la Tour d'Auvergne.[21] On July 9, Cazaux telegraphed Gramont: "In spite of the rather vague terms of Beust's instructions to Prince Metternich, my impression is that France can count absolutely on the chancellor, whatever the circumstances may be."[22]

Beust sensed danger in Gramont's statement to the council of ministers. To the outside world it might appear there was a prearranged deal with Paris.[23] In desperation Beust telegraphed Metternich: "The French government's method of proceeding completely paralyzes us. They give us one surprise after another. . . . It seems to me that by recklessness they have spoiled a magnificent position. . . . Gramont's words to the council were thoughtless."[24] In a dispatch the same day he interpreted Austria's obligation as nothing more than a promise not to conclude a separate treaty with Prussia and to give France diplomatic support. He also stressed that "public opinion in Austria also has to be managed and won over by wise measures. We cannot jump from one extreme to another, especially with no apparent motive."[25] Beust added: "They must understand that we must have time to find a pretext . . . to put out not only abroad but also in this country."[26] It is impossible to explain Beust's motives as wanting nothing but peace. While issuing one warning after another to France asserting his right to retain a free hand, he always inserted remarks that generated false hopes in Paris.

Gramont seemed to pay no attention to Beust's protestations. Quite apprehensive, Beust, while reiterating his earlier position, reminded the French chargé d'affaires: "The French government must remember that I shall walk with France, I shall not follow it."[27] To make sure that Paris understood him, Beust asked that Baron Bourgoing, the secretary of the French embassy in Vienna, be sent to warn Napoleon and

Gramont of the danger of exposing Austria through indiscretion.[28] Beust's trusted negotiator Vitzthum was also sent to Paris to try to reach an understanding with the French leaders.[29]

In the meantime, discouraging news continued to pour in from Paris.[30] Prompted by the ominous tidings from the French capital, Beust in a dispatch to Metternich declared on the evening of July 11 that Austria would not intervene unless Russia allied itself with Prussia. In a war limited to France and Prussia, Austria would remain neutral unless and until it was decidedly in its interest to enter the contest.[31] But this explicit letter, which would have made Vienna's position clear to the French leaders, was never passed on to Gramont.[32] It is evident that Beust intended to use it to cover his tracks in case the war ended badly for France.[33]

In a postcript to it, the chancellor chided Metternich for alluding to the secret agreement in his report of July 8. He advised the ambassador to be more careful in dividing his correspondence in two parts, one for his cabinet and Count Alfred Potocki[34] as well as Count Andrássy, the other for him and Francis Joseph.[35] It appears that Beust had no intention of honoring his agreement with Andrássy about Austria's foreign-policy objectives. Worse still, Beust's action was in clear violation of the law.[36]

A telegram of the Italian chargé d'affaires in Vienna, who met Beust on July 12, gives fresh evidence of the way the chancellor's mind was working. He told Curtopassi that Italy should accept the French proposal of a military alliance against Prussia once a definite settlement had been reached on the Roman question, which interested him for reasons of internal policy. To make the alliance even more attractive, he hinted at the possibility of satisfying Italian aspirations on the Austro-Italian frontiers.[37]

Beust's recklessness was tempered, however, by the French failure to consult him and provide him with the necessary pretext for rendering Austrian military aid.[38] Not surprisingly, therefore, when on July 13 he received news about the withdrawal of the candidacy and the new French demands for additional assurances from Prussia, Beust immediately cabled Metternich to urge the French government to accept the withdrawal without further ado.[39] That same morning William I of Prussia and Benedetti, the French ambassador, had their famous encounter at Ems. By the evening Bismarck had sent the edited version of the celebrated Ems telegram, in which the king gave an account of the meeting, to the newspapers, which published it on the morning of July 14.[40] War seemed absolutely inevitable; the Austrian statesman "was preaching to deaf ears."[41] Still there was a moment of hope that a congress would be called to avert open hostilities. Beust's instant readiness to mediate was, however, not taken advantage of.[42] The French rushed heedlessly ahead.

The Hungarian premier, in the meantime, was being kept regularly informed of the latest developments through Orczy's reports. An ominous communication from Orczy disclosing the background of Gramont's July 6 sword-brandishing performance deeply impressed on Andrássy the gravity of the situation.[43] Now that he had read the text of Gramont's declaration for himself, the premier realized that a Franco-Prussian War might well be imminent. His already acute apprehension about the possibility that Austria might be drawn into the long-brewing struggle was reinforced by Orczy's report that on July 8 Gramont had told a cabinet meeting that Austria would station an observer corps along the Prussian frontier.[44]

In the first flash of alarm, taking the same position as he had during the Luxemburg crisis of 1867 that Austria should stay clear of involvement in German affairs, he wrote emphatically to Orczy: "Only the policy of neutrality serves our interest."[45] It is evident that this was not intended merely for home consumption. "Hungary must prevent any military actions by Austria aimed at recovering its German status,"[46] Orczy told Schweinitz. After receiving the same information, the Italian chargé d'affaires reported that French efforts to bring Austria to war with Prussia were gaining ground. The sole obstacle, he stressed, was the Hungarians' opposition.[47] In an obvious reaction to a similar statement by Orczy, the French chargé d'affaires nervously exclaimed: "Have you thought over well what grave consequences a Prussian victory would mean for you?" When Orczy replied that it was another important reason for avoiding adventurous policy, Cazaux exploded threateningly that "France might make peace at the expense of the Austro-Hungarian Monarchy."[48] Just about the same time another report reached Andrássy from Orczy about the missions of Bourgoing and Vitzthum with the disheartening information that Beust was still leading the French on and making promises that he could not possibly fulfill.[49] Of equally great concern to Andrássy were the newspaper reports and the emotions they aroused in both halves of the monarchy. The nation was worried and restive. Reflecting the national mood, two questioners in Parliament, Ede Horn and Count T. Csáky, demanded a statement from the premier about the policy and aims of the common government, and expressed the fear that Vienna might already have taken irrevocable steps to aid France.[50]

These interpellations paralleled Andrássy's own qualms. More than anything else, Austria's vulnerability to French pressure preyed on his mind. There were the members of the Court party, the emperor and Beust, whose interventionist penchants posed a grave threat to the preservation of Austrian neutrality. Andrássy knew the monarchy could expect no political or economic gains commensurate with the sacrifices it would have to make if it joined France against Prussia. Furthermore, the monarchy was militarily unprepared, and public opinion was overwhelmingly opposed to joining a war against Prussia. Above all, victory or defeat could only detract from the position Hungary had attained in 1867.[51] Bismarck's secret communication to him confirmed his fears in this direction.[52] It was therefore with a particular sense of urgency that he hastened to allay the deputies' anxieties. Correct as always, Andrássy cleared the reply he intended to make with Beust.[53]

Late in the morning of July 14, Andrássy hurried to Parliament. There was an air of expectancy in the lower house as he rose to answer the questioners. On mounting the rostrum, his first care was to make clear that he regarded Parliament's desire for information as natural. Then addressing himself to the questions raised the previous day, he said: "The principal interest of Austria and Hungary in the present crisis has been the preservation of peace. The foreign ministry has been working in Berlin, Paris and Madrid along lines that seem especially conducive to the maintenance of peace."[54]

Andrássy went on: "By virtue of our laws, it follows as a matter of course that the common foreign ministry has to carry out its duties in such grave matters as this in concurrence with the ministries of both governments [of the monarchy]."[55] There was thus no danger, he declared, that the monarchy could be involved in a war without the consent of the Hungarian Parliament. The deputies of all parties evinced their satisfaction in a lively manner.[56] Andrássy had achieved his purpose: the nation had been reassured and its representatives had given their wholehearted approval to the policy that Andrássy had expounded. The premier's last remark, in spite of its diplomatic finesse, contained a well measured warning to Vienna that no policy but one of peace and neutrality was acceptable to Hungary. It was also an ingenious way of responding to Bismarck's confidential message. Beust understood the admonition. As Curtopassi pointed out, "the opposition he [Beust] is experiencing from the Hungarians" was restraining the chancellor's inclination to commit Austria to France.[57] If Russia intervened, the Hungarians would be only too willing to fight, Schweinitz reported.[58] These considerations appear to have continued to determine Andrássy's position on all the crucial questions now confronting the policymakers of the Dual Monarchy.

On July 15, the day after Andrássy's statement in favor of peace to Parliament, the French government reached its final decision for war.[59] Shortly afterwards, Gramont told Vitzthum: "War has been decided." He added: "If Austria understands its own interests it will march with us."[60] Andrássy learned that same evening that a virtual state of war existed between France and Prussia. Therefore on the morning of July 16 he hastened to Vienna to prevent developments contrary to his avowed policy of peace and neutrality. The premier knew enough from Orczy's reports not to trust Beust's intentions. He arrived in the Austrian capital full of strength and confidence, and with good reason.[61] Behind him he had left a united nation. Before his departure the premier had conferred with the leaders of the Deák party, who declared unanimously for strict neutrality.[62] Andrássy could thus speak in the councils of the monarchy from a position of unquestionable strength, a fact that was recognized not only by Vienna but also by the leading statesmen of Europe.[63]

By the time Andrássy reached Vienna, the clamor for a declaration of neutrality was at a new pitch in both parts of the Dual Monarchy. Its general popularity was tremendously encouraging to the Hungarian premier, and at the same time clear enough to Beust and the Court party that they scarcely needed to be reminded of it. Certainly, the domestic and international situation would have made it extremely difficult, if not impossible, for Vienna to pursue an openly aggressive policy.

It is evident that public opinion was a fairly constant and, on certain occasions such as the Franco-Prussian confrontation of 1870, even a determining factor in the foreign-policy decisions of the Dual Monarchy. In Hungary, both before and during this conflict, it seems to have served to advance both Hungarian and imperial interests simultaneously.

Magda Kégl and Diószegi, who concerned themselves with Hungarian public opinion during the July crisis, failed to reach satisfactory conclusions.[64] Both historians were, it seems, borne along by the ideological currents of their times: the conservative 1930s with its German orientation, and the Marxian socialist 1960s responding to France's attempt at accommodation with Eastern Europe. So their evaluations are frankly partisan and their interpretations in sharp conflict.

Kégl saw Hungarian public sentiment reflected in the contemporary press as decidedly pro-Prussian.[65] Newspapers were indeed the most effective vehicle for expressing public opinion, but by concentrating on newspapers that would support her thesis, she was forced to argue on the basis of partial evidence. Consequently, the case she advanced ends by misrepresenting public sentiment.

Diószegi also relied on contemporary newspapers but he was more cautious than Kégl. He seemed to feel that, because of its elusive character and the difficulty of arriving at acceptable conclusions, the depiction of the state of mind of any country, but especially of Hungary during the summer crisis of 1870, is a highly complex problem. In an attempt to avoid controversy, Diószegi concentrated only on the feelings of the Deák party and concluded emphatically that the "Hungarian ruling strata" were "unreservedly pro-French." His thesis was very definite: "The two main slogans of the Deák party were francophilism and neutrality."[66] He failed to differentiate between sentiment and viewpoint or saw them as virtually one and the same thing.

On top of all this, Diószegi tried to persuade his reader that national sentiment was synonymous with that of the Deák party. He cited the Prussian ambassador to this effect. Schweinitz, who had held his post only since the end of 1869, had noted: "The Hungarians are pro-French, only Count Szécsény speaks courageously and smartly in our interest."[67] But this is just as superficial as Diószegi's own opinion. Schweinitz was thoroughly familiar with the reports of the Prussian consul general in Pest, Wäcker-Gotter, who mentioned several pro-Prussian members of the Deák party, including General Klapka whom he hailed as "our most sincere friend." Since he had assumed his new position in the Austrian capital so recently, Schweinitz should have paid attention to these firsthand reports. His stay in Vienna was too short for him to become familiar with Hungary's internal politics, and the interests and ambitions that lay behind them. His judgment was evidently based on the pro-French articles in the Hungarian press and on rumor, and things looked black. His reports on Austria during those early days of the crisis were equally overstated. Schweinitz had witnessed the enthusiastic pro-Prussian demonstrations in Vienna and heard the Austro-Germans' loud demands for strict neutrality friendly to Prussia, yet "he felt as if he were in the enemy's country." He sounded the alarm so often that he almost drove his king to despair.[68] Finally, a highly irritated Bismarck stepped in and advised him what to do.[69]

To be sure, Diószegi unwittingly contradicted Schweinitz's opinion and his own when he indirectly admitted elsewhere that Tisza's Left-Center party was not at all pro-French but rather pro-Prussian.[70] Indeed it was.[71] In one of his reports, Wäcker-Gotter represented the Left-Center as the "party that has the greatest sympathy for Prussia."[72] With 140 deputies in the lower house of Parliament, the Left Center commanded the support of one-third of the nation. That substantially reduces Diószegi's suggested nationwide pro-French sentiment.

Notwithstanding the pro-French, and to a certain extent anti-Prussian, trend in most of the Hungarian press, Diószegi's version of the Deák party's "unreservedly pro-French" sentiment cannot be sustained either. At issue is not the existence but the extent of genuine sentiment for France. There can be no doubt about its presence both within and without the Deák party, deeply rooted in cultural and ideological affinity. The francophilism of the Deák party's small left wing was especially noticeable. With hostilities certain, its mouthpiece, *Reform,* coupled denunciation of Prussia with expressions of fervid support for France: "Every Hungarian patriot, who has at the same time just a little consideration, will follow the victory of French arms with wholehearted joy."[73]

Why then this pro-French tide, and the apprehension rather than hostility toward Prussia, in other papers like the *Pesti Napló?* Nothing but ignorance, suggested Halász.[74] Partly it was a function of the indifference Andrássy often showed. There was no inspired press that he could exploit to his own advantage.[75] Occasionally, to be sure, he commissioned well-known journalists to sketch his foreign-policy views through their papers. On such occasions, however, he strove for the greatest possible effect, as for example at the time of the *Pesti Napló* affair in December 1868.[76] His own governmental press office did not receive a steady flow of directives, had no carefully screened personnel, and was not kept under constant supervision. As a result the most vehement anti-Prussian and pro-French articles were often written by its members, and the premier would be the last to know about them. To Andrássy's embarrassment, the Prussian minister once reminded him of this fact.[77]

Partly the answer was also that most Europeans, including the Hungarians, were under the delusion of French invincibility.[78] The Hungarians' most immediate concern was to keep the victor's favor through gestures of sympathy, which cost them nothing. Thus, to a large extent, self-interest seems to have exaggerated francophilism.

A major reason is contained in the *Pesti Napló's* reaction to the Hohenzollern crisis. As already indicated, it was pro-French and rather apprehensive towards Prussia. "The right is on Napoleon's side,"[79] the paper had argued. A few days later, as the crisis became acute, the *Pesti Napló* explained its position: "Those who have a touch of feeling for the preservation of the European balance of power and see in the need to maintain it the possibility of the peaceful development of nations must at the same time admit the legitimacy of France's action."[80] Here the paper appears to have sympathized with France because it feared that, if the balance of power shifted further in-favor of Prussia, it would be encouraged to annex Austria's German provinces and so deprive Hungary of protection against hostile neighbors. The *Pesti Napló* had often voiced its opposition to such a development: "Even if the Pragmatic Sanction did not exist, we would not like it if, for instance, the Prussians were to advance to the Leitha instead of the Main."[81]

The final reason may be found in Wäcker-Gotter's report of December. "In their enmity toward Russia," wrote the Prussian consul general, "all Hungarian parties are united, and every hint of an understanding between Russia and Prussia would have the result that our friends in this country would become mute . . . and our enemies vocal."[82] The crisis had shown Prussia on the closest terms with Russia, and what Wäcker-Gotter predicted happened. The Italian chargé d'affaires reported sagaciously that the Hungarian press, anticipating Russian intervention on Prussia's side, had begun "to exhibit its sympathy toward France."[83] In other words, the Hungarian press was demonstrating its outrage toward Russia and Prussia through increased cordiality toward France. An explanation of this was provided by the *Pester Correspondenz:* "Russia's ally, whoever it may be, will be against us. Hungary has only one natural enemy and that is Russia. We will fight her wherever we may find her." It went on: "Whoever our ally against Russia may be will be welcomed."[84] It is clear that, since France would have to fight Russia, should the latter intervene in the forthcoming contest, France would be Hungary's ally. The *Pesti Napló* had enlarged on this theme a few years before: "If it were certain that Prussia would renounce its traditional friendship for Russia, we would advise any government commonly or exclusively conducting Hungary's foreign affairs to ally itself with Prussia," but otherwise to "be against the Prussian the moment he joins with the Russian."[85] Thus, without Russia as a disturbing element in the calculations, it seems quite possible that pro-Prussian sentiment would have been, if not dominant, at least on a par with pro-French sentiment, even in the Deák party.

As for Andrássy, a realist, he had sentiments only for Hungary, and for the Dual Monarchy as its bulwark against hostile neighbors.[86] Pro-French trends in the Hungarian press were thus a false portent. Public opinion made press sentiment irrelevant. The pressure of crisis most of the time generates emotional and practical unanimity or near unanimity — that is, it creates predominant sentiments and points of view. Usually both factors are united in their demands and actions. In Hungary during the July crisis, however, sentiment was one thing and viewpoint another. The sentiment, though it was touching, provided France with no help. The viewpoint was rational and practical, and it offered Prussia advantages. It came out strongly for strict neutrality. This viewpoint appears to have been the work of Andrássy, who had shaped and most effectively advocated it during the preceding years. Ever since the Luxemburg Crisis of 1867, he had kept hammering away at the necessity of remaining neutral in the event of a Franco-Prussian war[87] until he succeeded in winning the public over to his view.

The Hungarians were aware that they owed their success in the constitutional compromise of 1867 largely to Austria's defeat in 1866. They were not about to endanger their recently won position by a war of uncertain consequences. Bismarck, through a confidential agent, drew Andrássy's attention to the danger that, if Prussia were defeated by France with Austrian help, Hungary would have to choose between either the scrapping of the dualist arrangement or becoming independent only to be submerged in the "Slav-Rumanian ocean."[88] Very much alive to this, Andrássy dreaded a French victory which would surely be exploited by Austria. To avoid such a development, Andrássy was ready to thwart any military action by Austria aimed at recovering its German predominance.[89] The French chargé d'affaires in Vienna assessed the Hungarian position quite realistically: "The Hungarians clamor for the maintenance of neutrality. . . . They desire no extension of Cisleithania to break the equilibrium that exists today between the two parts of the monarchy."[90]

The moment war seemed imminent, Andrássy came out unhesitatingly for a policy of neutrality, which was echoed by the press.[91] The *Pesti Napló* invented the slogan: "Neutrality, namely, neutrality at peace."[92] This was seconded by the *Pester Lloyd*[93] and the *Hon,*[94] both of which demanded that the monarchy declare its neutrality real, not armed, neutrality. The majority of the press took the same stand.

Among the larger papers only the *Reform,* serving the small left wing of the Deák party, identified itself consistently with Beust's "policy of a free hand" by calling for armed neutrality.[95] This meant that under this cover preparations for war could be completed, and Austria might join France at the right moment against Prussia. Without premeditation the left wing of the party thus advocated a stand similar to that of its pro-French conservative faction.[96]

This was clearly contrary to the foreign-policy views of Andrássy, who desired German unification under Prussian leadership,[97] and hence "the policy and necessity of Austrian neutrality"[98] in the present Franco-Prussian confrontation. But as has already been indicated, there were conflicting tendencies in the faction-ridden Deák party, and the spokesmen of each could and did air their opposing views in the press.[99] It is beyond doubt, however, that the party's leadership, including Deák and Eötvös, supported Andrássy's policy of neutrality. Answering a question by the Left-Center deputy Keglevich, Deák himself made it pointedly clear to the Lower House that the government party did not identify itself with the anti-Prussian and pro-French statements of the so-called Deák party papers. He firmly rejected the notion entertained at home and abroad that the Deák party had any official organ.[100] Since Keglevich, expressing apprehension over the anti-Prussian and pro-French views of the press, had referred specifically to the *Pesti Napló,* Deák's statement meant the dethronement of this paper as his party organ. The views advanced by the *Pesti Napló* cannot therefore be regarded as the expression of the standpoint of the majority of the Deák party.

Not surprisingly, the pro-Prussian Left Center, in spite of its conceptual differences with Andrássy over Hungary's position within the monarchy, was more united in its support of the premier's policy of peace and neutrality than was his own Deák party.[101]

Public opinion in Hungary showed itself overwhelmingly in favor of strict neutrality, in full agreement with Andrássy who as in the past years insisted on making it contingent on what Russia might do.[102] The *Pesti Napló* emphasized that Russia's entry into the war would drastically alter the monarchy's foreign policy.[103] The *Pester Lloyd* said that Austria should abandon its neutrality only "if Russia intervenes."[104] On July 16, to the suggestion of John Jay, the United States ambassador in Vienna, "that, if Russia were to intervene in the war, Hungary would be ready to fight with a will," Andrássy gave his "emphatic assent."[105]

Since developments so far suggested that it would be a "localized" Franco-Prussian war, Andrássy insisted on a declaration of neutrality.[106] The premier's manifestly strong hand in dealing with the Court party was further reinforced by the sentiment and point of view of the Austro-German liberals and nationalists.

Unlike Hungary, Austria was deeply divided politically in the summer of 1870,[107] and the July crisis aggravated the existing situation by creating new divisions. The staunchly pro-French Court party made no secret of its eagerness for revenge on Prussia and showed its readiness to run the risk of war. "Everyone who wore uniform was enchanted with the idea of avenging Königgrätz,"[108] observed Przibram. "In aristocratic circles here, there is no want at all of voices that feel the occasion ripe for taking revenge for Königgrätz,"[109] the well-informed Saxon ambassador to Vienna reported. The Austrian bureaucracy took the same line.[110] Had the foreign policy of Austria depended on the Court party, the monarchy would have mobilized its army already in the early stage of the crisis. The Court party found considerable support among the Slav races of the monarchy, especially the Czechs, who resented and feared German domination in the Austrian half of the Dual Monarchy.[111]

The state of Austro-German liberal-nationalist opinion was, however, a serious obstacle to intervention against Prussia. As the crisis moved toward the point of no return, the *Neue Freie Presse* made the view of the *Verfassungstreue Partei* unmistakably clear: "The slogan of Austrian policy must be absolute neutrality."[112] Cazaux reported to Paris that the rest of the Viennese press, with a few exceptions, was either strongly in favor of neutrality or fervently pro-Prussian in sentiment, and definitely hostile to the idea of an Austrian alliance with France.[113] The generously measured Prussian bribes to the notoriously corrupt Viennese press no doubt accentuated its pro-German support.[114] Bismarck also advised the Prussian ambassador to try to get in touch with Austro-German youth in order to incite them to rebellion if necessary to prevent Austrian intervention on the French side.[115]

According to Cazaux, the Austro-German liberals feared that a victorious war against Prussia on the French side would prompt and enable Emperor Francis Joseph and the Court party to suspend the constitution and reestablish absolutism.[116] Furthermore, though unsympathetic to the Junker-dominated Prussia of the Hohenzollerns, the Austro-German liberals abhorred the idea of participating in a new *Bruderkrieg*.[117] They would not go against the German national movement. "Where the German defends his fatherland against the foreigner, our sympathy is also with him,"[118] the organ of the *Verfassungstreue Partei* declared.

The French declaration of war threw the Austro-German liberal-nationalists into unprecedented emotional uproar. While the government was still officially undecided, important bodies, including the municipalities of Vienna, Linz and Brünn (Brno), as well as various organizations in dozens of cities and towns presented resolutions to the emperor demanding a policy of strict neutrality friendly to Prussia.[119] Students organized demonstrations and collections for German wounded, and a good number of them volunteered to enlist in the Prussian army.[120] Though for different reasons, the Hungarians and the Austro-Germans thus had similar aims.

In marked contrast to the Austro-Germans and the Hungarians, the wartime sympathies of the major Slavic nationalities of the Dual Monarchy were decidedly pro-French.

The attitude of the Czechs seems to have been determined by their uneven struggle to secure autonomy for the lands of St. Wenceslaus (Bohemia, Moravia and Silesia), and by the rising specter of Pan-Germanism.

The Austro-Hungarian Compromise of 1867 had shown the Czechs that they could expect meager understanding from Vienna and little or no help from other Slavic groups in either Austria or Hungary. They would have to look elsewhere for help in their struggle for national autonomy within a federalized Habsburg monarchy. As early as 1860 Palacký felt that the Czech nation must secure allies against the Germans, particularly among the Slavs and the French. He confided to his son that "the defense of our national interest cannot take place in the Germans' lands. . . . We are therefore forced to turn to the French and Russians just to be heard."[121]

In their attempts to establish contacts abroad, the boldest gesture of Czech political leaders like Palacký and his son-in-law, František L. Rieger, was their journey to Moscow in 1867 on the occasion of the Pan-Slav Congress.[122] The highlight of their visit to Russia was the audience granted to the Czech delegation by Alexander II at Tsarskoe Selo on May 23, 1867,[123] but the Czech leaders failed to gain the tsar's moral support. Moreover, their journey aroused a storm of protest in the Austro-German press and governing circles.[124]

Following their visit to Russia, the Czech leaders turned their eyes toward France. When Prince Napoleon visited Prague in 1868, he received Palacký and Rieger, who tried to enlist France to mediate the Czech-Austrian dispute. The prince was sympathetic but noncommittal.[125] In mid-1869, Rieger went to Paris where he vainly sought help from Napoleon III, himself in desperate need of assistance from Vienna. The next year again, on the eve of the Franco-Prussian War, Rieger addressed a memorandum (the text of which leaked out) to the

French ambassador in Vienna, arguing in the interest of a strong and federalized Austria as a counterweight to the Prussian-German danger.[126]

In view of this, it is not surprising that, when the Franco-Prussian War broke out, the Czech leaders, both the spokesmen of the conservative nobility and of the National party, distinctly favored France, and benevolent neutrality was the least they expected from the foreign ministry.[127]

But the Czech leaders, by boycotting both the provincial diet of Bohemia and the *Reichsrat,* had maneuvered themselves into an awkward position by the late spring of 1870. Consequently they were deprived of any direct influence on the foreign policy of the Dual Monarchy. Their negative attitude, while it accentuated their demands for recognition of their historical rights, considerably weakened the pro-French elements in the *Reichsrat.*[128] The Czech leaders were reluctant to put France above their own national aspirations, take their seats in the *Reichsrat,* and support those more friendly to France than to Prussia.[129] The French disaster at Sedan moved Palacký deeply,[130] but he felt that whatever followed the Second Empire could only be more auspicious for the French as well as the Czechs. To one of his French friends Palacký expressed his belief that the French nation would rapidly recover its moral and physical strength.[131] He felt a Latin-Slavic alliance now a certainty against the Germans.[132]

Indeed, in spite of France's defeat, as time went on, the special Czech-French connections, which played so great a part in the disintegration of the Dual Monarchy little less than fifty years later, continued to become closer.

Like the Czechs, the Poles in Galicia expressed fervent pro-French sentiments. In spite of this, public opinion showed itself strongly in favor of unarmed neutrality. The Poles felt that no positive good for Galicia could result from the war. Galicia needed a long interval of peace in order to consolidate the political gains of the previous years and to regenerate Polish national strength.[133] Moreover, a strong, victorious Austria might encroach upon the newly gained Polish autonomy,[134] and in the case of Prussian victory "it would be only a matter of time before Galicia and Hungary would be swallowed up by Russia."[135] Thus the Poles were motivated by similar reasons and aims to the Hungarians'.

Among the southern Slav nationalities the Croats, especially the anti-Unionist and anti-Hungarian elements, although pro-French in outlook, aimed to advance their own national cause. The nationalist newspaper *Zatočnik* in an editorial in late July 1870 called on the *Grenzer* (the soldier-settlers of the Military Frontier Districts) to take advantage of any involvement of the Dual Monarchy in a foreign war to realize their national aspirations.[136]

In view of all this, the attitude of the Austro-Germans, the Hungarians and the Poles, as well as the possible repercussions of a foreign war in Croatia, dimmed the prospect for any other policy for Vienna than nonintervention.

Once it became known that to all intents and purposes a state of war existed between France and Prussia, attention was focused on Austrian policy.

Understandably France pursued the most active Austrian policy. The French were shocked to learn how gravely they had misjudged their diplomatic position. It had been believed in Paris that the attitude of Russia and Britain would favor France, and that Austria as well as Italy would enter the war on the French side.[137] These assumptions now appeared to be illusory.

Still the French hoped by threat or cajolery to bring Austria into the conflict. Knowing from experience that the opposition of Hungary was the major obstacle, the French leadership was ready to coerce the Hungarians into cooperation by creating disturbances in the Danubian Principalities.[138] But such tactics only deepened Andrássy's distrust of the French.[139] The representatives of France in Vienna compounded this with their overbearing and ill-advised arrogance: "The French are angry with me and are uncivil,"[140] wrote the enraged Andrássy to his wife. Naturally, both Beust and Andrássy issued stern protests against the French behavior.[141]

Gramont seemed to have little faith in the French pressure tactics because on July 17 he wrote directly to the Hungarian premier pleading for prompt action on Austria's part. Trying to gain Andrássy's support, he emphasized: "The motive for the war is not a German cause; it rests entirely on the dynastic ambitions of the King [of Prussia] and the procedures he has used to conceal from the eyes of his people the actual failure of his German policy." He assured Andrássy that France was not waging a war of aggression against Germany, that its intention was merely "to reduce the ambitions and the size of Prussia and to escape from the state of unease created by its earlier aggrandizement." As an inducement, Gramont drew Andrássy's attention to the benefits of the French campaign if aided by Austria.[142]

The French foreign minister also wrote a persuasive letter to Beust the same day, hoping to bowl the Austrians over with his enthusiasm and promise of great success. "If you aid us, if you permit Italy to move 70,000 to 80,000 men into Bavaria through your territory, if you send 150,000 into Bohemia, and later raise 200,000 to 300,000 more, then peace will be signed in Berlin, and with one glorious stroke you will efface all the memories and all the consequences of 1866." He then proceeded to describe in glowing terms France's military preparedness and the enthusiasm of its army, and ended by inviting Beust to come to a preliminary agreement that would be concluded "while the troops are advancing." [143] In view of the internal political situation, however, the only thing Beust could do to aid France was to keep Prussia on tenterhooks by trying to avoid issuing a declaration of neutrality.[144] But the latter was precisely what Andrássy pressed him to do.[145]

If the interest of France was in the widening of the war, St. Petersburg aimed to localize it, not so much for Prussia's as for its own sake.[146] The Russians were seriously alarmed at the possibility of a French victory in cooperation with Austria, a victory that would bring in its wake the revival of the Polish question.[147] Alexander II therefore summoned the Austrian ambassador, Count Bohuslav von Chotek, and after an impassioned plea for an Austro-Russian understanding, made some very conciliatory offers. The tsar told him that he would stay neutral so long as the Austrians remained at peace and avoided causing difficulties in Poland. He even guaranteed Austria's territorial integrity in the name of the Prussian king, promised to secure an Austrian protectorate over southern Germany, and undertook to keep his hands off the Danubian Principalities. Alexander strongly stressed, nevertheless, that, if Austria took threatening military measures, particularly in Galicia, then he would immediately take countermeasures, including concentrating troops along the Austrian frontier.[148] Beust, however, preferred to keep a free hand, and Andrássy remained deeply suspicious of Russia's real motives.[149]

The localization of the war was also Prussia's overriding concern. Bismarck was confident that without outside intervention Prussia could defeat the French. In his judgment Austria was the touchstone, because its understanding with France was close, and the two had repeatedly discussed contingencies like the one that had arisen. Bismarck, who earlier had referred to these serious negotiations as "conjectural rubbish,"[150] could not at this time afford to take a chance. Therefore on July 14 he sent a last-minute inquiry to St. Petersburg through the Russian ambassador, Baron Paul Oubril, whether, if Austria joined the French, Russia would come to Prussia's assistance.[151] The tsar's reply reached Bismarck on July 16, promising that, if Austria declared war on Prussia, he would concentrate an army of 300,000 men on the Galician frontier to paralyze the forces of the Dual Monarchy.[152] In a letter to William I, Alexander later repeated this promise and added that he had formally guaranteed Austria that a victorious Prussia would not move against it.[153] Bismarck at once accepted the tsar's assurances. "We have no interest in seeing the Austrian monarchy collapse and in involving ourselves in the insoluble question of what should take its place."[154] In a reassuring message to Andrássy, he again disclaimed any design of detaching German Austria.[155] The further course of events would now depend on Austria.

VI

The Council of Common Ministers of July 18, 1870

Now that France and Prussia to all intents and purposes were at war,[1] the all-important question confronting Vienna was the policy Austria-Hungary was to follow amidst opposing domestic and international influences. The conflicting views of the policymakers of the monarchy had a full airing at the Council of Ministers for Common Affairs in the Hofburg on July 18 under the presidency of Francis Joseph.

Attending were the ministers of common affairs, the prime ministers of Austria and Hungary, and the inspector general of the common army.[2] Thus all the major political interest groups with a voice in the shaping of the monarchy's foreign policy were represented in the council.

In numbers, the representation of the Court party was the most significant in the persons of Francis Joseph, Minister of War Franz Freiherr von Kuhn, and Inspector General Archduke Albrecht. Prime Minister Andrássy and Common Minister of Finance Count Menyhért Lónyay[3] were there to advance the viewpoint of the Hungarian liberals, and Common Foreign Minister Beust and Prime Minister Potocki, that of the Austro-German liberals. Naturally, the participants strove to promote the aspirations of the party they represented by integrating its viewpoint into the framework of their personal foreign-policy conceptions.[4]

The presence of Francis Joseph, who through the peculiar constitutional arrangement of the Dual Monarchy retained many of his absolutist prerogatives in the actual conduct of foreign policy, was of utmost importance. Well-founded sources unanimously attest that he was anxious for revenge.[5] "The Emperor desires war to compensate for Königgrätz,"[6] confided Andrássy to Kállay. On July 12 the monarch himself noted on the margin of a report describing French military preparations: "I beg to hasten banning the export of horses, lest we have no horses if the occasion arises."[7] A number of foreign diplomats also reported his desire to intervene in the war.[8] Beust himself admitted in the fall of 1870 that "the Emperor, the army, Austria even, wished to have their revenge."[9]

It has already been noted that the inspector general and the minister of war were among the leading proponents of a war of revenge.[10] Archduke Albrecht, who had recently visited France with a project for joint military action, returned from his mission with a rather unfavorable impression of the preparedness of the French war machine. Consequently he was quite anxious not to reveal the monarchy's military intentions prematurely. On July 12 Albrecht advised Beust that the monarchy must avoid anything that could be construed as provocation, including the concentration of troops.[11] Even the regular yearly maneuvers were abandoned for fear they might be interpreted as warlike preparations.[12]

The other irreconcilable, Kuhn, "the hotspur at the head of the War Ministry,"[13] considered the French army weak. In a memorandum of July 14 on preventing a speedy Prussian victory, he insisted that Austria intervene immediately, "even at the risk of setting all Europe afire," by sending 200,000 men to Warsaw against Russia, 200,000 to Berlin, and 200,000 to the Rhine to take William I prisoner. The monarchy would take as its prizes Bavaria, Württemberg, Baden, the Danubian Principalities and Bosnia. "Prussia on the Inn means *finis Austriae*,"[14] he prophesied.

Kuhn had based his strategic plan on the misapprehension that the common army was sufficiently prepared to undertake a full-scale war.[15] Other highly respected military experts like the ex-minister of war, Franz Freiherr von John, and Colonel Friedrich Ritter von Beck, head of the monarch's military chancellery, were strongly opposed to Kuhn's highly optimistic reports. Both John and Beck pressed on Francis Joseph most urgently that the army was in no state to take part in a war.[16]

Prime Minister Potocki of Austria, who had not yet participated in the foreign policymaking of the monarchy, was a *verfassungstreuer* great landowner who by predilection preferred the Court party. His attitude was thus anti-Prussian and pro-French. In spite of his Polish aristocratic background and the recent violent Russian attacks on him,[17] he was willing to cooperate even with Russia against Prussia.[18] At this juncture, however, bowing to Andrássy's strong pressure and clever reasoning, he agreed that the monarchy should stay neutral.[19]

Common Finance Minister Lónyay, an astute observer of foreign affairs but very limited in practical experience, belonged to the pro-

French conservative faction of the Deák party[20] that considered Prussia to be the major danger to the monarchy. He was only moderately anti-Russian. Lónyay looked forward to a French victory, but spurred by the Hungarian viewpoint, he rejected the idea of intervention. "God grant that the present war leave us untouched; we need peace badly,"[21] he wrote shortly after the council adjourned.

Foreign Minister Beust was one of the most important statesmen at the council whose interventionist tendencies matched those of the Court party. Due to his position, however, he had to chart a course that would not conflict with the interests of the Austro-German and Hungarian liberals who strenuously opposed a policy of intervention in favor of France.

Although Beust had misgivings about France for turning a Hohenzollern dynastic issue into a German national question that made an active anti-Prussian policy impossible,[22] he still hoped to profit from the situation. Like Russia's statesmen, Beust expected a French victory, but he strove increasingly to exploit it for the realization of his German policy. On the day the French government opted for war, Beust implied to Cazaux that he, unlike Francis Joseph and most of the ministers, would not be averse to provoking Russian — and hence Austrian — intervention at some future date. Speaking "very vaguely," Beust alluded to a plan that included among other things the resurrection of Poland.[23] The Austrian statesman had thus to scrutinize the prospects for the war and judge whether favorable internal and external conditions existed for changing the western war in the making into what he considered the optimum, an eastern war.[24]

Andrássy was without any doubt the other most important and also the most powerful statesman present at the council. His strength lay in the fact that by advocating a popular viewpoint, neutrality, he enjoyed mass support, while the Court party and its sympathizers did not.

Self-interest, stout opposition to a policy of revenge against Prussia, and fear of Russian aggression characterized Andrássy's attitude. Unlike the other members of the council, with the exception of Beust, the premier had an independent and purposeful concept of foreign policy. The various strategic plans he conceived were to answer the exigencies of both a western and an eastern war. To prevent Austria's participation in the Franco-Prussian war, he advanced a policy of strict neutrality. If complications arose in the east, if Russia intervened in behalf of Prussia, then the Dual Monarchy would have to fight. Andrássy's strategic considerations for dealing with the Russian danger were oriented to defensive purposes. His plans envisaged either a preemptive strike (which he feared to be forced into)[25] or a defensive-offensive strategy against Russia. In considering a suitable program of action, Andrássy had to weigh with care the pros and cons of his plans in order to ensure that no harm came to the vital interests of Hungary and the monarchy.

After Beust, Andrássy and the other ministers as well as Francis Joseph and Archduke Albrecht had stated their views, it emerged that all participants in the council favored a position of nonintervention.

In a broad scan of the situation, Beust defined the policy of the monarchy as *Passivitätpolitik*. He made it perfectly clear from the outset that Austria-Hungary was under no obligation to France. On the contrary, it was against Vienna's insistent advice that France had gone ahead and transformed the Spanish question into a German national issue. "For an alliance with France, it would first be necessary for us to reach agreement on all other points. But this has not happened and France itself has claimed that it has been surprised by events,"[26] Beust stated. The chancellor in effect stated that, since France had acted arbitrarily in spite of his warning, it had only itself to blame for going into the war unaided. It did not mean, however, that he had abandoned the idea of helping the French. Beust assured Cazaux fervidly: "I am your friend . . . even your ally, believe it well, an ally who has already given proofs of his sincerity and will do so again." Then he pleaded: "But let me do what is possible; let me ride out this flood of opposition which will perhaps spend itself."[27]

Faithful to his previous expressed convictions about the German question, Andrássy declared himself in favor of nonintervention. After expressing his qualms about Prussian agitation inside the monarchy and bitterly condemning French machinations in the Danubian Principalities, he stated firmly: "There are at the moment only two options open to us: either war with France against Prussia, or neutrality. We have not, however, been called to war in alliance with France, so only neutrality remains."

The minutes of the council reveal that Lónyay, after approving reference to Andrássy's views, likewise spoke in support of nonintervention: "The first thing we had to strive for was that no harm should befall the monarchy; deriving advantage from the crisis should be a secondary consideration. In the light of that, he also wished victory to French arms."

Count Potocki, Andrássy's Austrian counterpart, while expressing his personal sentiment in favor of France, admitted that he was bound by the pro-German sympathies of the Austro-German population: "If it was a question of peace or neutrality, he could not deny that, so far as public opinion was known, the former predominated in the German provinces. As prime minister, he felt obliged to recognize the sympathies for Germany that existed in Cisleithania." Then he warned that Prussian reverses would result in Russian intervention and occupation of Galicia, so Austria might as well decide for armed neutrality now rather than later.

Ignoring internal political factors, the revanchists gave up the idea of immediate intervention for military reasons. Francis Joseph resigned himself to provisional nonintervention because of the time factor. With the existing system of mobilization, he said, it would take six weeks for the army to be ready. Archduke Albrecht expanded on the time needed for the march to the theater of operations." In his esticall-up order was issued to when the men could be assembled at the mobilization centers [*Ergänzungsbezirke*], and it would take another fourteen days to get them to their regiments. To this should be added the time needed for the march to the theater of operations. In his estimation, "In the best circumstances, and if requisitioning horses went well, forty days would be needed." The complex and outmoded system of mobilization thus precluded prompt military action by the monarchy. Kuhn's arguments in favor of preparedness were based on his conviction that the monarchy would inevitably have to fight and that a Prussian victory was possible. Austria must therefore be ready "to throw its sword into the balance on France's behalf at the decisive moment." Albrecht, after once again citing the time factor, reminded the council about Russia, "which we must not forget while coming to our decision." He advised against immediate intervention because, accomplished strategist that he was, he knew that the strength of the monarchy alone would be inadequate against the eastern giant.

There was, then, unanimity on the basic issue: the monarchy could not at that moment go to war. But that was as far as agreement went. The council members differed quite substantially on the military and diplomatic steps to be taken in given circumstances.

During debate of the military course of action, four distinct points of view emerged. Beust voiced the first — passivity. "Anything that might even have hinted at deviating from the policy of passivity had so far been purposely avoided." At first glance it seems as though Beust was resolved to continue the policy of military inactivity, but the final question in his opening remarks reveals that he did not think passivity was a viable military course. "If one looked at the attitude of other states, that is, that of our neighbors in the east, it was a question whether the current policy of inaction could still be followed or whether it would not be preferable to put ourselves on such a footing that we would not be caught unprepared when confronted by events." From this, Beust's preference for the second alternative, military preparedness, is quite clear.

The second viewpoint was put forward by Andrássy. "The speaker, however, had in mind a state of neutrality similar to Holland's, which would allow us to make certain military preparations in order not to be surprised by events." The Hungarian premier explained the kind of military preparations he envisaged when he proposed that "horses and equipment should be bought, part of the army, *perhaps 300,000 men*[28] [italics supplied], readied, and other preparations made, so that we could be on alert within three weeks."[29] In other words, Andrássy favored "partial mobilization"[30] in order "not to be surprised by events."[31] Andrássy's plan for partial mobilization, however, was not what the members of the Court party wished, and it elicited a strong reaction. Francis Joseph himself launched the attack. After analyzing the state of the forces, the monarch stressed that "all this could not be done with only part of the army." He saw only two alternatives: either complete mobilization or inactivity. Albrecht's assessment of mobilization procedures underscored the monarch's contentions. Kuhn's comment that "war is inevitable for us," so "we must arm completely," was an indirect attack on Andrássy's plan in support of Francis Joseph's approach.

It is apparent that Andrássy's opponents realized the danger inherent in the Hungarian premier's alternative to their plan. Only general mobilization fitted in with the revanchists' ideas, for they were thinking in offensive terms, while Andrássy's considerations were defensive. The advocates of general mobilization could ensure the success of their own proposal only by discrediting Andrássy's partial mobilization plan. Indeed, the debate that ensued revealed the intensity of the feelings and irritation of the Hungarian premier's critics. This was obvious in Francis Joseph's initial remarks that he favored "complete mobilization" instead of "passivity."[32] Albrecht said emphatically: "If we cannot and do not wish to go into action by mid-September,[33] then no armaments are needed at all, but if we want to be ready by then, let us take measures immediately and energetically." The argument for general mobilization was expressed most explicitly, however, by Kuhn, who was "for immediate arming on a grand scale."

It has already been noted that Beust seemed to lean toward military preparations. When he spoke the second time, his remarks made it clear that he favored general mobilization. "We should secure ourselves against surprise by preparing for combat," he declared.[34] In his closing speech he was even more explicit: "When all is said and done, there is nothing for it but to mobilize." Beust thus supported the Court party.

A fourth alternative was suggested by Potocki when he made the point "that sooner or later we would come to armed neutrality." To this, only Andrássy reacted by stating "that he did not mean *neutralité armée* by the proposed neutrality." He reemphasized that he wished only "a partial mobilization of troops." Potocki's alternative, like "passivity" earlier, was disregarded.

It is to Andrássy's credit that he was the first to favor neutrality. It is curious, to say the least, that some Austrian and German historians have denied the Hungarian statesman even this credit on the flimsy ground that, since he was the first speaker — Beust had given only a routine introductory survey (to be sure, a detailed one) — it is natural that Andrássy should have been the first to advocate "neutrality."[35] This appears intentionally to disregard the questions Beust raised in closing his briefing: Should inaction continue or should preparations be made for any eventuality? It is evident that Beust ignored Andrássy's alternative because he did not include it in his calculations.

The council then turned to the other question of vital importance: whether the monarchy should issue a formal declaration of neutrality, and if so, how.

This issue was met with disapproving silence by the interventionist members of the council. Archduke Albrecht's negotiations with the French military specialists during the spring of 1870, the monarch's note in the margin of the report of July 12, and War Minister Kuhn's memorandum of July 14 show convincingly that they intended to enter the war.

On the other hand, reliable sources indicate that even before the council Andrássy, the advocate of the policy of neutrality, was in favor of such a declaration. Discussing the possibility of a Franco-Prussian war with Orczy in the fall of 1868, the premier had remarked: "We must declare openly that we want full neutrality."[36] Cazaux's report of July 17 shows that the Hungarian statesman remained true to his view.[37] It is evident that Andrássy approved the declaration of neutrality at the council, where he spoke about it as a question settled beforehand. He first mentioned it when describing the sort of neutrality he envisaged. It "ought not to be equated with passivity, but neither should it be declared as armed neutrality." He went on: "Without tying ourselves to any side, and after declaring our neutrality, we should offer as a motive our pure self-interest."[38]

Andrássy concluded by expressing the hope that Beust would find the opportunity to "make plain to the Prussians" that Austria would remain neutral as long as the war was limited to France and Prussia. It seems the Hungarian premier wanted a declaration of neutrality with a special clarification to Prussia. Apparently he hoped to gain Prussia's favor so that it would "desist from further agitation" in the monarchy. In discussing this proposal with Beust, Andrássy reminded him: "We must take care, because we have dangerous neighbors in Prussia and Russia." Andrássy thought, rightly, to be sure, that what was known in Berlin was also known in St. Petersburg. As for the other powers that posed no threat to Austrian security, Andrássy proposed "to admit openly to any who asked that we would not enter the war so long as Prussia was on its own."

Beust's attitude was by no means so unequivocal. Reliable documents indicate that up to the opening of the council he frowned on issuing a formal declaration of neutrality. Such a declaration would be a mistake, he told the Italian chargé d'affaires on July 15. "Because of the geographical proximity of Austria to Prussia and Italy to France," a declaration of neutrality by either Austria or Italy would amount to a gesture of hostility toward France.[39] A day later Cazaux was told practically the same thing:

> Come what may at this point, Monsieur Beust requested me to tell Your Excellency that, though he is under spirited pressure to issue an official declaration of neutrality, it is his explicit intention not to make this declaration. It is obvious, he told me, that on this question we cannot be Prussia's ally; if precisely on this basis we make this declaration, we would cease to be neutral, which would make it possible for the Prussians to withdraw their troops from their southern frontiers.[40]

Citing Andrássy's letter of May 1871, Wertheimer stated: "Beust has tried for two days to persuade him [Andrássy] to abandon neutrality."[41] Cazaux's report of July 17 supports this contention: "Count Andrássy is having frequent meetings with the chancellor, who hopes to bring him to a better disposition."[42]

Beust wanted to avoid issuing a declaration of neutrality because it could have been to the advantage of Prussia. His immediate aim seemed to be to retain French favor. By keeping Berlin in uncertainty about the attitude of the Dual Monarchy, he would be aiding Paris.

But whatever Beust had said before, at the council he supported the declaration of neutrality. Like Andrássy, he spoke about the issuance

of the declaration of neutrality as though it were a foregone decision:
"We must avoid everything that would give the impression of supporting France's enemies. Any declaration of neutrality would be of more
help to Prussia than to France, to which it must first be presented in
acceptable colors." His very next sentence shows his anxiety to keep
France's goodwill. "What matters now in this war, however, is that we
should secure ourselves against surprises by preparing for war, and
declare this without being provocative. It is of no importance what
name we give this declaration externally. Furthermore, we must
remain on good terms with Italy and, of course, with France, even
though we have to give the latter the bitter pill of a declaration of
neutrality to swallow." There is little doubt that, even though Austria
"could not march with France from the outset," Beust planned to enter
the war if the French were to win the initial encounters.

It is fairly clear that considerations of both domestic and foreign
policy played a part in Beust's attitude, but he seems to have attached
greater importance to the domestic aspects. When he spoke the second
time, Beust stressed that "he had intentionally confined himself for the
time being to discussing only the general situation and to making the
question of policy to be followed dependent on internal factors, for the
execution of the former would be conditioned by the latter." Three
days after the council, while defending his policy to the French, Beust
emphasized that neutrality was not declared out of choice but out of
necessity: "If at this time I declared myself against neutrality, I would
unite against me all of Hungary and all of the [Austro-]German liberal
party. I would not have either a cent or a man at my disposal."[43] Beust
cited the menacing pressure of Russia, "an ever more obvious enemy,"
as the external reason for the declaration of neutrality.

This leads to the important question when and why Beust changed
his position. Beust spoke against a declaration of neutrality to Curtopassi in the early evening of July 15 and to Cazaux in the afternoon of
July 16.[44] So as late as July 16, Beust was still opposed to the declaration, yet he spoke for it at the council on July 18. The change therefore
took place between July 16 and 18.

What prompted him to change his mind? It seems clear, from the
language of Beust's introductory survey, that he was not then aware of
Alexander II's offer to Prussia to concentrate a Russian army of
300,000 men to tie down the Austrian forces in Galicia, should the
Dual Monarchy decide to enter the war.[45] Beust's language at the
council betrays that he merely had general reasons for believing what
was indeed a strong possibility, that Austrian entry into the war might

lead to Russian intervention. Although the tsar made his promise of substantial manpower aid to Berlin, there was no evidence at this moment that Russia was moving forces to the Galician frontier.[46] Chancellor Gorchakov was quite candid when he declared: "Russia did not paralyze support that had no chance of being realized."[47] Anyway, Beust confided to Cazaux that he expected Austria's intervention to be prompted by Russia.[48] While mindful of Russia, it is obvious that Beust's decision was not dictated primarily by the possible threat from Russia. What was it then that made him revise his original position and integrate the idea of a declaration of neutrality into his foreign-policy line?

The question arises whether Andrássy had anything to do with the foreign minister's change of mind. The letter from Andrássy mentioned above suggests that he and Beust collided on the issue of neutrality. Two other documents point in the same direction and suggest that Beust and the Hungarian premier had come to an agreement on the question of neutrality before the opening of the council. Orczy indicated this in a letter to his mother on July 18,[49] and Andrássy himself wrote about it to his wife: "Beust was at first very rash. Right now, however, he is acting more correctly."[50] It is likely that this was when Andrássy and Beust agreed on a declaration of neutrality. Cazaux on July 17 reported "the not very reassuring news" that Andrássy arrived "in Vienna yesterday with the aim of taking up the matter [of neutrality] strongly with the central government in order to wring a formal declaration of neutrality from it."[51] Andrássy spent most of his time between his arrival and the opening of the council with Beust, his letter to his wife indicates.[52] All this strongly suggests that Andrássy's pressure was the major factor in making Beust change his position. With a united Hungary behind him, supported by the vociferous pro-German sympathies of the Austro-German liberals, Andrássy could not be ignored. Beust himself acknowledged this fact.[53] There were other background factors, too, such as Austria's military unpreparedness and the general political and financial chaos of the Dual Monarchy. The situation had seemed worse in 1866 when Austria burnt its fingers, and now in 1870, it appears, the members of the Court party would have liked to take the chance for revenge.

Andrássy's position was that, "if Russia were to intervene" on the side of Prussia, the Dual Monarchy "would have no choice." So to avoid this possibility, he suggested that the declaration of neutrality should be transmitted to Prussia by a "special note." Beust opposed this proposal because he did not trust the Prussians and because it would be to the disadvantage of France. He suggested the declaration should be effected through regular diplomatic channels in the form of a "circular note." The most spirited debate at the council turned precisely on this technicality. Both Andrássy and Beust spoke twice in favor of their own viewpoints. Andrássy argued that Prussia would reciprocate by ceasing its agitation in the monarchy aimed at preventing Vienna from entering the war on the French side.[54] Beust kept reiterating his view that a "special note" to Prussia would hurt the monarchy's prestige abroad without gaining anything in return from the Prussians. Finally Andrássy conceded to Beust's view and the argument came to an end.

What were the foreign-policy concepts and plans behind the council members' proposals? The concentric problems of their conflicting views lead to this central question. Because of the obscurity and complexity of the minutes of the meeting, the answer must be inferred from the document. An analysis of the proceedings of the Council of Ministers for Common Affairs in this manner helps to explain the participants' stances.

Andrássy's diplomatic and military proposals can only be appreciated in the light of the Russian-Pan-Slav problem, which was the mainspring of his foreign-policy ideas. Fear of Russian aggression emerges as the motivating force behind his suggestions. If Prussia's eastern ally intervened, Andrássy would have entered the war to thwart Russian ambitions, that is, to prevent a possible coalition of the Russian-Pan-Slav forces with the Slavic national movements in the Dual Monarchy.

Consequently, Andrássy's program of action consisted of four major phases: "wait-and-see neutrality," declaration of neutrality, partial mobilization, and finally counteraction.

"Wait-and-see neutrality" was a device that was simultaneously to achieve three objectives: first, to keep the monarchy in "watchful expectation" for "possible repercussions" in the east; secondly, to curb the revanchist ambitions of the Court party; and finally, to prevent making Prussia "feel itself threatened from the rear" so that it would not be provoked into a preemptive strike at the monarchy.

The declaration of neutrality, which Andrássy intended to make through a "special note," had to camouflage the monarchy's military preparations with regard to Prussia, in order to deny it "the excuse to move the theater of war onto our territory." It was also to serve as an inducement for Prussia "to desist from further agitation" within the Dual Monarchy. Finally, the "special note" was intended to warn

Berlin against inviting Russia to intervene because, "if a third power is drawn in," the Dual Monarchy would have to modify its position. The plan of partial mobilization was likewise a multipurpose expedient. Once completed, it was suitable for defense against both Russia and Prussia. In the event of a stalemate in the war, partial mobilization would have provided adequate forces for the monarchy to mediate peace.

Andrássy foresaw three scenarios for full-scale counteraction. The first was intervention by Russia, in which case "we have no choice"; the second, "Prussia and France will weaken each other to such an extent that we . . . can dictate peace to them as arbiter"; finally, a Prussian victory in the war.

With regard to the first possibility, Andrássy, deeply affected by the war psychology created by the crisis, feared a Russian attack on the Dual Monarchy. He confided to Kállay that "he does not want war [with Russia], but it will hardly be avoidable."[55] As already stated, in the summer of 1870, if Prussia suffered reverses, Russia would inevitably have intervened on Prussia's behalf. In Andrássy's estimation, counteraction by the Dual Monarchy would then be unavoidable not only because Russia, expecting another Polish revolt, would storm Galicia, but also because it would fulfill the precondition that the premier deemed necessary for war against Russia: "that Russia initiate the conflict."[56] Andrássy eschewed preventive war in favor of a defensive-offensive strategy. In the first phase, spirited Austrian defense would blunt the main Russian thrust. In the second phase, after the aggressor had exhausted its forces in fruitless assaults, the common army of the monarchy, reinforced by the Hungarian *Honvéd* forces, and in close cooperation with the victorious French army, would have launched a counteroffensive.[57]

As a second eventuality, Andrássy considered intervention by the monarchy "in favor of effective guarantees of the European balance of power." But as Diószegi has pointed out, mediation by the monarchy between mutually weakened parties was rather hypothetical.[58]

Andrássy, unlike the other members of the council, did not discount the third possibility — a Prussian victory. When the premier himself spoke about it, he struck a surprisingly anti-Prussian note by saying: "This would certainly not be a desirable outcome of the war for us." Andrássy believed, however, that "even if Prussia should win," partial mobilization and the "special note" would cover the monarchy militarily and diplomatically. But he considered a French victory more probable, so his tactical plan was shaped to this end.

Andrássy had to contend with very difficult and often conflicting problems. Consequently, many contradictory elements crept into his plans. In the first place, Andrássy wanted militarily and diplomatically to prevent the intervention against Prussia planned by the Court party. In the second place, he wanted to prepare the home front psychologically and militarily, and to take the necessary diplomatic precautions, for he was convinced there would be war with Russia. These efforts would have involved extremely difficult and contradictory, but not entirely irreconcilable, problems. The premier conceived the idea of partial mobilization to bridge the apparent contradiction between avoiding a Prussian war but accepting a Russian war. Andrássy's remarks and suggestions can only be understood in this light. This was the reason for his vigorous protest against the general mobilization advocated by the interventionists. His objection was directed primarily at the war minister, who wanted to go into combat as soon as preparations were complete. Andrássy considered it was still possible the monarchy might not have to go to war at all, and he predicted that the war would be of long duration. Andrássy drew the council's attention to the risk involved in collaborating with Napoleon III, who "has never carried an undertaking through to completion." Recalling the war of 1859, he warned against an alliance with France in case Napoleon suddenly made peace with Prussia, leaving the Dual Monarchy at the mercy of both Prussia and Russia.

Fear of war with Prussia prompted him repeatedly to press for his declaration of neutrality through the "special note," in order to prevent Prussia from initiating war. Besides, if Prussia were victorious against France, his approach was supposed to appease Prussia and make the security of the Dual Monarchy certain. But to face the possible emergency of war with Russia, partial mobilization was a necessary military precaution. Diplomatically, "in case of war with Russia," the monarchy had to obtain "assurances from Turkey," to prevent the proclamation of the "red republic" threatened by the Rumanian radicals in the Danubian Principalities, and neutralize Serbia, "whose attitude in a war with Russia is of the greatest importance."[59]

Not even this plan, however, could satisfactorily overcome all the contradictions inherent in the situation. Andrássy, after all, would have been forced to fight against Russia in alliance with France, the probable victor, without having to join in the war against Prussia. Since the Dual Monarchy and Prussia were immediate neighbors, the possibility of avoiding war with Prussia was rather remote. It was the course of events that saved Andrássy from having to deal with the difficulties of the situation that such a war would have created for the Dual Monarchy.

Andrássy's plan certainly offered no clear-cut solutions. Andrássy himself was firmly convinced that "he who makes no great mistakes has to have only a little luck to achieve success."[60] There is no doubt that Andrássy's performance in the past and at the council showed him to be a statesman with a bagful of tricks.

A further rather controversial question needs to be considered. What prompted Andrássy to call an eventual victory by Prussia undesirable?[61] One obvious reason was that he outwardly adapted himself to his anti-Prussian environment. In one of his letters to his wife from Vienna, Andrássy lamented: "Here matters do not entirely depend on me. I have to play four-handed, even eight-handed, and I am not quite sure in any direction. My position is very difficult, but I feel it is my duty, because I can prevent men from making a great mistake."[62] Since Andrássy's objective had been a formal declaration of neutrality, he evidently wished to reduce the expected opposition by making concessions in his mode of expression.

It is also possible that Andrássy was not then thoroughly familiar with Bismarck's foreign-policy ideas about Hungary and the monarchy. Consequently, he believed that, through "Prussia's agitation within our monarchy, which in the guise of liberalism and German nationality stirs up the Cisleithanian half of the realm," Bismarck was working against the integrity of the monarchy. It is quite certain, however, that whatever Andrássy said against Prussia at the council was against his own conviction. Nothing shows this better than Andrássy's own reply to the questions of József Madarász and Kálmán Tisza in the lower house of Parliament on July 28, 1870. Genuinely alarmed, the two deputies were demanding an answer from him whether or not Vienna contemplated exploiting the situation to recover the German position Austria had lost and renounced in 1866. Reiterating statements he had previously made, Andrássy asserted: "There is no such intention, either on the part of the government or decision-making circles, to restore the position abandoned in 1866, which would in my opinion be detrimental to the realm."[63]

Andrássy answered two of József Eötvös's letters in similar vein. In a letter of August 14, 1870, Eötvös observed: "Just because the Prussian policy is conducted by a man who is not troubled by sentimentality, we need not fear Prussia, unless we provoke it, and above all I consider it necessary to reestablish friendly relations with this power. It is beyond any doubt that Germany is the decisive factor in our policy."[64] A few days later, Eötvös elaborated on this theme:

> The unexpected growth of Prussia's power will create the conviction in every state that the continuance of the Austro-Hungarian realm is now needed doubly to curb Russian and Prussian ambitions. For these reasons, I do not consider a Prussian victory to be dangerous for us. Certainly, it is much less so than the contrary. Because, if Prussia had been defeated, this would have resulted in the reestablishment of the situation that existed in Germany before Sadowa, and in this case, I do not know who could check all those conducting Austria's affairs from continuing to play the old game and so dissipating all the strength of the monarchy in order to gain a minimal influence for Austria in Germany, even though this would most probably be the greatest blow for our country.[65]

Andrássy replied in a short but telling letter: "I agree with you in every respect."[66]

An additional and powerful reason for Andrássy's attitude was his deep distrust of Bismarck's Russian policy. On two separate occasions, before and after the council, Andrássy expressed to the Prussian minister his fear of a possible coalition of Prussia and Russia for the spoliation of the monarchy.[67] Bismarck reacted promptly and sent word to Andrássy that he had no such intention and, while Russia was a friend of Prussia, it nurtured no hostile intentions against Hungary and the monarchy.[68] This crisis of confidence, which was largely responsible for Andrássy's attitude at the council, ceased after Prussia's victory when it became clear that Bismarck meant what he said.

In view of Beust's past activities, his diplomatic and military program of action can only be understood in the framework of his "third force" concept. Beust's tactical plan was simply to apply his concepts to the concrete diplomatic and military situation. His immediate object was clearly to retain French favor and make his government's eventual course of action acceptable to Paris.

Beust's program was divided into the following phases: "watchful waiting," declaration of neutrality, preparation, and, finally, intervention.

The first phase of his plan, "watchful waiting," was based not on military considerations but primarily on his realistic judgment of the diplomatic situation. Beust realized that the monarchy could not openly back France because the latter was inflaming German opinion instead of isolating Prussia from Germany, as he had always suggested. "We had to exercise our duty of friendship toward France by warning it against a provocation of German national consciousness," Beust stated. The chancellor deemed it wise to remain neutral until the decisive battle had been fought, ending favorably for the French and thus for the Austrians.

The second phase of Beust's plan, the declaration of neutrality, was the direct outcome of the domestic and international situation. It was mainly imposed on him by internal opposition, which found a forceful and eloquent spokesman in Andrássy. After some reflection, however, Beust found it useful in the face of "an ever more obvious enemy, namely Russia," which "becomes more dangerous with every day." The chancellor wished to use the declaration of neutrality to conceal from Russia the monarchy's military preparations, which, he hoped, would culminate in general mobilization.

The third phase of Beust's plan was to mobilize in readiness for intervention, either diplomatically or militarily. There was not only the Russian enemy, "but it is also necessary to be armed if we wished to act as a peaceful mediator," he told the council. This, Beust believed, could be cited as a justifiable defense measure. It would be understood as such by the delegations, and public opinion would be assured that, "by ordering military preparations, the government is not acceding to the inspiration of frivolous war lust but rather to the imperative of securing the empire from all directions."

In the fourth phase of his plan, Beust considered both diplomatic and military intervention. Beust expected a French victory even after the first successes of the combined Prussian and allied German armies. "We want to believe notwithstanding," he wrote to Metternich, "that the brilliant qualities of the French army, the patriotic spirit of the nation and its immense resources, which are still intact, will not be slow in reestablishing the balance." Beust therefore stressed that "in the event of a French victory clever action could bring us profit." For this reason it was essential to keep France's favor. To this end, "we must avoid everything that would give the impression of supporting France's enemies."[69]

Meanwhile, military preparations could be completed. This, Beust hoped, would place the monarchy both diplomatically and militarily in an advantageous position to act effectively later, either to help administer the final blow to Prussia, or to restrain whichever power, France or Prussia, proved victorious. He would then be able to restore Austrian influence in southern Germany,[70] and his "third force" concept would become a reality.

Military intervention by the Dual Monarchy would become inevitable if Russia entered the war to rescue its Prussian ally. Russian intervention would transfer the theater of operations to the "eastern terrain" where the chancellor of the Dual Monarchy had suggested in the past that the German question could be solved. But since the war had started over western issues, Beust would fight an eastern war only out of necessity. In the existing circumstances, his intentions were to exploit the French victory in the west, if possible, either militarily or diplomatically.

While Beust's plan seemed impressive, it was by no means as good as it looked. In view of external and internal conditions, his plan for the reconstruction of Germany on Austria's terms was retrograde. Beust based his calculations so much on a French victory that he simply could not take a contrary possibility seriously. He thus failed to take the necessary diplomatic precautions toward Prussia to cover the projected military preparations of the Dual Monarchy. This neglect exposed the monarchy to the danger of falling victim to Prussia before sufficient preparations had been made. Andrássy's proposal, because it recognized the Russian-Pan-Slav problem as the basic question of the Dual Monarchy's foreign policy, was more realistic.

Beyond doubt, the political program of the Court party envisaged the restoration of Austrian hegemony in Germany through conquest. Its program of action was divided into three phases. The first was "watchful waiting," which was dictated by military considerations, that is, the time factor involved in the difficulties of mobilization and waiting for the decisive battle. The second phase was mobilization which was to be achieved concurrently with the first phase. The final phase was entry into the contest on the French side. The Court party excluded the declaration of neutrality from its plan as an obstacle to intervention. Its advocates found Andrássy's plan for partial mobilization an even greater impediment to intervention. Hence their heated reaction to Andrássy's proposals.

While the members of the Court party were agreed on the essential, intervention, they were far apart on the details of how it was to be carried out. Kuhn, the minister of war, considered a Prussian victory quite likely, so he was for immediate intervention to prevent it. His judgment of the military balance of forces was correct, but he sadly overestimated the common army's ability to mobilize for war speedily and launch a major offensive. Kuhn's proposal was also shortsighted because it totally disregarded the dynamism of German nationalism. It was based on the mistaken notion that the South German states would remain neutral.

Thinking in terms of a French victory, and anticipating a prolonged struggle in any case, Archduke Albrecht proposed prompt general mobilization and intervention only when the decisive battle had been fought. His estimate of the common army's ability to reach a state of readiness, supported by the monarch's analysis, was more realistic than Kuhn's, but his plan of action was basically faulty because it discounted totally the possibility of a Prussian victory. Similarly, the archduke's assessment of the military balance of forces was grossly inaccurate, and so were his geographical estimations.

On the whole, the Court party's program of action was one-sided and unrealistic. It showed total disregard of internal and international factors unfavorable to intervention. In view of the Hungarian and Austro-German hostility toward a conflict over German national issues, the resentful Slav minorities infected (with the exception of the Poles) by Pan-Slav propaganda, and the shaky financial condition of the monarchy, it was simply irrational to prepare for war against Prussia.

Worse yet, the plan made no provision to cover diplomatically the general mobilization that was to be directed against Prussia. It could have had grave consequences, since by then the mobilized Prussian armies were practically battle-ready. They could have dealt a death-blow to the Dual Monarchy even before it had called up its reserves. At the same time, the Russian forces available in Poland and the Ukraine could have overrun Galicia. Besides, the monarchy could not be sure about Italy's intentions toward the Tyrol and other segments of Austria.[71]

Diószegi has called attention to another serious shortcoming of the Court party's proposal: "The party had no positive German program within the 'great conception'" of reestablishing Austrian primacy in Germany.[72] Nor had any provision been made for what should be done with Germany after victory. The party had a strategy without the required tactical plans, that is, the superstructure had no infrastructure and could only collapse.

After lengthy discussions, Francis Joseph decided on a declaration of neutrality accompanied by limited military preparations, particularly work on fortifications and the purchase of horses. The powers were to be informed of the neutrality of the monarchy with an explanatory note about the nature of its military precautions. Military preparations had to be started on the day of the declaration of neutrality: this was July 20.

Francis Joseph, after carefully weighing the conflicting proposals, set aside his personal inclinations in favor of reason and in the end essentially adopted Andrássy's program. The outcome was an unmistakable triumph for the Hungarian premier, who had insisted on a formal declaration of neutrality, limited defensive measures, and no involvement in any conflict to which Russia was not a party. Beust's victory was over a formality: the declaration of neutrality was to be issued by a "circular note" to all powers instead of the "special note" recommended by Andrássy.

The monarch's decision that "for the time being neutrality would be observed" was of major significance for the immediate situation, since it leaned toward a policy of peace rather than war, without finally excluding either. The rival factions were all thus able to reconcile it with their own calculations. Every proposal presented to the council emphasized "eventuality," since each in the long run and under different circumstances envisaged the possibility of entering the war. The participants in the council, championing directly contradictory viewpoints, thus found it possible to reach a decision acceptable to all, at least for the moment. This tacit agreement was, however, deceptive because behind its façade basically antagonistic forces continued to exert their influence toward different ends. The result was that the Dual Monarchy could not pursue definite foreign-policy goals. The final outcome could only be hesitation and indecision.

VII

The Aftermath

With the conclusion of the council of ministers on July 18; a period of uneasy waiting began. As expected, reaction varied. Andrássy, of course, was highly satisfied. "Our game goes well," he told Orczy, "but let us not spoil it."[1] Andrássy clearly was acutely mindful of the difficulties ahead. He regarded the Dual Monarchy's neutrality as certain until Russia made an aggressive move against its territory.

The members of the Court party were no doubt displeased with the outcome, which scotched their carefully laid plan for intervention. Looking forward to much easier times, they kept a low profile for the time being. Among prominent Hungarian officials in Vienna it was generally believed that the struggle between Andrássy and the advocates of intervention was not over yet and that they would eventually manage to take the Dual Monarchy into the French camp. Vince Weninger, a Hungarian financial expert delegated to the common ministry of finance, conveyed his fears to his friend Antal Csengery, a confidant of Deák: "Archduke Albrecht is conducting himself correctly. How long this will be the case I do not know, but I am afraid they [the members of the Court party] will pull us in."[2] To prevent this, "Andrássy should not leave here [Vienna]."[3]

As for Beust, he chose to place a different interpretation on the monarch's decision from Andrássy's. Beust was clearly troubled by the idea that the Dual Monarchy might miss a great opportunity to benefit from a French victory. He expressed to Vitzthum his fear "that in eight days a French army of 300,000 could be on the Austrian border." Special care must therefore be taken not to offend Napoleon III.[4]

Laboring under this impression, Beust linked the Dual Monarchy's declaration of neutrality on July 20 with profuse assurances of Vienna's devotion to the French cause, although he must have known that his words would raise false hopes in Paris. "We consider the cause of France as our own," Beust wrote to Metternich, "and we will contribute to the successes of its arms within the limits of our possibilities."[5] Beust then added that the determined opposition of the Austro-Germans and the Hungarians was something that should not be overlooked.[6] It seemed plain, however, that, for the moment at least, Beust's "activist" policy had been suspended if not abandoned.[7]

To keep France's goodwill, Beust tried to clear the way for a French alliance with Italy. He advised Paris to obtain Italy's aid by evacuating Rome, for then Austrian assistance would be easier to secure.[8] Although anxious for Italy's help, Napoleon, for reasons of internal policy, could not comply with the Austrian suggestion.[9] In spite of Victor Emmanuel's personal desire for a Franco-Italian accord, the Italian government could not be persuaded to conclude an alliance with France and Austria. Throughout the July crisis, Foreign Minister Emilio Visconti-Venosta worked actively for a peaceful settlement of the Franco-Prussian dispute, and, when war broke out, he kept Italy neutral.[10]

The government of the Dual Monarchy meanwhile set its military preparations in motion. Between July 22 and July 24, three meetings of the Council of Ministers for Common Affairs, chaired by Beust, dealt with the financial measures made necessary by military dispositions.

Curiously, at the July 22 meeting War Minister Kuhn singled out Russia as the main danger to the monarchy, although on July 18 his main concern had been Prussia. Kuhn apparently intended to exploit Andrássy's fear of possible Russian aggression against the Dual Monarchy in order to win the Hungarian premier over to the idea of general mobilization and eventual intervention on the French side. Then Kuhn proceeded to ask for 45 or 50 million guldens to make such necessary preparations as the purchase of supplies, the fortification of border areas like Galicia, and the mobilization of reservists. Neither Andrássy nor the others present were taken in, however. Shocked by the sum requested by Kuhn, most of the ministers reacted negatively. Andrássy again proved to be the Court party's most formidable adversary. As noted, the Hungarian premier had himself proposed limited preparations to make the Dual Monarchy ready for any eventuality in the east. His considerations were defensive in nature, and he remained firm on going no further. Andrássy realized that the amount requested by Kuhn, if approved, would enable the Court party to effect a swift transition from partial to general mobilization, and from neutrality to intervention should the opportunity present itself.

Determined to have his way, Andrássy rebuked Kuhn sharply: "One must always keep in mind that the aim of our preparations is not aggression but our own security; that is why from now on one should act with the idea that we are not going beyond this degree of preparation."[11] The majority of the participants lined up behind Andrássy and, stiffened by him, refused to grant the amount of money requested by the war minister.[12] At the meeting of the council the next day Kuhn was given only 12 million guldens to make limited arrangements.[13]

That same day the Austrian ambassador in St. Petersburg telegraphed the Russians' conciliatory offer with its implicit warning.[14] A day later Chotek reported that Russia had formally declared neutrality as long as its interests remained uncompromised.[15] Chotek was impressed by Alexander II's evident sincerity, and implored Beust to welcome the tsar's proposal, arguing that to reject it would play into the hands of Austria's enemies both in Russia and in areas where Pan-Slav forces were working actively for the destruction of the Dual Monarchy.[16]

It was at once apparent that the policies of the Dual Monarchy and Russia were not identical. The government of Austria-Hungary continued its military preparations. At the July 24 meeting of the Council of Ministers for Common Affairs, Count Potocki expressed fears that the planned fortifications in Galicia would provoke Russia into launching an offensive against the Dual Monarchy. Andrássy disagreed; he had been very disappointed by the vagueness of the Russian reassurances given up to then. He was convinced that it was only Russia's military unpreparedness that had prevented it from attacking the monarchy up to that point. Andrássy argued that, while the monarchy should avoid any semblance of provocation, it should proceed with the proposed defensive measures, including fortification of strategic points in Galicia. In the end, the council agreed to go ahead with the defenses.[17]

Another meeting of the council under Francis Joseph decided on July 30 to grant the war minister's financial request by the immediate allocation of essential initial expenses. Subsequent sums were to be voted by the constitutional organs.[18]

Meanwhile, in an unenthusiastic reply to the tsar's call for unarmed neutrality, Beust pointed out that, unlike Russia, the Dual Monarchy, due to its geographical position, was surrounded by enemies on all sides, and this necessitated the continuation of military preparations.[19] On August 3 the Council of Ministers for Common Affairs decided to accelerate the construction of strategically important railways.[20] A day later the council discussed, among other pressing matters, the purchase of horses and partial mobilization of reservists.[21]

Undeterred by Beust's negative response, Alexander II persisted, and with good reason. On August 4 the French suffered a reverse near Weissenburg and two days later a major defeat near Wörth. The superiority of the German armies became apparent and their victory a strong possibility. Alarmed by the overwhelming strength of German arms, the tsar urged the Austrians to discontinue their military preparations and to join Russia and Britain in efforts to mediate between the warring nations.[22]

Vienna was no less surprised by the unexpected developments than St. Petersburg. As a result, the Council of Ministers for Common Affairs met on August 22, with Francis Joseph in the chair, to discuss the future policy of the Dual Monarchy. By now it was clear to all that there could be no question of intervention. The council deliberated instead whether the Dual Monarchy should support the tsar's mediation proposal and take a lead to restrain Prussia diplomatically in order to save France from ruin. This would please Alexander. The tsar could be further mollified with an assurance that Vienna had no intention of supporting a revolutionary movement in Poland. Andrássy, while not averse to some conciliatory gestures toward Russia, warned against undue optimism. He feared that improved relations with St. Petersburg would be only temporary. Andrássy therefore insisted most forcefully on the continuation of military preparations: "Austria's mission remains, as before, to constitute a bulwark against Russia, and, as long as it does, its existence will be a European necessity."[23] The council meeting ended on Beust's final plea to accept the Russian overtures.[24]

Beust's reply to St. Petersburg, which was positive in every respect but the question of the Dual Monarchy's military preparations,[25] was ill received by the Russian government. After repeated rebuffs from Vienna, Russia lost interest in strict Austro-Hungarian neutrality, and in the face of Prussia's swift victories, it went its own way. After Sedan, Russia abandoned its mediation efforts.

As for Vienna, whatever plans Beust and the Court party entertained for exploiting the Franco-Prussian War evaporated after the fall of Napóleon III, and in November 1870, all the Dual Monarchy's military preparations were halted. Sedan turned out to be as much an Austrian defeat as Königgrätz had been a blow to France. Beust's policy of cooperation with France had failed, and the attempts to restore Habsburg primacy in Germany were brought to a definitive end.

In the meantime, Vienna learned the real lesson for Russia's sudden loss of interest in joint steps by the neutrals to reach an acceptable peace. It exploited the victories of its Prussian ally by renouncing the humiliating Black Sea clauses of the Paris Treaty of 1856. A circular to this effect was sent to the powers on October 31, 1870.[26]

The Great Powers reacted to the unilateral Russian action with mixed feelings. Vienna's reaction was the most impulsive.[27] Although Beust himself had previously suggested the removal of restrictions on Russia in the Black Sea, he now protested on the technical grounds that Russia's action was arbitrary and illegal.[28] Britain and Prussia opted for the idea of an international conference.[29]

The London Conference (January 17–March 13, 1871), in spite of tough Austrian opposition, accepted the Russian move.[30] The decision revealed how seriously Beust had miscalculated, for the other powers were in no mood for drastic counteractions. His idea of a permanent western presence in the Black Sea was rejected.[31] Meanwhile, one day after the conference opened, the German Empire was proclaimed at Versailles. A unified Germany under Prussian leadership became a reality. Bismarck's victory over Beust was complete.

Under these circumstances, Beust undertook a thorough reappraisal of the Dual Monarchy's foreign policy, urging Francis Joseph in a memorandum to adopt a policy of friendship and close cooperation with the new German Empire.[32] Austro-German reconciliation was realized by a meeting of Beust and Bismarck at Gastein in August and of Francis Joseph and William I at Salzburg in September 1871. Andrássy's presence at the Salzburg meeting was an indication of the authority he wielded in the affairs of the Dual Monarchy.

The new policy was not forced on Beust, but it was mapped out for him by his chief external and internal rivals, Bismarck and Andrássy. Beust was not to be the man to complete this reorientation. The outcome of the Franco-German War had left his western-oriented foreign policy in ruins. His prestige suffered severe damage while that of Andrássy, whose past foreign-policy position had been justified by recent events, rose high. Yet it was a domestic question, his failure to reconcile the Slavs in the empire, that brought Beust down. After the fall of the pro-Slav Hohenwart ministry, which he had inspired in order to seek agreement with the Czechs and the Poles on constitutional reform along federal lines,[33] Beust was abruptly dismissed, and succeeded by Andrássy. The appointment of the Hungarian premier to the foreign ministry signaled Francis Joseph's acceptance of the new central European arrangement and his determination to uphold the dualist system, the fatal influence of which he never fully recognized. Fischof's dream of a harmonious, multinational empire was buried.

VIII

Conclusion

The Compromise of 1867, particularly the powerful position Hungary attained in the Austro-Hungarian partnership, profoundly affected the foreign policy of the Dual Monarchy. As a result, Andrássy, who weighed the security of Hungary and the Dual Monarchy in terms of foreign policy, could successfully impose his views on the common government.

The basic aim of Andrássy's foreign policy was to prevent developments that were contrary to particular Hungarian national interests. To achieve this, the premier wanted the status quo maintained within and the integrity of the Dual Monarchy, Hungary's shield against hostile neighbors, protected without. Andrássy understood that to realize his ambition required considerable Hungarian influence in the councils of the Dual Monarchy. So from the beginning of his prime ministry, Andrássy strove to achieve this. Between 1867 and 1870, with his well-planned, single-minded and aggressive drive, Andrássy succeeded in establishing Hungary's right to parity in the internal affairs and to decisive influence in the external affairs of the Dual Monarchy.

Andrássy's foreign policy was simple in its underlying principles. One of its fundamental axioms was (and he subjected the survival of the dualist system to this condition) that Austria renounce its attempts to regain its former position in Germany. Andrássy regarded a Prussian-dominated Germany as the best insurance against such a development. Alliance with France, whose policy was aimed at checking Prussia, held no attraction for Andrássy, for it spelled disaster.

The second axiom of Andrássy's foreign policy was the need to turn the Dual Monarchy's energies toward the east to check aggressive Russian expansionism. Andrássy saw in Russia and the Pan-Slav-inspired national movements the most dangerous enemy. In his view, if they joined forces, they would have endangered the territorial integrity of Hungary (and hence Hungarian domination of the nationalities) and the very existence of the Dual Monarchy.

Andrássy regarded friendship and alliance with Bismarckian Germany as the best guarantee against Russian expansion. This was the third axiom of his policy. It suited Bismarck's aims and this is why he endeavored to strengthen Hungary's voice in the councils of the Dual Monarchy.

Finally, Andrássy wished to maintain the territorial integrity of the Ottoman Empire and the political status quo in the Balkans. He betrayed no ambitions to inaugurate an imperial drive either to the east or the south. On the contrary, his attitude was conciliatory toward both the South Slavs (especially the Serbs) and the Rumanians. Andrássy hoped to gain their cooperation against Russia or, at least, to neutralize them. Andrássy's policy was thus limited in aim and defensive in nature.

The supreme aim of Andrássy's foreign policy, like Beust's, was the recovery and maintenance of the Dual Monarchy's position as a Great Power. Beust too recognized the danger that threatened the Dual Monarchy from the east but he failed to devote his full energies to containing it. Beust and the Court party gave priority to the German question, which they hoped to solve in alliance with France. This difference in priorities was one of the two principal elements of conflict between Beust and Andrássy. The other was Beust's continued provocation of Prussia.

Andrássy's stand took into full account the fact that the Dual Monarchy required a long interval of tranquility to adjust to its new internal structure. Moreover, he believed that Hungary needed peace in order to consolidate its special position within the monarchy. As Hungarian premier, Andrássy therefore devoted all his energies to the preservation of peace and to prevent the monarchy's involvement in the Franco-Prussian contest, which he foresaw as early as the spring of 1867.

While his timely countersteps between 1867 and 1870 forced the antidualist conservatives and military leaders of Austria onto the defensive, Andrássy consistently hindered Beust's anti-Prussian and pro-French policy. Time and again Beust was reminded that, unless he took into account Hungary's wishes on issues of foreign policy, he would lose its support. Occasionally Andrássy warned Paris not to entertain false hopes about an Austro-French combination against Prussia because Hungary would never consent to it. To avert a possible, drastic Prussian reaction against the Dual Monarchy, the Hungarian premier assured Berlin that Hungary would prevent any Austrian action against the North German Confederation.

Although Beust recognized the validity of Andrássy's arguments, under the unremitting pressure of the Court party and Paris, the chancellor of the Dual Monarchy pushed his policy on a collision course with Prussia. Beust hoped that he could eventually gain Andrássy's support for an Austro-French alignment. Therefore, throughout his negotiations with France, Beust tried to shift the focus of the projected alliance toward the east, the source of all Hungary's anxieties. But Andrássy was undeceived. In 1869, during the triple-alliance negotiations between Austria, France and Italy, Beust came close to committing the Dual Monarchy to a contractual anti-Prussian alliance, but when his consent was sought, it was Andrássy who vetoed the project.

By that time, Andrássy had emerged as the most powerful politician in the Dual Monarchy. Andrássy managed to attain his preeminence because he had all the aggressiveness, self-confidence and flexibility that Beust and the members of the Court party lacked. And more important, Andrássy enjoyed mass support in Hungary, and his policy corresponded to the ambitions of the Austro-Germans, and of the Poles in Galicia. Andrássy was always lucid and explicit, and was able to present his views with unshakable conviction, which helped him to convince Francis Joseph of the feasibility of the policy he suggested. Finally, the monarch perceived behind Andrássy's motives not only Hungarian but also imperial merit.

These were the motives and views that determined Andrássy's stand on all crucial questions confronting the Dual Monarchy during the July crisis of 1870. The Franco-German War forced on Andrássy a role he could not have enjoyed. Expecting a French victory, Beust and the Court party were eager to exploit it, but their careful plan was entirely frustrated. The Hungarians held the balance of power in the Dual Monarchy.

In line with his convictions, Andrássy refused to sanction any military action against Prussia. Unhesitatingly he demanded a policy of strict neutrality, with partial preparedness for defensive purposes in case complications arose in the east. If Russia had made a move in favor of Prussia, the Hungarian premier would have supported intervention on the French side. This was the position that Francis Joseph adopted in essence at the crucial meeting of the Council of Ministers for Common Affairs on July 18, 1870. Neither Francis Joseph nor Beust and the Court party could go against Hungarian and Austro-German public opinion.

As Andrássy probably rightly calculated, Hungary had everything to lose in victory or defeat in the war. The consequences of defeat were ominous, and of victory scarcely less so: an Austrian victory could have led to the abolition of the dualist system, defeat to the collapse of the monarchy. Consequently, Andrássy remained adamantly true to his avowed position throughout the critical months of the war. Not sentiment but sound recognition of internal and external factors guided his foreign policy.

The victorious thundering of the German guns at Sedan terminated Andrássy's ordeal; the neutrality of the Dual Monarchy was assured for the duration of the war. Andrássy's opposition was thus one of the major considerations that prevented Austria's entry into the war. The other was Russia's menacing attitude. Among a host of contributory factors were the unpreparedness of the armed forces, inadequate financial resources, and unrest in both Bohemia and Croatia.

The prevention of the monarchy's intervention in the war contributed not only to the localization of the war but also significantly to the defeat of France and the victory of Prussia. France's defeat magnified the bankruptcy of Beust's foreign policy. Beust's failure was thus Andrássy's success. With Andrássy in the foreign office, alliance with Germany, the issues of the "Eastern Question," and relations with the Russian Empire became the major themes of the foreign policy of the Austro-Hungarian Monarchy, masking the tragic premonitions of a not too distant future.

Notes

Introduction

1. Since it was not merely a Franco-Prussian contest but a German national war against France, the event may rightly be called the Franco-German War.

2. Ede Wertheimer, *Gróf Andrássy Gyu'z élete és kora* [Life and Times of Count Julius Andrássy] (3 vols.; Budapest, 1910–13).

3. Imre Gonda, *Bismarck és az 1867-es osztrák-magyar kiegyezés* [Bismarck and the Austro-Hungarian Compromise of 1867] (Budapest, 1960), p. 7.

4. See Erik Fügedi, "The War Losses of Hungarian Private Archives," *Journal of Central European Affairs,* VIII, No. 3 (October 1948), 282–84.

5. Wertheimer, *Andrássy,* I, 589 ff.

6. Wertheimer, "Franz Joseph u. Napoleon III in Salzburg; nach ungedruckten Akten," *Österreichische Rundschau,* LXII (1920), 164–74, 224–29; and "Zur Vorgeschichte des Krieges von 1870," *Deutsche Rundschau,* CLXXXV (1920), 1–26, 220–41, and CLXXXVI (1921), 35–76.

7. Manó Kónyi, *Beust és Andrássy 1870 és 1871-ben* [Beust and Andrássy in 1870 and 1871] (Budapest, 1890).

8. Imre Halász, *Egy letűnt nemzedék* [A Bygone Generation] (Budapest, 1911); see also his *Bismarck és Andrássy* [Bismarck and Andrássy] (Budapest, 1913); and Adolf Kohut, *Bismarck és Magyarország* [Bismarck and Hungary] (Budapest, 1915).

9. Richard Charmatz, *Geschichte der auswärtigen Politik Österreichs im 19. Jahrhundert* (2 vols.; Leipzig, 1914), II, 80; see also his *Österreichs innere Geschichte von 1848 bis 1907* (2 vols.; Leipzig, 1911–12), I, 74, and II, 148; Heinrich Friedjung, *The Struggle for Supremacy in Germany, 1859–66* (New York, 1966).

10. Julius Graf Andrássy, *Ungarns Ausgleich mit Österreich vom Jahre 1867* (Leipzig, 1897).

11. Heinrich von Sybel, *The Founding of the German Empire by William I* (7 vols.; New York, 1890–98).

12. *Ibid.,* VII, 462–64.

13. Hans Delbrück, *Erinnerungen, Aufsätze und Reden* (Berlin, 1902). See also Herman von Petersdorff, "Der Streit über den Ersprung des deutschenfranzösischen Krieges," *Forschungen zur brandenburgischen u. preussischen Geschichte,* IX (1897), 55–100.

14. Erich Brandenburg, *Die Reichsgründung* (Leipzig, 1916), II, 308–13.

15. This is used only as a term of convenience. In Hungarian it is without the idealist connotations of the German. The Hungarian equivalent of the

German school is called *szellemtörténet*, meaning "intellectual history" or
"history of ideas." It was a rather happy mixture of French- and English-
inspired historical criticism and German *Geistesgeschichte*. Thus, the new
school, though German in name, was essentially a Hungarian phenomenon.
16. Gyula Szekfű, *Három nemzedék: Egy hanyatló kor története* [Three
Generations: History of a Declining Age] (Budapest, 1922), p. 338. In spite of
the availability of new documentary sources, Szekfű in his later works maintained his earlier point of view. Cf. Bálint Hóman and Gyula Szekfű, *Magyar
történet* [Hungarian History] (5 vols.; Budapest, 1936), V, 490.
17. Jenő Horváth, *Magyar diplomácia, 1815-1918* [Hungarian Diplomacy,
1815-1918] (Budapest, 1928), pp. 94-98; Gusztáv Gratz, *A dualizmus kora*
[The Age of Dualism] (Budapest, 1941), I, 99; D. G. Kosáry, *A History of
Hungary* (Cleveland, 1941), p. 296.
18. Loránt Hegedüs, *Két Andrássy és két Tisza* [Two Andrássys and Two
Tiszas] (Budapest, 1941).
19. Victor Bibl, *Der Zerfall Österreichs: Von Revolution zu Revolution*
(Wien, 1924), II, 343; Joseph Redlich, *Emperor Francis Joseph of Austria*
(2d ed.; Hamden, 1968), p. 385.
20. Bibl, *Der Zerfall Österreichs,* II, 343.
21. Hermann Oncken, *Die Rheinpolitik Kaiser Napoleon III: von 1865 bis
1870 und Ursprung des Krieges von 1870/71* (hereafter cited as Oncken)
(2d ed.; 3 vols.; Stuttgart, 1967), I, 113; see also Ernst Grob, *Beusts Kampf
gegen Bismarck* (Turbenthal, 1930), pp. 1-5, 46. While deploring that historians have viewed Beust "too onesidedly from the *kleindeutsch* point of view,"
Grob also concludes that his goal was to "nullify the Treaty of Prague."
22. Ernst Erichsen, *Die deutsche Politik des Grafen Beust im Jahre 1870,
ein Beitrag zur Geschichte der Reichsgründung* (Kiel, 1927).
23. Alfred Stern, *Geschichte Europas von 1848 bis 1871* (Berlin, 1924),
X, 358-63. Friedrich Engel-Jánosi in one of his noted articles observed that
Stern's and Wertheimer's interpretations were biased in favor of Bismarck and
Andrássy, and against Beust. But Engel-Jánosi neither raised nor solved the
problem in its entirety. See Friedrich Engel-Jánosi, "Austria in the Summer of
1870," *Journal of Central European Affairs,* V, No. 4 (January 1946), 335-53.
24. Wäcker-Gotter, the consul of the North German Confederation in Pest,
summarizing the summer events of 1870, wrote of Andrássy: "*Russland* ist
sein Gedanke früh und spät, wie jeder seiner Landsleute halt er den Zusammen-
stoss mit dieser Macht für unvermeidlich und glaubt, dass man nichts besseres
tun könnte als sich darauf vorzubereiten und den Moment richtig zu wählen"
(Wäcker-Gotter to Bismarck, Pest, 22 Nov. 1871, Deutsches Hauptarchiv des
Auswärtige Amts (hereafter cited as DHAA), IAA 1 (Österreich) 58, Acta
betr. Schriftwechsel mit dem Consulat in Pest über Ungarische Zustände
(hereafter cited as Austria, File 58), II, No. A4730.
25. Walter Platzhoff, "Die Anfänge des Dreikaiserbundes," *Preussische
Jahrbücher,* CLXXXVIII (June 1922), 305.
26. Eric Eyck, *Bismarck: Leben und Werk* (3 vols.; Zürich, 1941-44),
III, 394.
27. The decline and fall of the Habsburg Monarchy haunted Srbik all his
life. Contemplating the tragic destiny of his country in the light of the German
nationalist spirit that dominated Austria after 1918, he reached the conclusion

that Austria was essentially a German state (Srbik, *Deutsche Einheit: Idee und Wirklichkeit vom Heiligen Reichs bis Königgrätz* [4 vols.; Münich, 1935–42], I, 10). To Austria Srbik assigned a supranational mission, the unification of Central Europe under undisputed German leadership. He envisaged the Third Reich as "der feste nationalstaatliche Kern der Erdteilsmitte, mit ihm in festester nationaler Lebensgemeinschaft verbunden das heutige rein deutsche Österreich, ferner angegliedert auf der Grundlage der Achtung ihrer *Staatlichkeit und der Achtung ungehemmten Lebensrechtes* ihrer Völker die ostmitteleuropäische Staatenwelt" [italics supplied] (Srbik, "Zur gesamtdeutschen Geschichtsauffassung," *Historische Zeitschrift*, CLVI [1937], 229–62). In view of this, it is by no means surprising that Srbik greeted with zest the Nazi rape of Bohemia (Srbik, "Deutsche Führung — der Segen des Böhmischen Raums," *Völkischer Beobachter,* 19 March 1939).

28. Heinrich Ritter von Srbik, *Aus Österreichs Vergangenheit von Prinz Eugen zu Kaiser Franz Joseph* (Salzburg, 1949), p. 68. Austrian conservative historians, from Hugo Hantsch to Novotný, unreservedly accepted, if not his irreverent expressions, Srbik's conclusions. See Hugo Hantsch, *Die Geschichte Österreichs* (2 vols.; Graz, 1962), II, 401–402; and Alexander Novotný, "Aussenminister Gyula Graf Andrássy der Altere," *Gestalter der Geschichte Österreichs,* ed. by Hugo Hantsch (Innsbruck, 1962), pp. 457–71. Students followed the examples of their sponsors. Cf. Walter Wagner, "Kaiser Franz Joseph und das Deutsche Reich von 1871–1914" (unpublished Phil. dissertation, University of Vienna, 1950). Recently, Heinrich Potthoff and Hans A. Schmitt provided a corrective to the prevailing picture of Beust as an unqualified revanchist, but neither of them has changed substantially the standard view of Austro-Hungarian foreign policy from 1866 to 1870 as anti-Prussian and aimed at recovering Habsburg primacy in Germany. Cf. Heinrich Potthoff, *Die deutsche Politik Beusts: Von seiner Berufung zum österreichischen Aussenminister Oktober 1866 bis zum Ausbruch des deutsch-französischen Krieges 1870/71* (Bonn, 1968); and Hans A. Schmitt, "Count Beust and Germany, 1866–1870: Reconquest, Realignment or Resignation?" *Central European History,* I (March 1968), 20–34. For a recent critical view of Beust, see Robert A. Kann, *A History of the Habsburg Empire, 1526–1918* (Berkeley, 1974), pp. 277, 332.

29. A. J. P. Taylor, *The Struggle for Mastery in Europe, 1848–1918* (Oxford, 1963), pp. 208–10, and *The Habsburg Monarchy, 1809–1918* (New York, 1965), pp. 144–45. A more balanced and modified interpretation of the policy of Andrássy and Beust is given by Nicholas Der Bagdasarin, *The Austro-German Rapprochement, 1870–1879* (Rutherford, 1976), pp. 24–68.

30. István Diószegi, *Ausztria-Magyarország és a francia-porosz háború, 1870–1871* [Austria-Hungary and the Franco-Prussian War 1870–1871] (Budapest, 1965).

31. See, for example, Béla Lederer, ed., *Gróf Andrássy Gyula beszédei* [Speeches of Count Julius Andrássy] (2 vols.; Budapest, 1891), I, 306.

32. Kállay Béni, Belgrádi Napló, XXXI–XXXIV, Magyar Országos Levéltár [Béni Kállay, Belgrade Diary, XXXI–XXXIV, Hungarian National Archives] (hereafter cited as Kállay diary, MNA), XXXI, entries of August 19 and October 15, 1868. A copy of this highly valuable unpublished diary is in the possession of the present writer. Béni Kállay, a distinguished diplomat, his-

torian and expert on Balkan affairs, had been a close friend of Andrássy, who pressed Beust to appoint Kállay to the sensitive position of consul general in the Serbian capital, Belgrade (1868–75).

Chapter I

1. On Bismarck's insistence a preliminary peace treaty was signed at Nikolsburg on July 24–25 and the final treaty at Prague on August 23, 1866. The treaty's major terms were included in Articles IV and VI. Article IV: "His Majesty the Emperor of Austria acknowledges the dissolution of the Germanic Federation as hitherto existing, and gives his assent to a new organization of Germany, in which the Austrian Imperial State shall not participate. He also promises to recognize the closer federation which the King of Prussia intends to establish north of the Main [River]." In Article VI, Prussia declares itself ready not to interfere with the integrity of Saxony. "His Majesty the Emperor of Austria promises in return to recognize the new settlement which His Majesty the King of Prussia will make in Northern Germany, including territorial changes" (Staatsarchiv XI, No. 2369, p. 177).

2. On February 23, 1866, a palace coup forced Hospodar [Prince] Alexandru Ion Cuza of the United Rumanian Principalities to abdicate. The vacant throne was offered to Count Philip of Flanders, the second son of King Leopold of the Belgians, and on his refusal to accept the uncertain position, the choice of the Rumanian Chamber fell upon Prince Charles of the Catholic and South German branch of the House of Hohenzollern. On March 30, 1866, the throne was offered to Charles by Ion C. Brătianu, one of the leaders of the Liberal party. The election was confirmed by a plebiscite on April 15, by 685,969 votes to 224. On May 22, Prince Charles entered Bucharest. His election, although contrary to the Treaty of Paris of 1856, and to the wishes of the conference assembled in that city, had by the end of the year been accepted by the Sultan and the powers. For details of the events in Bucharest, see P. Henry, *L'Abdication du Prince Cuza* (Paris, 1930), pp. 60ff.; T. W. Riker, *The Making of Rumania* (London, 1931), pp. 491ff.; W. E. Mosse, "England, Russia and the Rumanian Revolution of 1866," *Slavonic and East European Review,* XXIX (1960–61), 73–94; consult also his *The Rise and Fall of the Crimean System, 1855–71* (London, 1963), pp. 132ff.

3. General Helmuth von Moltke himself regarded the "fratricidal war [Bruderkrieg]" — and rightly — merely as a cabinet war, and contrasted it with the modern national war's "struggle for existence [Existenzkampf]." Cf. Gerhard Ritter, *Staatskunst und Kriegshandwerk* (München, 1959), I, 252.

4. Max von Gagern (son of Heinrich, secretary to the Hessian legation in Vienna) to Baron Reinhard von Dalwigk (minister-president of Hesse-Darmstadt), Aug. 15, 1866, Staatsarchiv Darmstadt (hereafter cited as SAD), Abt. Gesandschaftsakten, Berichte aus Wien 1866–1870 (hereafter cited as Reports).

5. *Der Zerfall Österreichs, von einem Deutschen-Österreicher* (Leipzig, 1867), p. 8.

6. Cf. Friedrich Cornelius, *Der Friede von Nikolsburg und die öffentliche*

Meinung in Österreich (München, 1927), p. 50. Cf. Potthoff, *Die deutsche Politik Beusts,* p. 39.

7. Auersperg wrote under the pseudonym of Anastasius Grün. *Ibid.,* n. 66.

8. See Herbert Michaelis, "Königgrätz: Eine geschichtliche Wende," *Die Welt als Geschichte,* XII (1952), 180–92. The foreign minister of Württemberg, Friedrich Gottlob von Varnbüler, noted during his stay in Vienna that "Biegeleben and the others belonging to the Augur's caste [officials of the Foreign Ministry] made faces as if the rope were around their necks and they would be immediately hanged." Cf. Julius Fröbel, *Ein Lebenslauf: Aufzeichnungen, Erinnerungen und Bekenntnisse* (Stuttgart, 1891), p. 441.

9. Max von Gagern to Dalwigk, July 20, 1866, SAD, Reports; see also Michaelis, "Königgrätz: Eine geschichtliche Wende," p. 183.

10. *Pester Lloyd,* Dec. 22, 1866.

11. Cited by Potthoff, *Die deutsche Politik Beusts,* p. 40.

12. As quoted in Heinrich Friedjung, *Der Kampf um die Vorherrschaft in Deutschland 1859 bis 1866* (2 vols.; Stuttgart, 1916), II, 418; see also Ulrich von Stosch, ed., *Denkwürdigkeiten des Generals und Admirals Albrecht v. Stosch ersten Chef der Admiralität: Briefe und Tagebücher* (Stuttgart und Leipzig, 1904), p. 104.

13. Metternich to Mensdorff, Paris, Oct. 24, 1866, Oncken, II, 117.

14. Rpt., Oct. 25, 1866, Baron Eugène G. Stoffel, *Rapports militaires, écrits de Berlin, 1866–70* (Paris, 1871), p. 45.

15. See Douglas W. Houston, "The Negotiations for a Triple Alliance Between France, Austria, and Italy, 1869–70" (unpublished Ph.D. dissertation, University of Pennsylvania, 1959), pp. 20–21. Cf. Friedjung, *The Struggle for Supremacy in Germany, 1859–66,* p. 252; Fran Zwitter, "Causes et conséquences du Compromis austro-hongrois," in *Der österreichisch-ungarische Ausgleich 1867: Materialien (Referate und Diskussion) der internationalen Konferenz in Bratislava, 28.8–1.9.1967,* ed. Ľudovít Holotík, compiled by Anton Vantuch (Bratislava, 1971), p. 68.

16. See Potthoff, *Die deutsche Politik Beusts,* p. 40.

17. Lederer, *Gróf Andrássy,* I, 136; and Hans Lothar von Schweinitz, *Denkwürdigkeiten* (Berlin, 1927), I, 297. Many Austro-Germans expressed similar opinions. Cf. Adolph Fischhof, *Österreich und die Bürgschaften seines Bestandes* (Wien, 1869), p. 9.

18. Cf. Manó Kónyi, *Deák Ferenc beszédei* [Speeches of Francis Deák] (2d ed.; Budapest, 1903), III, 764. Reporting the hostility of the populace to the Chancellery for Hungary in Vienna, the *főispán* (High Sheriff) of Csongrád County stated that the people "stand ready for anything but to let their children be taken to be massacred" for the Habsburgs. According to the report of Upper Hungary's Royal Commissioner, "It may also be feared in certain counties that [the people] would use the arms, if given into their hands, for other purposes" than against Austria's enemies. Quoted in József Galántai, *Az 1867-es kiegyezés* [The Compromise of 1867] (Budapest, 1967), p. 99.

19. *Ibid.,* p. 98.

20. For details see Andreas Kienast, *Die Legion Klapka* (Wien, 1900); and Otto Pflanze, *Bismarck and the Development of Germany: The Period of Unification, 1815–1871* (Princeton, 1963), pp. 302–08. Cf. Jiří Kořalka, "Die preussisch-deutsche Politik, der Ausgleich von 1867 und die nationalen Fragen

in Mitteleuropa," in *Der österreichisch-ungarische Ausgleich 1867,* ed. Holotík, pp. 88–89.

21. Disappointed by the armistice of July 26, General Klapka and his legion invaded northern Hungary on August 3, 1866, but the appearance of his troops did not evoke much enthusiasm among the largely Slovak population. After a few hours on Hungarian soil the legion withdrew into Bohemia. Gonda, *Bismarck,* p. 58.

22. In contrast to the general interpretation, Béla K. Király rightly asserts that the *Ausgleich* "was not a unique event in the history of Hungarian-Habsburg relations," because "nothing was more characteristic of these relations than the sequence: tension — clash — compromise." Király cites as precedents the Vienna Peace Treaty of 1606, the Sopron Compromise of 1681, and the Szatmár Peace Treaty of 1711. "All these agreements had one feature in common — they were compromises in the proper sense of the word. By each of them the estates acknowledged the validity of the crown's rather broad prerogatives and the hereditary rights of the Habsburgs (except in the cases of the 1606 and 1681 compromises, for at those times the kingdom was still elective). The dynasty, for its part, recognized the privileges of the estates." Béla K. Király, *Hungary in the Eighteenth Century: The Decline of Enlightened Despotism* (New York, 1969), pp. 238–39.

23. The constitutional problems, effects and legal premises of the settlement are presented from the Hungarian point of view in Gyula Andrássy [the Younger], *Az 1867-iki kiegyezésről* [About the Compromise of 1867] (Budapest, 1896); Mihály Réz, *A kiegyezésről* [About the Compromise] (Budapest, 1905); Henrik Marczali, *Ungarisches Verfassungsrecht* (Tübingen, 1911). The best recent survey is by József Galántai, *Az 1867-es kiegyezés,* pp. 95ff. The following works represent the Austrian viewpoint: Edmund Bernatzik, *Die österreichischen Verfassungsgesetze* (2d ed.; Wien, 1911); and Josef Redlich, *Das österreichische Staats- und Reichsproblem* (2 vols.; Leipzig, 1926). For a balanced interpretation see R. A. Kann, *The Multinational Empire: Nationalism and National Reform in the Habsburg Monarchy, 1848–1918* (2 vols.; 2d ed.; New York, 1964), II, 88ff.

24. Robert A. Kann, *The Austro-Hungarian Compromise of 1867 in Retrospect: Cause and Effect.* Report to the International Conference on the *Ausgleich* of 1867, Bratislava, Aug. 28 to Sept. 2, 1967 (Bratislava, 1967), pp. 18–19.

25. Hungarian text in *Corpus Juris Hungarici, 1836–1868 évi törvénycikkek* [Acts of the years of 1836–1868] (Budapest, 1896), pp. 333–52. German text in Bernatzik, *Die österreichischen Verfassungsgesetze,* pp. 289–306. For the most recent treatment of Law 1867:XII, see A. Radvánszky, "Das ungarische Ausgleichgesetz vom Jahre 1867," in *Der österreichisch-ungarische Ausgleich von 1867,* ed. Peter Berger (Wien, 1967), pp. 90–112.

26. The term "Austria" will be used throughout this study instead of the more accurate but inconvenient name "those kingdoms and lands represented in the Reichsrat," as the non-Hungarian half of the Monarchy was officially designated.

27. Galántai, *Az 1867-es kiegyezés,* p. 121. For details, see Gustav Turba, *Die Pragmatische Sanktion mit besonderer Rüchsicht auf die Länder der Stefanskrone* (Wien, 1906).

28. The common minister of finance could only present the common-affairs expenses to the finance ministers of the two halves of the monarchy, and these had to devise the necessary taxes. After the occupation of Bosnia and Hercegovina in 1878, the management of these provinces was entrusted to the common minister of finance. Cf. Galántai, *Az 1867-es kiegyezés,* pp. 125–26.

29. His most recent and definitive biography is Béla K. Király, *Ferenc Deák,* (Boston, 1975).

30. Cf. Erich Zöllner, *Geschichte Österreichs: Von den Anfängen bis zur Gegenwart* (Wien, 1961), p. 411.

31. Cf. Sándor Okolicsányi, "Adalékok gróf Andrássy Gyula jellemrajzához" [Additional Data to the Character Study of Count Julius Andrássy] *Budapesti Szemle* [Budapest Review], LXII (1890), 119.

32. On this, see Gusztáv Beksics, *A dualismus története* [The History of Dualism] (Budapest, 1892), pp. 209–10.

33. This right was never actually exercised.

34. On the provisions concerning the Delegations, see Law 1867:XII, Arts. 29–53, in *Corpus Juris Hungarici, 1836–1868,* pp. 339–45.

35. Professor May states rightly that the Delegations were insignificant. They were certainly not organs of "Hungarian rule." Arthur J. May, *The Habsburg Monarchy, 1867–1918* (Cambridge, Mass., 1960), p. 41.

36. The government party from 1867 to 1875. It was a coalition of moderate-liberal Hungarians: aristocracy, gentry and bourgeoisie, united in support of the Compromise of 1867 with Austria. In 1875, the Deák party fused with Tisza's Left-Center party, thus establishing the Liberal party. For details, see Viktória M. Kondor, *Az 1875-ös pártfúzió* [The Party Fusion of 1875] (Budapest, 1959).

37. The Left-Center party developed from the radical Resolution party of 1861. It was controlled firmly by Kálmán Tisza, the shrewdest political organizer in contemporary Hungary. The educated gentry constituted the mainstay of the party. In 1868, Tisza set forth his platform in the so-called "bihari pontok" [Bihar Points], demanding a separate national army, commerce and finance. With this program Tisza contributed to the intensification of antipathies against the Compromise of 1867, but he supported Andrássy's foreign policy more than the faction-ridden Deák party. Cf. *ibid.,* pp. 62–67.

38. The German Liberal party in Austria was the party of the new bourgeoisie, the modern business elements and the high tariff party. For further information see Kann, *The Multinational Empire,* I, 90–95.

39. Because of their close association with the dynasty and their adherence to the imperial idea, the conservative social elements, such as the aristocracy, the bureaucracy, the military circles and the Catholic Church may informally be called the "Court party." This term was also used by Prussian diplomatic personnel. Wäcker-Gotter to Bismarck, Pest, Nov. 22, 1871, DHAA, Austria, File 58, II, No. A 4730.

40. See, especially, Diószegi, *Ausztria-Magyarország,* pp. 17–24, 29–33, and 40–63. It is the best, though one-sided and often generalized, treatment of political party aspirations from the standpoint of foreign-policy tendencies in the monarchy.

41. For details, see May, *The Habsburg Empire,* pp. 93, 369–70.

42. In accordance with the constitutional changes, the emperor, reacting to

objections in the Hungarian Delegations to the use of the old terms, decreed the new designations "Austro-Hungarian Monarchy" and "Austro-Hungarian Empire" for the monarchy. Francis Joseph to Beust, Vienna, Nov. 14, 1868, cited in Kónyi, *Deák*, IV, 82–83.

For details about the controversy, see Miklós Komjáthy, "Die organisatorischen Probleme des Gemeinsamen Ministerrates in Spiegel der Ministerratsprotokolle," in *Studien zur Geschichte der Österreichisch-Ungarischen Monarchie* (Budapest, 1961), pp. 392–98.

43. *Ibid.*, p. 396.

44. For an evaluation of Hungary's position in military affairs and in the economic life of the monarchy, see Péter Hanák, "Hungary in the Austro-Hungarian Monarchy: Preponderance or Dependency?" *Austrian History Yearbook* III, Pt. 1 (1967), 266–84, 295–99.

45. *Corpus Juris Hungarici, 1836–1868*, p. 335.

46. *Supra*, p. 12. Beust was the last foreign minister of the empire with the title of Imperial Chancellor.

47. Several historians have cautioned that a student of Austro-Hungarian diplomacy must always consider the extent of the influence that various common foreign ministers exerted on the emperor and to what extent the foreign ministers themselves were influenced by officials of the Foreign Ministry. Cf. Soloman Wank, "Foreign Policy and the Nationality Problem in Austria-Hungary, 1867–1914," *Austrian History Yearbook* III, Pt. 3 (1967), 41; and Friedrich Engel-Jánosi, *Geschichte auf dem Ballhausplatz* (Graz, 1963), p. 10.

48. *Corpus Juris Hungarici, 1836–1868*, p. 335.

49. Hanák, "Hungary in the Austro-Hungarian Monarchy," p. 294.

50. Stephen [István] Burián, *Austria in Dissolution* (London, 1925), p. 245.

51. Wäcker-Gotter to Bismarck, Pest, May 15, 1869, DHAA, Austria, File 58, I, No. A 1930.

52. Quoted in Galántai, *Az 1867-es kiegyezés*, p. 124.

53. Wäcker-Gotter to Bismarck, Pest, July 31, 1870, DHAA, Austria, File 58, I, Abschrift.

54. Cf. *Corpus Juris Hungarici, 1836–1868*, p. 335.

55. See especially, Galántai, *Az 1867-es kiegyezés*, p. 124; and Hanák, "Hungary in the Austro-Hungarian Monarchy," pp. 293–94.

56. Text in Bernatzik, *Die österreichischen Verfassungsgesetze*, pp. 379–89. For the most recent treatment of Law No. 146 of 1867, see E. C. Hellbling, "Das österreichische Gesetz vom Jahre 1867 über die gemeinsamen Angelegenheiten der Monarchie," in *Der Österreichisch-Ungarische Ausgleich von 1867*, pp. 64–89.

57. It should be noted that the Diet of 1790/91 had extracted from Leopold II (1790–1792) a pledge not to resort to such a device. See especially, Király, *Hungary in the Late Eighteenth Century*, p. 237.

58. "Lónyay naplójából" [From Lónyay's diary] (hereafter cited as Lónyay diary), Vienna, May 30, 1867, published in Kónyi, *Deák*, V, 97–98.

59. For details on his family, see Gróf Sándor Vay, "Az Andrássyak" [The Andrássys] in *Magyarország vármegyéi és városai: Gömör-Kishont vármegye* [Counties and Cities of Hungary: Gömör-Kishont County], ed. S. Borowsky, VIII (Budapest, n.d.), 593–613; Wertheimer, *Andrássy*, I, 18.

60. On Andrássy's youth and education see Etele Matolay, "Emlékezés

Andrássyról" [Remembrance of Andrássy], *Zemplén,* March 30, 1890. The intimate and revealing details contained in this article are of special interest because Matolay, who served as Andrássy's private secretary, received most of his information from his chief. Further valuable details can be found in Manó Kónyi, "Visszaemlékezés Andrássy Gyula grófra" [Recollections of Count Julius Andrássy], *Nemzet* [Nation], Feb. 19–21, 1890.

61. See, for instance, Manó Kónyi, "Andrássy Gyula gr. politikai első fellépése" [Political Debut of Count Julius Andrássy], *Budapesti Hírlap* [Budapest Journal], Feb. 19, 1890; and Wertheimer, *Andrássy,* I, 11–20.

62. See especially [Sándor Takács], "Andrássy az 1847–48-iki országgyűlésen" [Andrássy at the Diet of 1848–49]; *Budapesti Hírlap,* Nov. 29, 1906; and Lederer, *Gróf Andrássy,* I, 5–105.

63. Cf. Hegedüs, *Két Andrássy és két Tisza,* p. 37; Wertheimer, *Andrássy,* I, 21–24.

64. On Andrássy's mission, see B. Reiner, "Graf Julius Andrássy als Diplomat der Revolution," *Neue Freie Presse,* Feb. 21, 22, 23, 1890; Wertheimer, *Andrássy,* I, 27–60; and Eszter Waldapfel, *A független magyar külpolitika, 1848–1849* [Hungary's Independent Foreign Policy] (Budapest, 1962), pp. 266–71.

65. Cf. Michael B. Petrovich, *The Emergence of Russian Panslavism, 1859–1870* (New York, 1956), pp. 273–76.

66. Certain indiscreet utterances by Palacký are quoted in Joseph F. Zacek, *Palacký and the Austro-Hungarian Compromise of 1867,* A Report to the International Conference on the *Ausgleich* of 1867, Bratislava, Aug. 28 to Sept. 2, 1967 (Los Angeles, 1967), pp. 8–10, 24–25, n. 16. For the latest monograph on Palacký, see Zacek's *Palacký: The Historian as Scholar and Nationalist* (Paris, 1970).

67. [Count Julius Andrássy], "The Present Position and Policy of Austria," *The Eclectic Review,* XXVIII (November, 1850), 604–29. It was written ostensibly as a comment on the works of E. Zsedényi, *Ungarn Gegenwart* (Wien, 1850); and Paul von Somssich, *Das legitime Recht Ungarn und seines Königs* (Wien, 1850), but since the article contains no reference to these works, it may be regarded as an independent study.

68. See, especially, *Mednyánszky Cézár emlékezései és vallomásai az emigrációból* [Recollections and Confessions of Caesar Mednyánszky from Exile] (Budapest, 1930), p. 88. In 1852, Andrássy wrote to one of his friends that some day he would reconquer his confiscated parental estates by force of arms "if only God gives an opportunity." Andrássy to Miklós Nemeskéri Kiss, Paris, Feb. 8, 1852, quoted in Zoltán Horváth, *Teleki László, 1810–1861* [László Teleki, 1810–1861] (Budapest, 1964), I, 384. In 1858, after his return from exile, at a meeting of former émigrés he declared that "if a revolution becomes unavoidable, he will also be there among the others." Cf. Kónyi, *Deák,* III, 113–14.

69. For a complete collection of documents relating to Kossuth's visit in the United States, see Denis Jánossy, *The Kossuth Emigration in America* (Budapest, 1940).

70. Andrássy refused to give an oath of allegiance after he appealed for clemency and signed only a profession of allegiance. The full text is printed in Wertheimer, *Andrássy,* I, 90.

71. On Andrássy's role in the Compromise negotiations see, especially, Wertheimer, *Andrássy,* I, Chaps. IV–XI. For his most important, powerful and revealing speeches between 1861 and 1867, see Lederer, *Gróf Andrássy,* I, 109–232; and Kónyi's *Deák,* II–V which contain political polemics, conversations, addresses, letters and memoirs providing valuable details on Andrássy's thinking and activities, too.

72. Louis Eisenmann, "Austria-Hungary," *Cambridge Modern History* (Cambridge, 1910), XII, 183. Cf. Király, *Ferenc Deák,* pp. 177–179.

73. See Lederer, *Gróf Andrássy,* I, 149–50.

74. According to Eisenmann, Deák, brought up in the old school, was the representative of the policy of continual protest against infringements of Hungarian rights; Andrássy, on the other hand, represented a new voice, who believed that Austria's existence was a European necessity, that Hungary could only gain by joining hands with her. Cf. L. Eisenmann, *Le compromis austro-hongrois de 1867* (Paris, 1904), p. 413.

75. Its composition was: Andrássy, Premier and Minister of Defense; Count Menyhért Lónyay, Finance; Boldizsár Horváth, Justice; Baron Béla Wenckheim, Interior; István Gorove, Trade; Count Imre Mikó, Communications; Baron József Eötvös, Education; Count György Festetics, Minister *a latere* to the Crown. On the résumé of the ministers, see Ágnes Kenyeres, ed., *Magyar életrajzi lexikon* [Hungarian Biographical Encyclopedia] (2 vols.; Budapest, 1967–69).

76. See George Barany, "Hungary: The Uncompromising Compromise," *Austrian History Yearbook,* III, Pt. 1 (1967), 252–54; Iván T. Berend and György Ránki, "The Hungarian Manufacturing Industry, Its Place in Europe, 1900–1938," in *Nouvelles études historiques* (Budapest, 1965), II, 423–36.

77. For details, see Tibor Papp, "A magyar honvédség megalakulása a kiegyezés után, 1868–1890" [Establishment of the Hungarian Army after the Compromise, 1868–1890], *Hadtörténelmi Közlemények* [Review of Military History] II (1967), No. 2, 311–322. See also Gunther E. Rothenberg, *The Army of Francis Joseph* (West Lafayette, 1976), pp. 75–78.

78. Act XXX/1868 in Hungarian legislation. Text in *Corpus Juris Hungarici, 1836–1868,* pp. 422–39. See also Király, *Ferenc Deák,* pp. 184–86, and p. 219, n. 51.

79. For details, see Wertheimer, *Andrássy,* I, 476–501. The best and most recent monograph on the military frontier is Gunther E. Rothenberg, *The Military Border in Croatia, 1740–1881* (Chicago, 1956).

80. For the text of the law, see Foreign Office, *Foreign Policy of Austria-Hungary* (London, 1920), pp. 115–20; see also Paul BöDy, *Joseph Eötvös and the Modernization of Hungary, 1840–1870: A Study of Ideas of Individuality and Social Pluralism in Modern Politics* (Philadelphia, 1972), pp. 111–15; Oscar Jászi, *The Dissolution of the Habsburg Monarchy* (4th ed.; Chicago, 1966), pp. 314ff.

81. Cf. Király, *Ferenc Deák,* p. 188. Baron József Eötvös (1813–71), Hungarian Liberal statesman and author, was born and died in Budapest. He became a lawyer in 1833, but soon devoted himself to literature. In the revolution of 1848 Eötvös was minister of education, and again under Andrássy from 1867 to 1871.

82. R. A. Kann, "Hungarian Jewry During Austria-Hungary's Constitu-

tional Period (1867–1918)," *Jewish Social Studies,* VII (1945), 357–86.

83. Francis Joseph to Empress Elisabeth, July 18, 1866, as quoted in Egon Count Corti, *Elisabeth, Empress of Austria* (New Haven, Conn., 1936), p. 127.

84. Francis Joseph to Frau Schratt, Ofen [Buda], Feb. 23, 1890, in Jean de Bourgoing, ed., *The Incredible Friendship: The Letters of Emperor Franz Joseph to Frau Katharina Schratt* (New York, 1966), p. 162.

85. As quoted in Franz von Krones, *Moritz von Kaiserfeld; Sein Leben und Wirken* (Leipzig, 1888), p. 271.

86. Cf. Gyula Szekfű, "Andrássy," *Napkelet* [Sunrise], I (1923), 418–22.

87. Lederer, *Gróf Andrássy,* I, 124.

88. Lytton to Granville, Vienna, Nov. 23, 1871, as quoted in May, *The Habsburg Monarchy,* p. 113.

89. For the details of the speech, see Wertheimer, *Andrássy,* III, 406–10; see also Henry W. Steed, *The Habsburg Monarchy* (London, 1914), p. 33, and Okolicsányi, "Adalékok gróf Andrássy Gyula jellemrajzához," p. 121.

90. See Wertheimer, *Andrássy,* III, 426, and Andrássy, *Bismarck, Andrássy and their Successors,* p. 48.

91. Lord Augustus Loftus, *Diplomatic Reminiscences* (London, 1894), I, 359.

92. Lytton to Granville, Vienna, Nov. 23, 1871, as quoted in May, *The Habsburg Monarchy,* pp. 112–13.

93. It is evident from the contents of the ambassador's letter that he did not refer to Andrássy's slyness in a negative sense. Meeting with the premier at the embassy, Schweinitz hoped to make Andrássy talkative by serving him his best French wine. He tried to learn some secret information from him. Evidently, Andrássy realized his aim and, while he refused to drink, Schweinitz became intoxicated. Cf. General von Schweinitz, *Denkwürdigkeiten,* I, 282.

94. This revealing incident is quoted in Wertheimer, *Andrássy,* III, 437–38.

95. Cf. Lederer, *Gróf Andrássy,* I, 137.

96. See, for instance, Okolicsányi, "Adalékok gróf Andrássy Gyula jellemrajzához," p. 122.

97. Cited by Wertheimer, *Andrássy,* III, 431; see also Count Julius Andrássy, Jr., *Bismarck, Andrássy and their Successors* (London, 1927), pp. 43–44.

98. Cited by Wertheimer, *Andrássy,* III, 436.

99. Quoted in Okolicsányi, "Adalékok gróf Andrássy Gyula jellemrajzához," p. 122.

100. This contention is well demonstrated by Andrássy's speech in the Hungarian Delegation in 1882. See *A magyar delegáció naplója* [The Minutes of the Hungarian Delegation], IV, April 23, 1882.

101. Quoted in Zoltán Ferenczi, *Báró Eötvös József* [Baron Joseph Eötvös] (Budapest, 1903), II, 273.

102. Deák to Andrássy, Rátót, Aug. 11, 1872. The text of this letter is published in Lederer, *Gróf Andrássy,* I, 193.

103. M. G. de Blowitz, "Austria and the Congress," *The Times* (London), July 26, 1878.

104. Lytton to Granville, Vienna, Nov. 23, 1871, as quoted in May, *The Habsburg Monarchy,* p. 113.

105. Béni Kállay testified to this in his memorial speech. See Béni Kállay,

"Gróf Andrássy Gyula emlékezete" [Remembrance of Count Julius Andrássy] *Akadémiai Értesítő* [Bulletin of the Academy], II, June 15, 1891, 341; see also Andrássy, *Bismarck, Andrássy and their Successors*, p. 43.

106. Cited by Okolicsányi, "Adalékok gróf Andrássy Gyula jellemrajzához," p. 121.

107. *Ibid.*

108. See, for instance, General von Schweinitz, *Denkwürdigkeiten*, I, 282.

109. Bernard Prince von Bülow, *Memoirs* (Boston, 1932), IV, 401.

110. Lord Odo Russell to Granville, Berlin, Sept. 12, 1872. Cf. Winifred Taffs, "Conversation Between Lord Odo Russell and Andrássy, Bismarck and Gorchakov in September, 1872," *Slavonic and East European Review*, VIII, March 1930, 704.

111. Quoted in R. W. Seton-Watson, *Disraeli, Gladstone and the Eastern Question* (2d ed.; London, 1962), p. 224. Italicized in the original.

112. Russell to Granville, Berlin, Sept. 12, 1872, in Taffs, "Conversation Between Lord Odo Russell and Andrássy, Bismarck and Gorchakov," p. 706. The two latter meetings with the Hungarian statesman more than confirmed Gorchakov's good impression of him, and he fully agreed with Novikov's (the Russian legate in Vienna) estimate of Andrássy as *"le rival honnête."* At this time Gorchakov honored Andrássy with the highest compliment that a conceited person can make: he regarded Andrássy as a "younger reincarnation of himself, exclusively concerned with the consolidation of the monarchy and not at all with territorial expansion." *Ibid.,* p. 401.

113. Andrássy, *Bismarck, Andrássy and their Successors*, p. 46.

114. Lónyay diary, Sept. 13, 1867, published in Kónyi, *Deák*, V, 230–31.

115. See Szekfű, "Andrássy," p. 419; cf. Wertheimer, *Andrássy*, III, 440–41.

116. *Ibid.*

117. *Supra*, p. 7.

118. See Lederer, *Gróf Andrássy*, I, 170.

119. Eötvös and others thought highly of this ability of Andrássy. Cf. Wertheimer, *Andrássy*, III, 439.

120. Quoted in Wertheimer, *Andrássy*, III, 440.

121. *A magyar delegáció naplója*, IV, April 23, 1882.

Chapter II

1. The former minister Ignatz von Plener, in one of his letters to his son, wrote that "at that time the idea of revenge existed in Austria and indeed was quite influential." Paul Molisch, ed., *Briefe zur deutschen Politik in Österreich von 1848-1918* (Wien, 1934), p. 68. "From the highest commander down to the youngest lieutenant, there was one paramount goal: Revenge for Sadowa!" Theodore von Sosnosky, *Die Balkanpolitik Österreich-Ungarns seit 1866* (Stuttgart, 1913-14), I, 95.

2. Wank, "Foreign Policy and the Nationality Problem in Austria-Hungary," p. 42. Resentment over Königgrätz was stronger among the archdukes than in the emperor himself; they could not resign themselves to regard its outcome as definitive. Bannewille to Remusat, Vienna, Jan. 5, 1873, E. Bourgeois and E. Clermont, *Rome et Napoléon III* (Paris, 1907), p. 360.

3. "When all the world is against you and you have no friends at all," he lamented after the war, "there is not much chance of success, but we must resist as long as possible, do our duty to the last, and finally perish with honor." Francis Joseph to his mother, Aug. 22, 1866, Franz Schnürer, ed., *Briefe Kaiser Franz Josephs I. an seine Mutter, 1838–72* (Munich, 1930), p. 358. But the emperor tried to hide his breakdown behind a courageous façade. "I have a bitterly hard crust to eat, and only my trust in God and an honest will to do my best can give me the strength to keep afloat." *Ibid.*

4. Referring to a conspiracy between Berlin, Paris and Florence, the monarch wrote about the conflict that "it is prepared with our complete destruction in view." *Ibid.*

5. Gordon W. Prange, "Beust's Appointment as Austrian Foreign Minister," *Iowa Studies in the Social Sciences,* II, No. 2 (1941), 223.

6. Gagern to Dalwigk, Vienna, Sept. 24, 27, 1866, SAD, Reports.

7. Werther to King William, Sept. 20, 1866, No. 207, Prange, "Beust's Appointment as Austrian Foreign Minister," p. 223. See also Eduard von Wertheimer, *Bismarck im politischen Kampf* (Berlin, 1930), pp. 250 ff.

8. See A. Bezecny, ed., *Die Thronreden Sr. Majestät des Kaisers Franz Josef I. bei der feierlichen Eröffnung und Schliessung des österreichischen Reichsrates* (Wien, 1908), p. 88. See also the special edition of the *Wiener Zeitung,* May 22, 1867.

9. As quoted in Srbik, *Aus Österreichs Vergangenheit,* p. 61.

10. Kállay diary, XXXI, entry of Aug. 19, 1868, MNA.

11. Adolphe Thiers, *Memoirs of M. Thiers, 1870–1873* (London, 1916), p. 29.

12. Gagern to Dalwigk, Vienna, Sept. 24, 27, 1866, SAD, Reports. The Bavarian ambassador held the same view, Bray to Pfordten, Vienna, Oct. 30, 1866, Bayerisches Geheimes Staatsarchiv München (hereafter cited as BGSA), Abt. Gesandschaftsakten, Berichte aus Wien 1866–1870 (hereafter cited as Reports). Cf. Rothenberg, *The Army of Francis Joseph,* pp. 87–88.

13. *Ibid.,* p. 88. Cf. Srbik, *Aus Österreichs Vergangenheit,* pp. 192–93.

14. Gagern to Dalwigk, Vienna, Sept. 24, 27, 1866, SAD, Reports. See also Wilhelm Schüssler, *Bismarcks Kampf um Süddeutschland 1867* (Berlin, 1929) p. 183.

15. Platzhoff, "Die Anfänge des Dreikaiserbundes," pp. 286, 304.

16. Bismarck, *The Memoirs* (2 vols.; New York, 1966), II, 50. Cf. Hans A. Schmitt, "Prussia's Last Fling: The Annexation of Hanover, Hesse, Frankfurt, and Nassau, June 15–October 8, 1866." *Central European History,* VIII, December, 1975, 330.

17. *Ibid.*

18. As quoted in Eyck, *Bismarck,* II, 262. See also Endre Kovács, "Der österreichisch-ungarische Ausgleich vom Jahre 1867 und die europäischen Grossmächte," *Der österreichisch-ungarische Ausgleich 1867,* ed. Holotík, pp. 117–122.

19. Loftus to Stanley, Jan. 18, 1868, Veit Valentin, *Bismarcks Reichsgründung im Urteil englischer Diplomaten* (Amsterdam, 1937), pp. 535–37.

20. Cf. Langer, *European Alliances and Alignments, 1871–1890* (2d ed.; New York, 1950), p. 19. A few months earlier Bismarck had refused to accept Beust as the head of the Saxon peace delegation. See Richard V. Freisen,

Erinnerungen aus meinem Leben (Dresden, 1910), II, 331–32, 338–40. Beust, as Saxon foreign minister since 1849, and minister-president since 1853, had supported Austria in every international question. No wonder that Prince Schwarzenberg called him "mon meilleur lieutenant." Cf. Margarete Berger, "Österreichs auswärtige Politik (Die Ministertätigkeit des Grafen Beust 1866–1870/71) und das Vaterland"(unpublished Phil. dissertation, University of Vienna, 1947). On top of all this, he brought Saxony into the war of 1866 on the side of Austria.

21. Some of his contemporaries regarded the Saxon capital, Dresden, to be too provincial and narrow an environment for a man of Beust's abilities. His admirers there considered him "a giant in an entresol." See Baron L. J. Beyens, *Le second empire vu par un diplomate Belge* (2 vols.; Paris, 1924–1926), II, 226. In Vienna Beust was equally recognized. Francis Joseph wrote of him that in difficult moments, the foreign minister rose to the occasion "in outstanding fashion." Quoted in Schnürer, *Briefe Kaiser Franz Josephs,* p. 375. A leading contemporary journalist hailed him as one of Europe's most distinguished statesmen because of "his high intelligence and experience in diplomacy." See Jules Hansen, *Les coulisses de la diplomatie: Quinze ans à l'étranger, 1864–79* (Paris, 1880), p. 189. Lord Bloomfield, the British ambassador in Vienna, considered Beust "a most remarkable character" whose "lightheartedness and confidence carries him through all his trouble." Cited by Georgiana Bloomfield, *Court and Diplomatic Life* (2 vols.; London, 1883), II, 288.

But not everyone thought of him so highly. To Bismarck Beust was "nothing but an ambitious, intriguing *Hauspolitiker.*" See Wertheimer, *Andrássy,* I, 288. The French statesman, Émile Ollivier, described him as a man of "one-fourth intelligence and three-fourths wind." Émile Ollivier, *L'Empire libéral* (18 vols.; Paris, 1895–1918), XV, 458. Cf. Houston, "France, Austria and Italy, 1869–70," pp. 22–23, nn. 16, 17.

22. Friedrich Ferdinand, Graf von Beust, *Aus drei Vierteljahrhunderten* (2 vols.; Stuttgart, 1887), II, 19–20.

23. For a detailed study of this issue see Prange, "Beust's Appointment as Austrian Foreign Minister," pp. 215–20.

24. Taylor, *The Habsburg Empire, 1809–1918,* p. 131. A similar opinion is advanced by F. Engel-Jánosi, "The Roman Question in the Diplomatic Negotiations of 1869–70," *The Review of Politics,* III (1941), 325. Historians of German unity support the thesis that Beust was brought to Vienna to prepare Austria for revenge against Prussia. See especially, Charmatz, *Österreichs Innere Geschichte,* I, 71; Wertheimer, *Andrássy,* I, 291; Eisenmann, p. 438; Heinrich Friedjung, *Historische Aufsätze* (Stuttgart, 1919), p. 136; Joseph Redlich, *Francis Joseph of Austria,* pp. 339–40. This rather extreme view gained wide acceptance among English-speaking historians. See among others, R. W. Seton-Watson, "The Emperor Francis Joseph," *History,* XVII, July and Oct., 1932, 222; May, *The Habsburg Empire,* p. 98; Otto Pflanze, *Bismarck,* p. 420.

In opposition to these historians there is a school of thought that discounts the revenge motive. See especially, Srbik, *Aus Österreichs Vergangenheit,* p. 61; Novotný, "Aussenminister Gyula Graf Andrássy der Altere," p. 467; Wagner, "Kaiser Franz Joseph und das Deutsche Reich," p. 37. For a more recent advocate of this view, who clearly aims at transforming the wounded lion into a pussycat, see Schmitt, "Count Beust and Germany, 1866–1870," I, No. 1, 20–21. Schmitt's assertion that after 1866 Austria pursued a "policy of peace at any price" is, to say the least, curious.

25. Prange, "Beust's Appointment as Austrian Foreign Minister," p. 221.

26. *Ibid.,* p. 222.

27. Werther to Bismarck, Vienna, Nov. 6, 1866, Erich Brandenburg *et al.,* eds., *Die auswärtige Politik Preussens, 1858–1871* (hereafter cited as *APP*) (10 vols.; Oldenburg, 1933–1939), VIII, No. 79; Beust himself laments this. Beust, *Aus drei Vierteljahrhunderten,* II, 30f. A diplomat in Paris prophesied: "Il a enterré la Saxe, il a enterré la Confédération, il va enterrer l'Autriche." *Ibid.*

28. Ministerrath, Oct. 29, 30, Redlich, *Das österreichische Staats- und Reichs-problem,* II, 515. The former Austrian foreign minister, Alexander, Count von Mensdorff-Pouilly, advised the emperor in September against the nomination of Beust. "I consider it decidedly not to Austria's advantage," he wrote. Mensdorff believed that as a foreigner and a Protestant Beust would hurt the feelings of the native Austrians and evoke the opposition of the Catholics; he would, furthermore, be *non grata* to the Hungarians who opposed Austria's German involvement; his Polish predilections would offend Russia; and above all, his selection would be regarded by Prussia as an open act of hostility. In his conclusion, he pointed out that Beust's French connections would probably result in following a policy of revenge in cooperation with Napoleon III, who "is a broken man," and it would be "unwise to seek safety on a sinking ship." Mensdorff to Francis Joseph, Vienna, Sept. 21, 1866, Haus-, Hof-, und Staatsarchiv (hereafter cited as HHSA), Kabinettsarchiv (hereafter cited as KA), Geheim Akten, Karton 6, File Mensdorff-Pouilly.

29. Plener writes in his memoirs: "My good Austrianism was deeply offended that only a foreigner could be found qualified for the position." Plener, *Erinnerungen* (3 vols.; Stuttgart, 1911–21), I, 98. Count Blome, Austrian ambassador to Munich, remarked to his Prussian colleague, Baron Werthern, that "The Prussians in Bohemia were a calamity, but the Saxon in the *Staatskanzlei* is a much greater misfortune." Reuss to Bismarck, Munich, Nov. 3, 1866, *APP,* VIII, No. 72.

30. Ministerrath, Oct. 29, 30, 1866, Redlich, *Das österreichische Staats- und Reichs-problem,* II, 514ff.

31. See Berger, "Österreichs auswärtige Politik, 1866–1870/71," p. 31; and Gramont to Moustier, Vienna, Oct. 28, 1866, France, Ministère des Affaires Étrangères, *Les origines diplomatiques de la guerre de 1870–71* (hereafter cited as *ODG*) (29 vols.; Paris, 1910–32), XIII, No. 3707.

32. Bray to Pforden, Vienna, Oct. 30, 1866, BGSA, Reports.

33. Reuss to Bismarck, Munich, Nov. 3, 1866, *APP,* VIII, No. 72.

34. Plener, *Erinnerungen,* I, 98. Prince Richard, the son of the former Chancellor of Austria, thought that Beust meant a new future for Austria, and now he was sure that he would "no longer encounter the hesitations of Buol [foreign minister, 1852–59], Rechberg [foreign minister, 1859–64], and Eszterházy [minister without portfolio, 1861–66]. The reign began with Felix [Prince zu Schwarzenberg, prime minister, 1848–52] and, after passing through adversities . . . , is now given to a new pilot who I wish may be even more 'Felix' than the first." Metternich to Beust, Paris, March 1, 1869, Oncken, III, 119–20.

35. *Neue Freie Presse,* Oct. 28, 30, 1866.

36. *Pesti Napló,* Nov. 1, 1866.

37. *Ibid.*

38. Diószegi, *Ausztria-Magyarország,* p. 34.

39. Beust to Dalwigk, Vienna, Nov. 23, 1866, Wilhelm Schussler, ed., *Die Tagebücher des Freiherrn v. Dalwigk zu Litchtenfels aus den Jahren 1860–71* (hereafter cited as Dalwigk) (Osnabrück, 1967), p. 305.

40. Beust to Wimpffen, Vienna, April 27, 1867, HHSA, KA, Geheime Akten, Karton 17.

41. Beust to Francis Joseph, Gastein, May 18, 1871, HHSA, Politisches Archiv (hereafter cited as PA), XL, 54.

42. Bray to Pfordten, Vienna, Oct. 30, Nov. 13, 1866, BGSA, Reports; and Gagern to Dalwigk, Vienna, Nov. 3, 1866, SAD, Reports.

43. Gramont to Moustier, Vienna, Nov. 5, 1866, *ODG,* XIII, No. 3726. See also Schüssler, *Bismarcks Kampf,* p. 188.

44. For an excellent survey of this problem see especially Diószegi, *Ausztria-Magyarország,* pp. 20–24; and Wank, "Foreign Policy and the Nationality Problem in Austria-Hungary," p. 43.

45. Ministerrath, Oct. 29, 1866, Redlich, *Das österreichische Staats- und Reichs-problem,* II, 519–20.

46. Memorandum of Beust to Francis Joseph, Salzburg, Aug. 13, 1867, Oncken, II, 448.

47. *Ibid.,* p. 449.

48. Ministerrath, Oct. 29, 1866, Redlich, *Das österreichische Staats- und Reichs-problem,* II, 520.

49. *Ibid.*

50. Cf. Hantsch, *Die Geschichte Österreichs,* II, 415f.; Wagner, "Kaiser Franz Joseph und das Deutsche Reich," p. 36, n. 8.

51. Memorandum of Beust to Francis Joseph, Salzburg, Aug. 13, 1867, Oncken, II, 448.

52. Beginning in the early 1850s, Beust sought to establish within the German Confederation a "third force *(Triastaaten),"* consisting of the middle states that wished to remain independent of both Austria and Prussia. These were to pursue an independent policy along with the two major states, which in turn were to preside over the German Diet on an equal footing. For detailed studies on this point see H. H. Thumann, "Beusts Plan zur Reform des deutschen Bundes von Oktober 1861," in *Neues Archiv für sächsische Geschichte,* XLVI (1925), 46–47; and Martin Daerr, *Beust und Bundesreform-plane der deutschen Mittelstaaten im Jahre 1859* (Dresden, 1931).

53. Gramont to Moustier, Vienna, Feb. 17, 1867, *ODG,* XIV, No. 4212.

54. Beust to Metternich, Vienna, Nov. 6, 1868, HHSA, PA, IX, Karton 177.

55. Ladenberg to Bismarck, Vienna, Sept. 16, DHAA, I. A.A. 1 (Österreich) 54, Acta betr. Schriftwechsel mit der Kgl. Gesandschaft in Wien, sowie mit anderen Kgl. Missionen und fremden Kabinetten über die innere Zustände und Verhältnisse Österreichs, III (hereafter cited as Austria, File 54), No. A 3896.

56. Platzhoff, "Die Anfänge des Dreikaiserbundes," pp. 298–306. See also William Langer, *European Alliances,* p. 20.

57. Lederer, *Gróf Andrássy,* I, 92.

58. *Ibid.,* p. 101.

59. For details, see especially, Zoltán Horváth, *Teleki László,* I, 205–11. Further information may be found in E. Waldapfel, *A független magyar külpolitika, 1848–1849,* pp. 13–46; and István Hajnal, *A Batthyány-kormány külpolitikája, 1848–49* [The Foreign Policy of the Batthyány Government, 1848–1849] (Budapest, 1957). The idea of German-Hungarian cooperation against Russia and the Pan-Slav danger was the legacy of the Hungarian liberals of the reform period. Cf. Barany, "Hungary: The Uncompromising Compromise," pp. 245–47. The events of 1848/49 only reinforced the need for such cooperation.

60. One of Andrássy's letters, written in exile to a close friend, Arthur, Count Scherr-Thoss, explained this new concept: "Common sense dictates that if Prussia wants to preserve the independence of Germany, it has to begin first of all by securing its supremacy in the German lands." Andrássy to Scherr-Thoss, March 13, 1855. The full text of the letter was published in *Pester Lloyd,* May 20, 1897. In the 1861 debate on the Address to the Throne, he declared bluntly that "Prussia's future is in German unity." Lederer, *Gróf Andrássy,* I, 130. To the German consul general the premier confided that "He [and] his government have the greatest interest in maintaining close relations with Prussia." Wäcker-Gotter to Bismarck, Pest, May 15, 1869, DHAA, Austria, File 58, II, No. A 1930.

61. Repeatedly during his many meetings with the German consul general Andrássy expressed his displeasure and advised that instead of agitation within the monarchy and support of his opponents, "he would consider it equally advantageous to Prussia itself if it stood in Hungary on the side of his ministry." Wäcker-Gotter to Bismarck, Pest, May 15, 1869, DHAA, Austria, File 58, II, No. A 1930. For further details see Gonda, *Bismarck,* pp. 88–92, 139.

62. It is of special interest to consult the reports sent by the Austrian consul general in Bucharest to Beust about the allegedly Prussian-supported irredentist activities of the Rumanians in Transylvania. Baron von Eder to Beust, Bucharest, Aug. 24–28, 1868, *Korrespondenzen des K. u. K. Ministeriums des Äussern, 1866–1871; Österreichisches Rothbuch* (Vienna, 1868), No. 2, 80. It is clear from the correspondence of Beust to Andrássy that the foreign minister used these reports to deepen Andrássy's suspicion about Prussia's intentions in order to be able to win him over to his pro-French policy. Cf. Horváth, *Magyar diplomácia, 1815–1918,* pp. 112–15, and p. 184, nn. 694–700; see also Wertheimer, *Andrássy,* I, 550–51.

63. Schweinitz to Bismarck, Vienna, Jan. 5, July 20, 1870. Otto Prinz von Bismarck-Schönhausen, *Die Gesammelten Werke* (hereafter cited as *GW*) (19 vols.; Berlin, 1924–1926), VIb, Nos. 1474 and 1701. Bismarck reacted promptly and sent word to Andrássy that he had no such intention. Bismarck to Schweinitz, Berlin, Jan. 12, July 23, 1870. *GW,* VIb, Nos. 1474, 1475, and 1701. Cf. Wertheimer, *Andrássy,* I, 637. Hans Lothar von Schweinitz (1822–1901), a distinguished and highly cultivated military man and respected diplomat, was Prussia's ambassador in Vienna between 1870 and 1876.

64. See the dramatic account of Arthur, Graf Scherr-Thoss, "Erinnerungen aus meinem Leben," *Deutsche Rundschau* (Berlin, 1881), p. 78. Count Scherr-Thoss, a former Prussian army officer, inherited an estate in Zemplén County (northern Hungary) of the Andrássys and settled there in 1839. He became a

close friend of the three Andrássy brothers and a patriotic citizen of Hungary. He participated in the Hungarian War of Independence of 1848/49, and after Hungary's defeat by the combined Habsburg and tsarist Russian forces, he fled the country. In exile, he lived mostly in Paris and kept up his old friendship with Andrássy. In 1862, he became acquainted with the Prussian ambassador to Paris, and the newly designated minister-president of that nation, Count Bismarck, whose confidence he won. At Bismarck's request, from that time on he sent him confidential reports about Hungary and its prominent political figures. In 1866 he fought in the Klapka Legion. He was captured by the Austrians, and only Bismarck's intervention saved him from execution. After the Compromise of 1867, he returned to Hungary and performed confidential services for Andrássy and Bismarck on several occasions. The details of his short memoir seem to be reliable.

65. Wäcker-Gotter to Bismarck, Pest, May 15, 1869, DHAA, Austria, File 58, II, A 1930.

66. Thiers, *Memoirs,* p. 29.

67. Graf Scherr-Thoss, "Erinnerungen aus meinem Leben," pp. 79–80.

68. The idea of Hungary becoming the Austrian center of gravity did not originate with Bismarck. Talleyrand in a note dated October 1805 advised Napoleon to persuade Austria to accept the loss of Germany and Italy, and to seek compensation in the east at the expense of Turkey. Talleyrand to Napoleon, Strasbourg, Oct. 17, 1805, Pierre Bertrand, ed., *Lettres inédites de Talleyrand à Napoléon* (Paris, 1889), pp. 156–68. Frederick von Gentz, the German publicist, advocated a similar solution. "Vienna must cease to be the seat of government, which must be removed to the center of Hungary, and this country be given a constitution. With Hungary, Bohemia, Galicia, and whatever else remained of Germany it would still be able to face the world," he wrote in 1806. These plans in some ways are similar to those Bismarck carried through successfully in the 1860s. As a diligent student of history during his university years in Göttingen, and during the years he spent in isolation (1839–47), Bismarck undoubtedly became acquainted with these plans.

69. Leopold von Gerlach, *Denkwürdigkeiten aus seinem Leben* (Berlin, 1891–92), II, 722.

70. Bismarck to Schleinitz, St. Petersburg, March 13, 1861, *GW,* III, No. 65.

71. Graf Scherr-Thoss, "Erinnerungen aus meinem Leben," p. 64.

72. Bismarck, *The Memoirs,* II, 50.

73. There is not a scrap of evidence to support the allegation made by Count Paul Breda, a French diplomat, to the Hessian minister Dalwigk that "Andrássy had, prior to the war of 1866, maintained treasonable relations with Prussia." Diary entry of April 3, 1868, Dalwigk, p. 369.

74. Conversation with the Austrian ambassador, Count Károlyi, Berlin, Dec. 4, 1862, *GW,* VII, No. 54. Bismarck's harsh words caused no alarm, only indignation in Vienna, although Francis Joseph and Rechberg did their best to stir things up. Cf. Chester W. Clark, *Francis Joseph and Bismarck: The Diplomacy of Austria before the War of 1866* (New York, 1968), p. 18.

75. See especially, Pflanze, *Bismarck,* pp. 302–08.

76. Landenberg to Bismarck, Vienna, Sept. 16, 1867, DHAA, Austria, File 54, III, No. A 3896; for further details see especially, Kállay diary, XXXI, entry of Oct. 15, 1868, MNA.

77. *Ibid.*

78. Artom to Visconti-Venosta, Vienna, July 29, 1870, private and unnumbered, Ministero degli affari esteri, Archivio storico (hereafter cited as MAE, AS), Archivi di gabinetto (1861-1887), busta 219: guerra franco-prussiana e trattative segrete 8 luglio-14 settembre 1870, fascicolo 4. Emilio Visconti-Venosta, one of Italy's foremost diplomats, served his country as foreign minister three times, 1863-64, 1869-78, and 1896-1901.

79. Curtopassi to Visconti-Venosta, Vienna, July 22, 1870, No. R. 212, MAE, AS, Serie politica (1867-1888), Austria-Ungheria, busta 1253: 1867-1870.

80. Werther to Bismarck, Vienna, June 18, 1867, *APP*, X, Nachtrag, No. 159. Werther's report deals with the coronation of Francis Joseph as king of Hungary. The Prussian ambassador included a penetrating analysis of Hungary's internal situation and the positive disposition of Hungarians of all classes toward Prussia. The report suggests the eagerness of the Prussians to have Hungarian support against the German aspirations of Austria. This document fell somehow into the hands of the Austrian government and it led to serious diplomatic complications. For a detailed account see Gonda, *Bismarck,* pp. 85-93.

81. Wäcker-Gotter to Bismarck, Vienna, Nov. 22, 1871, DHAA, Austria, File 58, II, No. A 4730.

82. *Ibid.*

83. Béla Orczy diary, entry of Oct. 31, 1868, in Wertheimer, *Andrássy,* I, 569. To make his opposition to Beust's anti-Prussian, pro-French policy more effective, Andrássy arranged to have his confidant, Baron Béla Orczy, appointed head of a department in the foreign ministry. The latter served in this capacity between 1868 and 1879. It was Orczy's duty, among others, to uphold Andrássy's views against Beust. Cf. Karl Tschuppik, *The Reign of Emperor Francis Joseph* (London, 1930), p. 205.

84. Kállay diary, XXXI, entry of April 4, 1869, MNA. Andrássy made it clear to Kállay that he "wants to avoid the French alliance," against Germany. *Ibid.* See also Nikola Petrović, "Der österreichisch-ungarische Ausgleich und die Orientalische Frage," in *Der österreichisch-ungarische Ausgleich 1867,* ed. Holotík, p. 201.

85. Wäcker-Gotter to Bismarck, Pest, Nov. 23, 1871, DHAA, Austria, File 58, II, No. 4730.

86. Salvini to Visconti-Venosta, Pest, Nov. 3, 1870, No. R. 10, MAE, AS, Serie politica (1867-1888), Austria-Ungheria, busta 1253: 1867-1870.

87. Salvini to Visconti-Venosta, Pest, Nov. 13, 1870, No. R. 11, *ibid.*

88. See for instance, Diószegi, *Ausztria-Magyarország,* pp. 42-43; and Barany, "Hungary: Uncompromising Compromise," pp. 245-46.

89. Cited by Florence Foster-Arnold, *Francis Deák Hungarian Statesman: A Memoir* (London, 1880), pp. 301-07.

90. See, for instance, Srbik, *Aus Österreichs Vergangenheit,* pp. 77, 80, 90. Srbik's contentions seem to represent a delayed revenge of the Austrian conservatives and reactionaries of 1866-1870, who were pushed aside by Andrássy.

91. Despite his extreme animosity toward the Magyars, even A.J.P. Taylor agrees with this proposition. See his *The Habsburg Monarchy, 1867-1918,* p.

126. For a realistic and highly scholarly appraisal consult May, *The Habsburg Monarchy*, pp. 34, 84, 109, 112–14; see also R. B. Mowat, "Andrássy," *The Hungarian Quarterly*, III, No. 2 (Summer 1937), 268–76.
92. Wäcker-Gotter to Bismarck, Pest, Nov. 22, 1871, DHAA, Austria, File 58, II, A 4730. See also Protokoll vom 22 Aug. 1870. Ministerrath für gemeinsame Angelegenheiten (hereafter cited as Ministerrath), HHSA, PA, XL, 285.
. 93. Thus Andrássy expressed himself to the special emissary of the·Italian Foreign Minister. Artom to Visconti-Venosta, Vienna, Aug. 7, 1870, private and unnumbered, MAE, AS, Archivi di gabinetto (1861–1887), busta 219: guerra franco-prussiana e trattative segrete 8 luglio–14 settembre 1870, fascicolo 3.
94. Salvini to Visconti-Venosta, Pest, Nov. 13, 1870, No. R. 11, MAE, AS, Serie politica (1867–1888), Austria-Ungheria, busta 1253: 1867–1870.
95. For the anti-Magyar orientation of the Pan-Slavists, see Petrovich, *Russian Panslavism*, pp. 273–76.
96. Kann, *The Austro-Hungarian Compromise of 1867 in Retrospect*, p. 15.
97. Thiers, *Memoirs*, p. 30.
98. [Andrássy], "The Present Position and Policy of Austria," p. 628.
99. Ministerrath, Aug. 22, 1870, HHSA, PA, XL, 285.
100. Personal notes of Andrássy, published in Roland Hegedüs, "The Foreign Policy of Count Julius Andrássy," *The Hungarian Quarterly*, III, No. 4 (Winter 1937/38), 633.
101. *Ibid.*, pp. 632–33. Cf. István Diószegi, "Honvédőrnagy Metternich íróasztalánál: 150 éve született Andrássy Gyula" [A Major at Metternich's Desk: Julius Andrássy Was Born One Hundred Fifty Years Ago], *Élet és irodalom* [Life and Literature], 1973, No. 9, p. 7.
102. "The integrity of the Turkish Empire" is a must, the Premier told Kállay. Kállay diary, XXXI, entry of Aug. 19, 1868, MNA. To the Russian chancellor Andrássy declared emphatically that "we desire the preservation of Turkey as it is." Gorchakov to Alexander II, Berlin, Aug. 28/Sept. 9, 1872. The full text of the report is printed in Baron A. F. Meyendorff, "Conversation of Gorchakov, Andrássy and Bismarck in 1872," *Slavonic and East European Review*, VIII, December 1929, 405.
103. I. Diószegi, *Ausztria-Magyarország és Bulgária a San Stefanoi béke után, 1875–1878* [Austria-Hungary and Bulgaria after the Treaty of San Stefano, 1875–1878] (Budapest, 1961), pp. 7–8.
104. *Ibid.*
105. Kállay diary, XXXI, entry of Aug. 19, and Dec. 30, 1868, MNA. See also David MacKenzie, *The Serbs and Russian Pan-Slavism, 1875–1878* (Ithaca, N.Y., 1967), p. 13. For more details see R. W. Seton-Watson, "Les Relations de l'Autriche et de la Serbie entre 1868 et 1874: La mission de Benjamin Kállay à Belgrade," *Le Monde Slave*, I, No. 2 (1926), 210–30; II, No. 5 (1926), 186–204; III, No. 8 (1926), 273–88.
106. As quoted in Hegedüs, "The Foreign Policy of Count Julius Andrássy," p. 630.
107. Anton, Freiherr von Mollinary, *Sechsundvierzig Jahre im österreichischen-ungarischen Heere* (2 vols.; Zürich, 1905), II, 257. Cf. Nikola Petrović,

"Der österreichisch-ungarische Ausgleich und die Orientalische Frage," in Holotík, pp. 202–211.

108. Kállay diary, XXXII, entry of July 29, 1870, MNA.

109. Artom to Visconti-Venosta, Vienna, July 20–21, 1870, private and unnumbered, MAE, AS, Archivi di gabinetto (1861–1887), busta 219: guerra franco-prussiana e trattative segrete 8 luglio–14 settembre 1870, fascicolo 3.

110. Artom to Visconti-Venosta, Vienna, Aug. 7, 1870, private and unnumbered, ibid.

111. Kállay diary, XXXI, entry of Aug. 19, 1868, MNA.

112. Ibid.

113. Ibid.

114. Wäcker-Gotter to Bismarck, Pest, Nov. 22, 1871, DHAA, Austria, File 58, II, No. A 4730.

115. Gerhard Ritter, "Das Bismarckproblem," Merkur, IV (1950), 663.

116. Moustier to Gramont, Paris, July 3, 1867, ODG, XVII, No. 5263.

117. May, The Habsburg Monarchy, p. 92.

118. See, for instance, Diószegi, Austria-Magyarország, pp. 42–43.

119. Hans Lothar von Schweinitz, Denkwürdigkeiten, I, 297.

120. Memorandum of Andrássy to Beust, Vienna, June 22, 1877. The full text is printed in Miksa Falk, Kor és jellemrajzok [Time and Character Studies] (Budapest, 1903), pp. 286–89.

Chapter III

1. Quoted in Wertheimer, Andrássy, I, 293.

2. With the constitutional reorganization of Austria Beust hoped to gain the sympathy of the South German states. Freiherr von Thumb, a sagacious observer of Austrian national policy, had clearly recognized that in his liberal concessions Beust saw the most appropriate means for the recovery of Austria's German position. Thumb to Varnbüler, Vienna, Feb. 6, 1867, Württembergisches Hauptstaatsarchiv Stuttgart (hereafter cited as WHSA), Abt. Gesandschaftsakten, Berichte aus Wien, 1866–1870 (hereafter cited as Reports). On Feb. 1, 1867, Beust explained publicly to Belcredi, the prime minister, that "through the appeasement of the German party in Austria," he hoped "to draw South Germany away from Prussia and make it sympathetic toward Austria." Quoted in Ludwig, Graf Belcredi, ed., "Fragmente aus dem Nachlass des ehemaligen Staatsministers Richard Graf Belcredi," Die Kultur (1907), p. 295.

3. As one of Beust's agents observed: "France was defeated more at Sadowa than Austria, because it felt its security compromised." Klindworth to Beust, Paris, Jan. 16, 1869, HHSA, PA, IX, 174.

4. For a brief résumé of this problem see E. Malcolm Carrol, Germany and the Great Powers, 1866–1914 (2nd ed.; Hamden, Conn., 1966), pp. 28–44; cf. Taylor, Struggle for Mastery in Europe, pp. 173–80.

5. Beust to Metternich, Vienna, Nov. 10, 1866, Oncken, II, 119.

6. Ibid. Cf. Gramont to Moustier, Vienna, Nov. 5, 1866, ODG, XIII, No. 3726.

7. Metternich to Beust, Paris, Nov. 14, 1866, Oncken, II, 119, n. 2.

8. In his report, Gramont only hinted at, but gave no details of, his own remarks. It seems that the French ambassador said more than his government desired him to say. Gramont to Moustier, Dec. 20, 1866, *ODG,* XIII, No. 3952. For details of Gramont's speech see Gagern to Dalwigk, Vienna, Dec. 16, 1866, SAD, Reports.

9. *Ibid.* For the press report on Beust's response see, for example, *Fremdenblatt,* Dec. 16, 1866.

10. Gagern to Dalwigk, Vienna, Dec. 16, 1866, SAD, Reports.

11. Goltz to Bismarck, Paris, Dec. 17, 1866, Oncken, II, 137.

12. La Gorce's assertion that Napoleon and his close circle viewed Austria as an Old Regime and so showed reluctance for an alliance with it is quite probable. Cf. Pierre de La Gorce, *Histoire du Second Empire* (7 vols.; Paris, 1903), VI, 150.

13. Metternich to Mensdorff, Paris, Oct. 24, 1866, Oncken, II, 117.

14. The French project of an offensive alliance between France and Prussia, drafted ca. Aug. 23, 1866, is published in Oncken, II, 94–95.

15. Moustier to Talleyrand, Paris, Feb. 18, 1867, *ODG,* XIV, No. 4180.

16. Gagern to Dalwigk, Vienna, Dec. 27, 1867, SAD, private letter, Nachlass Dalwigk.

17. Quoted in Endre Kovács, *Ausztria útja az 1867-es kiegyezéshez* [Austria's Road to the Compromise of 1867] (Budapest, 1968), p. 268.

18. Napoleon III tried, as early as the summer of 1860, to convince Vienna that it should strive to reconcile the Hungarians because it would open up new possibilities for Austria in the east. Metternich to Rechberg, Paris, June 25, 1860, HHSA, Nachlass Rechberg.

19. Metternich to Beust, Paris, Oct. 24, 1866, HHSA, PA, IX, 92.

20. For details of Beust's visit to the Hungarian capital, see Kónyi, *Deák,* IV, 142–55.

21. [Prince Jérôme Napoléon] to Andrássy, Paris, Dec. 16, 1866, *ibid.,* p. 151.

22. Andrássy to his wife, Buda, Dec. 21, 1866, *ibid.,* IV, 155–56.

23. Cf. Taylor, *The Habsburg Monarchy,* p. 126. Taylor appears to have an almost psychic dislike for Andrássy. And it is, to say the least, curious that he never substantiates his sweeping remarks of condemnation.

24. Werther to Bismarck, Vienna, Dec. 10, 1866, *APP,* VIII, No. 126. During the Christmas holidays, Beust complained to Richard, Freiherr von Friesen, the Saxon minister, about the reputation and low prestige of Austria. To restore its position in the councils of Europe, Austria needed some important diplomatic success, Beust maintained. Freisen, *Erinnerungen aus meinem Leben,* III, 4f.

25. For the genesis of the Cretan Revolt see *ODG,* XII, 72 n. k. On the course of events see Mosse, *The European Powers and the German Question,* pp. 253–90.

26. Cf. David MacKenzie, *The Serbs and Russian Pan-Slavism, 1875–1878* (Ithaca, N.Y., 1967), pp. 7–29.

27. Talleyrand to Drouyn, St. Petersburg, Aug. 30, 1866, F. Charles-Roux, *Alexandre II, Gortchakoff et Napoléon III* (Paris, 1913), p. 398; cf. Keyserling to Bismarck, St. Petersburg, Aug. 29, 1866, *APP,* VIII, No. 9.

28. Already before Beust's appointment as foreign minister of Austria,

diplomats called attention to a significant shift in Vienna's Balkan policy providing partial support for the Christian peoples of the Ottoman Empire. Wagner to Bismarck, Oct. 6, 1866, *APP,* VIII, No. 54.

29. Revertera to Beust, St. Petersburg, Nov. 7/Oct. 26, 1866, HHSA, PA, X, 57.

30. Revertera to Beust, St. Petersburg, Dec. 3/Nov. 21, 1866, HHSA, PA, X, 57.

31. Cf. Edmund von Glaise-Horstenau, *Franz Josephs Weggefährte: Das Leben des Generalstabchefs Grafen Beck* (Vienna, 1930), p. 176. See also the report on Austria's Balkan policy by Engelhardt, the French consul general in Belgrade, of Feb. 4, 1872, *Documents diplomatiques français* (hereafter cited as *DDF*) (Paris, 1929), pp. 128–29. Engelhardt identified Archduke Albrecht and General Wagner, the former governor of Dalmatia, as the chief proponents of a Russian-oriented policy.

32. Cf. Diószegi, *Ausztria-Magyarország,* p. 25.

33. Werther to Bismarck, Vienna, Dec. 10, 1866, *APP,* VIII, No. 126.

34. Speaking to the German ambassador about the inauguration of a new era in Austrian policy, Beust remarked that it was a mistake for Austria to attach itself to such dying causes as the legitimate Italian princes, the German Confederation or *the integrity of the Turkish Empire* [italics supplied], Werther to Bismarck, Vienna, Dec. 10, 1866, *ibid.*

35. Cf. Mosse, *The European Powers and the German Question,* p. 258.

36. Beust to Metternich, Vienna, Jan. 1, 1867, HHSA, PA, IX, 86.

37. Metternich to Beust, Paris, Jan. 5, 1867, telegram, *ibid.* The Austrian ambassador, seeking support for the new Austrian policy, explained it in detail to Napoleon III but to no avail. The French emperor doubted that either England or Russia would respond positively to Beust's plan. Metternich to Beust, Paris, Jan. 7, 1867, *ibid.* Moustier argued that public opinion in France would reject such a plan and also doubted whether Turkey or England would accept it. Metternich to Beust, Paris, Jan. 8, 1867, *ibid.*

38. The French leaders proved to be correct. England would not consider the Austrian proposal. Lord Stanley, the British foreign secretary, replied emphatically that "England and France would never consent to abandon the principle of the neutralization of the Black Sea." And without England in the 1860s no decision could be reached on the "eastern question." Apponyi to Beust, London, Jan. 30, 1867, HHSA, PA, VIII, 75. Cf. Richard Millman, *British Foreign Policy and the Coming of the Franco-Prussian War* (Oxford, 1965), p. 61.

39. Metternich to Beust, Paris, Jan. 11, 1867, telegram, HHSA, PA, IX, 86.

40. Metternich to Beust, Paris, Jan. 7, 1867, *ibid.*

41. Bismarck to Goltz, Berlin, Jan. 30, 1867, *APP,* VIII, No. 213.

42. Benedetti to Moustier, Berlin, Jan. 26, 1867, *ODG,* XIV, No. 4115.

43. The French foreign minister sneered at Bismarck's offer of friendship in the east by stating: "You offer us spinach without salt; Luxemburg is the salt." Goltz to Bismarck, Paris, March 1, 1867, *APP,* VII, No. 266.

44. Beust to Revertera, Vienna, Jan. 22, 1867, HHSA, PA, X, 54.

45. Werther to Bismarck, Vienna, Jan. 8, 1867, *APP,* VIII, No. 173.

46. Cf. Diószegi, *Ausztria-Magyarország,* pp. 22–24.

47. Kállay diary, XXXI, entry of Aug. 19, 1868, MNA.

48. Quoted in M. D. Stoyanovich, *The Great Powers and the Balkans,* *1875–1878* (Cambridge, 1939), pp. 30–31.

49. Kállay diary, XXXI, entry of April 4, 1869, MNA.

50. *Ibid.*

51. *Ibid.*

52. Diószegi, *Ausztria-Magyarország,* p. 25.

53. These developments led to mutual recriminations between Vienna and St. Petersburg. See, for example, Revertera to Beust, St. Petersburg, Nov. 7/ Oct. 26, 1866, HHSA, PA, X, 57; Beust to Revertera, Vienna, Dec. 1, 1866, *ibid.,* X, 58. Cf. Schoenhals, "The Russian Policy of Count Beust,"pp. 18–32.

54. See Taylor, *Struggle for Mastery of Europe,* pp. 173–83. Cf. Carrol, *Germany and the Great Powers,* pp. 28–47.

55. French public opinion regarded a united Germany as contrary to the interest of France and it inevitably opposed further strengthening of Prussia in Germany. After his trip in Southern France, Metternich noted: "The whole country is animated by a single feeling, and that is hatred for Prussia. Far and wide people are aware of the mistakes that have been committed and of the great chance that would never come back. They are longing for a *revanche éclatante.*" (italicized in the original) Metternich to Beust, Paris, March 7, 1867, Oncken, II, 230.

56. Cf. Metternich to Beust, Paris, Jan. 7, 12, 1867, *ibid.,* pp. 163, 178.

57. Metternich to Beust, Paris, Feb. 3, 1867, *ibid.,* p. 194.

58. Freiherr von Thumb's prognosis of the previous November had been realized: "Should the Danubian Monarchy succeed once in internal consoli-dation, then more than ever it would have a reinforced interest in breaking South Germany away from Prussia and bringing it under Austrian influence." Thumb to Varnbüler, Vienna, Nov. 26, 1866, WHSA, Reports.

59. Instead of a more sober attitude, for which Bismarck had hoped, it caused consternation in France. See, for example, *Liberté,* March 22, 1867; cf. Perglas to Louis II, Paris, March 25, 1867, Oncken, II, 259.

60. Beust to Wimpffen, Vienna, March 28, 1867, HHSA, PA, III, 97.

61. Lónyay diary, entry of March 29, 1867, Kónyi, *Deák,* IV, 379.

62. Lónyay diary, entry of Sept. 9, 1867, *ibid.,* p. 221; cf. Wäcker-Gotter to Bismarck, Budapest, May 15, 1869, DHAA, Austria, File 58, I, No. A 1930.

63. Lónyay diary, entry of March 19, 1867, Kónyi, *Deák,* V, 377.

64. Lónyay diary, entry of March 28, 1867, *ibid.,* p. 379.

65. A report of a Hungarian agent, written most likely in April, 1867, told Bismarck: "The particular attention of the Hungarian government is focused on Russia and the Danubian countries, and the fact that they believe in the existence of a secret agreement between Prussia and Russia influences greatly the policy of the statesmen to be followed towards Prussia." Usedom to Bismarck, Florence, April 16, 1867, *APP,* VIII, No. 492, n. 2.

66. Cf. Fröbel, *Ein Lebenslauf,* II, 536.

67. By a treaty made with the Netherlands in 1816, Prussia gained the right to garrison the fortress of Luxemburg, which was one of the strongholds on the eastern frontiers of France organized to prevent any future French aggression. The Grand Duchy of Luxemburg in which the fortress was located was the personal property of William III, King of the Netherlands, but at the same time it was also a member of the German Confederation and the *Zollverein.* Though

the Treaty of Prague dissolved the former, Prussia continued garrisoning the fortress. For details, see Pflanze, *Bismarck,* pp. 378–91; Carrol, *Germany and the Great Powers,* pp. 35–42; and K.A. Schierenberg, *Die deutsche-französische Auseinandersetzung und die Luxemburg Frage* (Luxemburg, 1933).

68. Wertheimer, *Andrássy,* I, 546.

69. See Lederer, *Gróf Andrássy,* I, 170.

70. Theodor von Bernhardi, *Aus dem Leben Theodor von Bernhardis* (9 vols.; Leipzig, 1893–1906), entry of May 4, 1867, VIII, 365–66.

71. Usedom to Bismarck, Florence, April 16, 1867, *APP,* VIII, No. 492, n. 2.

72. Cf. Schmitt, "Count Beust and Germany," p. 25.

73. Beust to Metternich, Vienna, April 27, 1867, Oncken, II, 361–65.

74. Beust to Metternich, Vienna, April 8, 1867, Oncken, II, 301.

75. Reuss to Bismarck, St. Petersburg, April 13, 1867, *APP,* No. 471.

76. Wimpffen to Beust, Berlin, April 12, 1867, HHSA, PA, III, 95.

77. Tauffkirchen to Ludwig II, Berlin, April 13, 1867, *APP,* VIII, No. 474.

78. Bismarck to Werther, Berlin, April 14, 1867, *APP,* VIII, No. 478.

79. Tauffkirchen to Ludwig II, Vienna, April 16, 1867, *APP,* VIII, No. 498; cf. Werther to Bismarck, Vienna, April 18, 1867, *ibid.,* No. 507. Francis Joseph gave his answer in a sharper manner: "I can assure you," he said to Tauffkirchen, "that Austria will be very selfish and set as high a price as possible for its cooperation." Tauffkirchen to Ludwig II, Vienna, April 22, 1867, *ibid.,* No. 522.

80. Beust to Wimpffen, Vienna, April 19, 1867, HHSA, PA, III, 95. Beust had also reminded Bismarck that not more than six months ago Napoleon had saved Austrian territories from Prussia. Austria could hardly be expected to make an alliance against him now. Cf. Gramont to Moustier, Vienna, April 27, 1867, *ODG,* XVI, No. 4866.

81. Beust, II, 119–23.

82. In his opinion: "Between the two great empires, Latin and Slav, only a federation of all the German elements can maintain the balance of power. Hungary can be independent and regain its strength and influence on the Sub-Danube under the wings of the German Federation." Lónyay diary, entry of March 28, 1867, Kónyi, *Deák,* IV, 379.

83. *Pesti Napló,* Oct. 28, 1866.

84. *Ibid.*

85. The offer came as no surprise to Beust, for Metternich had already reported about the new French speculations. Metternich to Beust, Paris, April 18, 1867, Oncken, II, 338. In a conversation with the Prussian ambassador, Gramont denied that he had proposed an alliance to Beust. Werther to Bismarck, Vienna, May 7, 1867, *APP,* VIII, No. 600. Reporting his negotiations with Beust, Gramont does not reveal the extent of his offer, and mentions only that he told Beust how far France was willing to support Austria in case of a common war with Prussia. Gramont to Moustier, Vienna, April 28, 1867, *ODG,* XVI, No. 4875. Gramont seems to have been more blunt than authorized by Napoleon III. In his opening remarks to Beust he confessed that he was empowered only to "sound out the terrain," but added that he preferred to talk "frankly."

86. A report of the Austrian military attaché in Paris provided Vienna with

contrary information about the state of the French army and public morale, which no doubt contributed to Gramont's failure to move Beust. For the report, see Major Graf Welsersheimb to K. K. Armee-Oberkommando, Paris, April n.d., 1867, Oncken, II, 290–92.

87. Beust to Metternich, Vienna, April 27, 1867, HHSA, PA, IX, 86.

88. Beust to Wimpffen, Vienna, April 27, 1867, HHSA, KA, Geheim Akten, Karton 17.

89. Under the influence of Beust's pompous promises and assertions, Gramont, contrary to other French diplomats, suggested even in 1868 that Andrássy's influence did not affect whatsoever Beust's views and actions. Gramont to La Valette, Vienna, Dec. 2, 1867.

90. Usedom to Bismarck, Florence, April 16, 1867, *APP,* VIII, No. 492, n. 2.

91. Ágoston Trefort, a confidant of both Andrássy and Deák, delegated by the former to assist Beust in the early stage of dualist transformation, told Lónyay that he "found the situation such that Andrássy should of necessity stay here [in Vienna] after the coronation; the Hungarian influence must be pregnant, otherwise, the centralists might overthrow the thoughtless Beust and seize the leadership of the government." Lónyay diary, entry of May 30, 1867, Kónyi, *Deák,* V, 97–98.

92. Echoing Andrássy, Lónyay also advised Beust to "strive for the preservation of peace . . . and not to pledge himself at the Salzburg meeting." Lónyay diary, entry of July 31, 1867, *ibid.,* p. 145.

93. According to the original plan Francis Joseph was to visit Napoleon III on the occasion of the Great Exhibition. However, the death of Maximilian, the younger brother of the Austrian monarch, in Mexico, for which Napoleon bore a large share of responsibility, made Francis Joseph's trip an impossibility. The French emperor was naturally embarrassed but he did not give up hope of meeting Francis Joseph. "Nothing divides us and everything must draw us together," he wrote the Austro-Hungarian sovereign. Napoleon III to Francis Joseph, Tuileries, July 11, 1867, Oncken, II, 436. Napoleon's trip to Salzburg was encouraged by both Beust and Metternich. Metternich to Beust, Paris, July 15, 1867, *ibid.,* p. 438; Beust, II, 131.

94. Gagern to Dalwigk, Vienna, July 7, 1867, SAD, Nachlass Dalwigk.

95. Cited by Wertheimer, *Andrássy,* I, 546.

96. For details on the Salzburg visit, see Oncken, II, 447–57; Beust, II, 132–36; and J. Redlich, "L'Entrevue de l'Empereur François-Joseph et de l'Empereur Napoléon à Salzbourg le 18 Aout, 1867," *Le Monde Slave,* Nouvelle Serie, III (1926), 143–51.

97. For the draft of an Austro-French alliance, see Oncken, III, 454–56. The document published by Oncken is missing from the archives. It was, however, made public in several European newspapers, including the *Bethlens diplomatischer Wochenschrift,* a German language monthly in Hungary. Oncken believes in its authenticity. *Ibid.,* p. 454, n. 1.

98. Explaining his rejection of the French offer to his old friend Dalwigk, the Hessian minister, Beust made clear his reasons for doing so. The eight million Austro-Germans would never agree to the transfer of German territory to France. Dalwigk, entry of Oct. 26, 1867.

99. The correspondent of a North German newspaper in Vienna, scruti-

nizing the Hungarian national scene, observed that Hungary's renewed political life must be considered and in Austria siding with France the Hungarians saw only a new source of danger. *Norddeutsche Allgemeine Zeitung,* May 8, 1867.

100. Bamberg to Bismarck, Paris, Sept. 12, 1867, *APP,* IX, No. 167, n. 2.

101. Lónyay to Andrássy, Vienna, Aug. 12, 1867, cited by Wertheimer, *Andrássy,* I, 550.

102. *Pesti Napló,* Aug. 27, 1867.

103. Kállay diary, XXXI, entry of Aug. 19, 1868, MNA. The Hungarian liberals would have considered an entente with France in the east because they were convinced, as the organ of the Deák party expressed it: "Be it an imperial, republican or Orleanist government beyond the Rhine — each considers it its best interest to fight against Russian expansion." *Ibid.,* Oct. 28, 1866.

104. Faithful to his policy, Andrássy absolutely declined to pledge cooperation on the part of Austria in a Franco-German conflict, even in his later years as foreign minister. See the Treaty of Alliance between Austria-Hungary and Germany, Oct. 7, 1879, A. F. Przibram, *The Secret Treaties of Austria-Hungary* (2nd ed.; 2 vols.; New York, 1967), I, 25–31.

105. Beust's memorandum to Francis Joseph, Vienna, Aug. 1867, Oncken, II, 447–50.

106. Draft in Beust's handwriting with marginal notes by Napoleon III. Oncken, II, 457–58.

107. Cf. Mosse, *The European Powers and the German Question,* pp. 280–81.

108. Bamberg to Bismarck, Paris, Sept. 12, 1867, *APP,* IX, No. 167, n. 2.

109. Ladenberg to Bismarck, Vienna, Sept. 8, 1867, DHAA, I.A.A. 1 (Österreich), 55, Acta betr. den von dem Kaiser und der Kaiserin der Franzosen dem Kaiser von Österreich in Salzburg abgestatteten Besuch (hereafter cited as Austria, File 55), I, No. A 3821. Bismarck to Ladenberg, Berlin, Sept. 15, 1867, *ibid.,* I, No. 1805. Cf. Walterskirchen to Beust, Florence, Aug. 23, 27, 1867, telegrams, HHSA, PA, II, 96.

110. Lefebvre de Behaine to Moustier, Berlin, Aug. 29, 1867, *ODG,* XVIII, No. 5603.

111. Bismarck to Rosenberg, Berlin, Aug. 20, 1867, *GW,* VIa, No. 17.

112. Lefebvre de Behaine to Moustier, Berlin, Aug. 29, 1867, *ODG,* XVIII, No. 5603.

113. Ladenberg to Bismarck, Vienna, Sept. 2, 1867, GHAA, I.A.A. 1 (Österreich), 54, Acta betr. Schriftwechsel mit der Kgl. Gesandschaft in Wien, sowie mit anderen Kgl. Missionen und fremden Kabinetten über die innere Zustände und Verhältnisse Österreichs (hereafter cited as Austria, File 54), III, No. A 3746. Ladenberg's analysis of Austrian public opinion reveals overwhelming sentiment against an alliance with France against Prussia. The report finds that a small circle of mostly influential conservative aristocracy desired close cooperation with France, fearing that German unification under Prussian leadership would bring about the destruction of Austria. A second group wished to avoid an alliance with France for fear of antagonizing Germany. In the event of a successful French thrust into South Germany, Austria should, however, take advantage of the situation and side with the highest bidder so that Austria would regain its position in Germany. The largest group which

included the majority of the bourgeoisie was sympathetic to German unity under Prussian leadership for it had seen no threat in it to Austrian interests. But the latter, deeply suspicious of Russia with respect to the Slav problem, was disturbed about the recently renewed Prussian-Russian amity.

114. Two weeks later, the same diplomat very well summarized Hungarian public opinion. The preservation of peace is the decided and urgent desire of the Hungarians to be able to consolidate and strengthen their gains. They watch with deep anxiety the eventuality of a Franco-Prussian war in which Austria could get involved. All parties and factions are decidedly opposed to Austria's participation in such a war for they fear that it would restore its power in Germany and thus deprive Hungary of its gains. The only war they would fight, as allies of France, would be one against Russia. This attitude is represented chiefly by Andrássy and the most prominent leaders of the Deák party. The organ of the party, the *Pesti Napló,* favors such a combination, but stresses that it is not in the interest of the Hungarians to frustrate German unity. Ladenberg to Bismarck, Vienna, Sept. 16, 1867, *ibid.,* No. A 3896.

115. Cf. Gonda, *Bismarck,* p. 130.

116. Lónyay diary, entry of Sept. 9, 1867, Kónyi, *Deák,* V, 211.

117. *Ibid.*

118. Werther to Bismarck, Vienna, Aug. 27, 1867, GHAA, Austria, File 55, I, No. A 3655. Cf. Beust to Wimpffen, Berlin, Aug. 28, 1867, *APP,*IX, No. 141.

119. Moustier's circular to legations, Paris, Aug. 25, 1867, *ODG,* XVIII, No. 5596.

120. Bismarck's circular to missions, Berlin, Sept. 7, DHAA, Austria, File 55, I, No. 1754.

121. Wimpffen to Beust, Berlin, Oct. 5, 1867, HHSA, PA, III, 96.

122. Ladenberg to Bismarck, Vienna, Oct. 6, 1867, GHAA, Austria, File 54, III, No. A 4117.

123. Bismarck to Werther, Berlin, Oct. 15, 1867, *ibid.,* No. 1922.

124. Wimpffen to Beust, Berlin, Oct. 12, 1867, HHSA, PA, III, 96. Concluding his conversation with the ambassador, Bismarck declared: "Austria can be threatened only from two sides, from France or from Russia. If Prussia and Austria are allied, the French danger ceases of itself; and as for the Russian menace to Austria, it would then be our duty to keep the latter quiet." *Ibid.*

125. Gonda believes that illegal connections existed between Prussia and certain Hungarian circles. However, he fails to marshal convincing evidence to prove his contention. Cf. Gonda, *Bismarck,* pp. 86–92.

126. Cf. Lónyay diary, entry of July 31, 1867, Kónyi, *Deák,* V, 145.

127. Cf. Gonda, *Bismarck,* p. 126.

128. See, for example, Freisen, *Erinnerungen aus meinem Leben,* III, 57–59.

129. Goltz to Bismarck, Paris, Nov. 4, 1867, DHAA, I.A.A. 1 (Österreich), 41, Akten betr. zur Haltung Österreichs Preussen gegenüber (hereafter cited as Austria, File 41), XI, No. A 4577.

130. Beust, *Aus drei Vierteljahrhunderten,* II, 136.

131. Auguste Ducrot, *La vie militaire du général Ducrot d'après sa correspondence, 1839–71* (2 vols.; Paris, 1895), II, 195.

132. Beust's circular to missions, Paris, Nov. 1, 1867, *APP,* IX, No. 278.

133. Beust to Metternich, Vienna, Nov. 19, 1867, Oncken, II, 479.

134. From Andrássy's personal notes, Paris, n.d., 1867, cited by Wertheimer, *Andrássy,* I, 549.

135. Ducrot, II, 195.
136. Cf. Wertheimer, *Andrássy,* I, 547.
137. Quoted in D. Jánossy, *A Kossuth-emigráció Angliában és Amerikában* [The Kossuth Emigration in England and America] (2 vols.; Budapest, 1940–48), II, 453–54. It contradicts the opinion of the Prussian legate in Vienna that Andrássy sympathized very much with French interests and was an ardent admirer of Napoleon III's policies. Ladenberg to Bismarck, Vienna, t. 10, 1867, GHAA, Austria, File 54, III, No. A3825.
138. Cf. Ministerrath, July 18, 1870, HHSA, PA, XL, 285.
139. For details, see Mosse, *The European Powers and the German Question,* pp. 270–75.
140. Brassier de St. Simon to Bismarck, Constantinople, Nov. 18, 1867, *APP,* IX, No. 336.

Chapter IV

1. Count Friedrich Wilhelm von Quadt, the Bavarian envoy in Paris, describing the general mood, observed: "Everyone is conscious of the unstable state of affairs and above all of the impossibility of indefinitely maintaining the ruinous system of armed peace." Quadt to King Ludwig II, Paris, July 30, 1868, Oncken, III, 15–16.
2. Memorandum by Vitzthum, Vienna, January, 1868, HHSA, PA, 177. The author of this policy, Count Karl Friedrich von Vitzthum, like Beust, was a Saxon diplomat. At Beust's request he was brought into the Austrian diplomatic service in the fall of 1867. Vitzthum was an able intriguer, who devoted a great deal of energy to frustrating Prussia's efforts in unifying Germany. After the Franco-German War he made his peace with Bismarck, a fact he demonstrated in the foreword of his book. Cf. Vitzthum, *London, Gastein, and Sadowa* (Stuttgart, 1889). For commentaries see, Oncken, II, 497–98.
3. Metternich to Beust, Paris, Jan. 16 and 19, 1868, HHSA, PA, IX, 177.
4. Moustier to Gramont, Paris, Jan. 18, 1868, *ODG,* XX, No. 6354.
5. Vitzthum to Beust, Paris, Feb. 1, 1868, *ibid.,* No. 6415.
6. Moustier to Benedetti, Paris, Jan. 26, 1868, *ibid.,* No. 6390.
7. *Ibid.;* Benedetti believed that Bismarck might support France in the Near East in return for guarantees of Prussia's position in Germany. Benedetti to Moustier, Berlin, March 3, 1867, *ibid.,* XXI, No. 6540. He repeatedly stressed at this time that Bismarck's aim was to unite South Germany with Prussia but without evoking the wrath of Paris. Benedetti emphasized that "no one on this side of the Rhine" entertained hostile feelings toward France. Benedetti to Moustier, Berlin, Jan. 5 and Feb. 4, 1868, *ibid.,* XX, Nos. 6297, 6432.
8. Reuss to Bismarck, St. Petersburg, Jan. 11 and 17, 1868, *APP,* IX, Nos. 487 and 515. Cf. Schweinitz to William I, St. Petersburg, Jan. 23, 1868, *ibid.,* No. 528.
9. Bismarck to Reuss, Berlin, Feb. 4, 1868, *ibid.,* No. 550.
10. Reuss to William I, St. Petersburg, Feb. 5, 1868, *ibid.,* No. 560. Cf. Alexander II to William I, St. Petersburg, Feb. 14, 1868, *ibid.,* No. 593.
11. Bismarck to Reuss, Berlin, Feb. 16, 1868, GW, VIa, No. 1064. King William's answer to his nephew was equally cautious and noncommittal. William I to Alexander II, Berlin, end of Feb., 1868, *APP,* IX, No. 630.

12. Reuss to William I, St. Petersburg, March 4, 1868, *ibid.,* No. 644. Three days later Alexander II repeated his offer and expressed his deep distrust of Beust as well as his hope that in the Polish question he could count on the absolute support of Prussia. Cf. Schweinitz to William I, St. Petersburg, March 19, 1868, *ibid.,* No. 644.

13. Bismarck to Reuss, Berlin, March 22, 1868, *GW,* VIa, No. 1108.

14. Bismarck to Reuss, Berlin, March 23, 1868, *APP,* IX, No. 680.

15. Reuss to Bismarck, St. Petersburg, March 25, 1868, *ibid.,* No. 688.

16. Reuss to Bismarck, St. Petersburg, March 27, 1868, *ibid.,* No. 690.

17. Count István Tisza, "Wertheimer 'Andrássy'-ja" [Wertheimer's 'Andrássy'], *Magyar Figyelő* [Magyar Observer] I, January–March, 1911, 337. Cf. Kondor, *Az 1875-ös pártfúzió,* pp. 62–66.

18. Lederer, *Gróf Andrássy,* I, 283.

19. *Ibid.,* pp. 283–88.

20. *Ibid.,* pp. 289–90.

21. *Ibid.,* p. 304.

22. *Ibid.,* pp. 305–06.

23. Orczy diary, entry of March 17, 1868, Wertheimer, *Andrássy,* I, 563–64.

24. It is rather amusing that Beust, who knew very well the nature of Orczy's mission, explains the latter's appointment simply by stating that he was in need of an interpreter in the Hungarian Delegation. Cf. Beust, *Aus drei Vierteljahrhunderten,* I, 175.

25. Kállay's appointment as consul general in Belgrade was officially announced on Feb. 2, 1868. Cf. Horváth, *Magyar diplomácia,* p. 105 and p. 178, n. 628.

26. Seton-Watson, "Les relations de l'Autriche-Hongrie et de la Serbie," pp. 215–18.

27. See, for instance, Kállay diary, XXXI, entry of Aug. 19, 1868, MNA.

28. See *ibid.,* entry of Oct. 31, and Nov. 11, 1868. Cf. Horváth, *Magyar diplomácia,* pp. 106–08, and Nikola Petrović, "Der österreichisch-ungarische Ausgleich und die Orientalische Frage," ed. Holotík, pp. 202–215.

29. Due to the recognition of this phenomenon, by the summer of 1868 most of the Great Powers accredited diplomatic agents to the Hungarian capital. Cf. *ibid.,* pp. 89–93.

30. Vitzthum to Beust, Paris, March 21, 1868, HHSA, PA, IX, 90.

31. Metternich to Beust, Paris, April 1, 1868, *ibid.,* p. 91.

32. Beust to Metternich, Vienna, April 4, 1868, Oncken, II, 549–51.

33. Metternich to Beust, Paris, April 9, 1868, *ibid.,* pp. 553–54.

34. Quadt to Ludwig II, Paris, March 28, and April 1, 1868, *ibid.,* pp. 542–45. The reports of the Bavarian envoy in Paris were based on his conversation with Prince Napoleon. Cf. Goltz to Bismarck, Paris, April 3, 1868, *APP,* IX, no. 705.

35. Metternich to Beust, Paris, April 9, 1868, Oncken, II, 553–54.

36. Beust to Metternich, Vienna, April 14, 1868, HHSA, PA, IX, 91.

37. Metternich to Beust, Paris, April 18, 1868, *ibid.,* p. 90.

38. Beust to Metternich, Vienna, May 12, 1868, *ibid.,* p. 91.

39. The passage of the Austrian army reorganization bill in June seemed to have subdued Napoleon's recurring concern over the opposition of the Hungarians. Vitzthum to Beust, Paris, June 17, 1868, *ibid.,* p. 90.

40. Beust to Metternich, Vienna, May 12, 1868, *ibid.,* p. 91.
41. Francis Joseph to Napoleon III, Vienna, May 27, 1868, *ibid.,* p. 177. Cf. Vitzthum to Beust, Paris, June 17, 1868, *ibid.,* p. 90.
42. See Friedrich Engel Jánosi, "The Roman Question in the Diplomatic Negotiations of 1869–70," *The Review of Politics,* III (1941), 327.
43. Orczy diary, entry of May 4, 1868, Wertheimer, *Andrássy,* I, 564.
44. See Plener, *Erinnerungen,* I, 351.
45. Cf. Gonda, *Bismarck,* p. 126.
46. Orczy diary, entry of May 4, 1868, Wertheimer, *Andrássy,* I, 564.
47. *Ibid.,* p. 565.
48. Beust to Vitzthum, Vienna, June 20, 1868, HHSA, PA, IX, 92.
49. Metternich to Beust, Paris, July 3, 1868, *ibid.,* p. 91.
50. Metternich to Beust, Paris, July 20, 1868, Oncken, III, 12–13.
51. Beust to Francis Joseph, Gastein, July 20, 1868, *ibid.,* pp. 13–14.
52. Beust to Francis Joseph, July (n.d.) 1868, *ibid.,* pp. 14–15.
53. *Ibid.* Another evident motive behind Beust's proposal was his need for public support for the enactment of the projected army reform bill. Had the Austro-German and Hungarian liberals been convinced that its aim was an aggressive war against Prussia, they would have rejected it beyond doubt. Realizing the value of Beust's proposal, Francis Joseph approved it. Beust to Metternich, Wildbad Gastein, Aug. 13, 1868, Oncken, III, 16–17.
54. Metternich to Beust, Paris, Aug. 19, 1868, Oncken, III, 19–22.
55. Napoleon told Metternich that, according to his cousin, Prince Napoleon (the prince visited Andrássy in June), the Hungarians were plotting the revival of an independent Poland against Russia, and they feared nothing more than "la reprise de la grande position en Allemagne." Their ambition was to win Prussia to a "coalition contre la Russie." *Ibid.,* p. 21. The day Metternich had his audience with Napoleon, Andrássy made similar statements to Kállay. Kállay diary, XXXI, entry of Aug. 19, 1868, MNA.
56. Metternich to Beust, Paris, Sept. 14, 1868, HHSA, PA, IX, 177.
57. Vitzthum to Beust, Paris, Sept. 24, 1868, *ibid.,* and the same to the same, Paris, Sept. 25, 1868, *ibid.,* p. 90.
58. Metternich to Beust, Paris, Oct. 28, 1868, Oncken, III, 53.
59. Metternich to Beust, Compiègne, Dec. 2, 1868, HHSA, PA, IX, 177.
60. See Potthoff, *Die deutsche Politik Beusts,* pp. 175–85.
61. Beust's speech may be found in his *Aus drei Vierteljahrhunderten,* II, 208–11. On the reaction of the Prussian press, see Münch to Beust, Berlin, Aug. 5, 1868, APP, X, No. 104, n. 3.
62. *Pesti Napló,* Aug. 8, 1868. The article is attached to the report of the envoy of Hesse-Darmstadt. Gagern to Dalwigk, Aug. 27, 1868, SAD, Reports.
63. Beust himself admitted that his participation was a mistake. Beust, *Aus drei Vierteljahrhunderten,* II, 207.
64. Beust to Andrássy, Gastein, Aug. 13, 1868, Wertheimer, *Andrássy,* I, 566–68.
65. The articles of the *Pesti Napló* drew the attention of diplomats to the differences of views between Andrássy and Beust. See, for example, Tessin to Taube, Vienna, Aug. 10, 1868, WHSA, Reports; and Gagern to Dalwigk, Vienna, Aug. 27, 1868, SAD, Reports.
66. Orczy immediately reported the new speculations to Andrássy. Orczy

diary, entry of Sept. 19, 1868, Wertheimer, *Andrássy,* I, 568. The memorandum is in Oncken, III, 28–31.

67. Kállay diary, XXXI, entry of Oct. 15, 1868, MNA.

68. *Ibid.*

69. *Ibid.* Cf. Orczy diary, entry of Oct. 31, 1868, Wertheimer, *Andrássy,* I, 570.

70. Andrássy emphasized that he desired complete and not an armed neutrality. In his view the latter would have been "the most idiotic position." To prove his point, he cited the failure of Napoleon III's armed neutrality in 1866. *Ibid.,* p. 569.

71. *Ibid.*

72. Brătianu, Ion, the elder (1822–1891), Rumanian statesman, minister of interior (1868), minister president (1876–81 and 1881–88).

73. Cf. Bismarck to Prince Charles, Berlin, Feb. 27, 1868, *Aus dem Leben König Karls von Rumänien* (4 vols.; Stuttgart: Deutsche Verlags-Anstalt, 1894), I, 239–43. Cf. Bismarck to Werther, Berlin, April 18, 1868, DHAA, Austria, File 41, XIa, No. A 1341; and D'Avril to Moustier, Bucharest, March 24, 1868, *ODG,* XXI, No. 6602.

74. For details, see Gábor G. Kemény, *Iratok a nemzetiségi kérdés történetéhez Magyarországon a dualizmus korában* [Documents on the History of the Nationality Question in Hungary in the Era of Dualism] (4 vols.; Budapest: Tankönyvkiadó, 1952–66), I, 83.

75. Eder to Beust, Bucharest, Aug. 24, 1868, HHSA, PA, X, 204; and Vetsera to Beust, Jassy, Sept. 2, 1868, *ibid.* Cf. *Aus dem Leben König Karls,* I, 284, 299.

76. Eder to Beust, Bucharest, Sept. 12, 1868, HHSA, PA, X, 204. Cf. Horváth, *Magyar diplomácia,* pp. 113, 184, n. 700, and Vasile Maciu, "La Roumanie et le Pacte Dualiste austro-hongrois de 1867," ed. Holotík, pp. 260–264.

77. R. W. Seton-Watson, *History of Rumania* (Cambridge: The University Press, 1934), p. 331.

78. See especially, Kai Peter Schoenhals, "The Russian Policy of Friedrich Ferdinand von Beust, 1866–1871" (unpublished Ph.D. dissertation, University of Rochester, 1964), pp. 17–36.

79. Gramont to Moustier, Vienna, Sept. 16, 1868, *ODG,* XXII, No. 6885. Beust declared to Fröbel that "the decision will come from the east." Fröbel, *Ein Lebenslauf,* II, 538.

80. Beust to Metternich, Vienna, Nov. 6, 1868, Oncken, III, 60.

81. *Ibid.*

82. Metternich to Beust, Paris, Dec. 17, 1868, HHSA, PA, IX, 177.

83. Beust to Metternich, Vienna, Nov. 6, 1868, Oncken, III, 60–61.

84. See, for instance, Horváth, *Magyar diplomácia,* pp. 112–15; Schoenhals, "The Russian Policy of Friedrich Ferdinand von Beust," pp. 58–66; and Potthoff, *Die deutsche Politik Beusts,* pp. 220–30.

85. Walter Rogge, *Geschichte Österreichs von Világos bis zur Gegenwart* (3 vols.; Leipzig-Wien: Brockhaus, 1872–73), III, 198.

86. Ladenberg to Thile, Vienna, Nov. 3, 1868, DHAA, Austria, File 56, V, No. A 3474.

87. Gramont to Moustier, Vienna, Oct. 30 and Nov. 3, 1868, *ODG,* XXII, Nos. 6956 and 6961. Cf. Przibram, *Erinnerungen,* I, 221.

88. Cf. *Rothbuch,* II, Nos. 47–110.

89. Werther to Bismarck, Vienna, Dec. 9, 1868, DHAA, Austria, File 56, V, No. A 3891. Cf. Rogge, III, 198 f.

90. *Ibid.*

91. Wertheimer, *Andrássy,* I, 551.

92. Officially Bismarck maintained that "Prussia's interests were 'not stronger than that of England and France, but not less strong than the neighboring Great Powers,' Austria, Russia, and Turkey." Bismarck to Goltz, Berlin, Feb. 26, 1868, *GW,* VIa, No. 1077.

93. Bismarck to Werther, Berlin, April 18, 1868, DHAA, Austria, File 41, XIa, No. A 1341. Beust understood the role Rumania played in Bismarck's game and complained about it to the French ambassador. Gramont to Moustier, Vienna, Sept. 16, 1868, *ODG,* XXII, No. 6885.

94. Potthoff, *Die deutsche Politik Beusts,* p. 229.

95. Bismarck to Goltz, Berlin, April 11, 1868, *GW,* VIa, No. 1123.

96. Thile to Bismarck, Berlin, Nov. 4, 1868, *ibid.,* No. 1204, n. 1.

97. Thile to Bismarck, Berlin, Nov. 10, 1868, *ibid.*

98. Thile to Keyserling, Berlin, Nov. 14, 1868, *ibid.*

99. Wesdehlen to Bismarck, Firenze, Nov. 18, 1866, APP, X, No. 1123.

100. *Aus dem Leben König Karls,* I, 309. Cf. Vasile Maciu, "La Roumanie et le Pacte Dualiste austro-hongrois de 1867," ed. Holotík, p. 264.

101. *Norddeutsche Allgemeine Zeitung,* Nov. 21, 1868.

102. Bismarck to Keyserling, Berlin, Nov. 22, 1868, *GW,* VIa, No. 1214. Bismarck followed up his message with a personal letter to Prince Charles emphasizing that "the confidence of the Hungarians is a guarantee of peace for us, an obstacle to Austria's participation in a coalition directed against us." Bismarck to Prince Charles, Berlin, Feb. 2, 1868, *GW,* VIa, No. 1304. Cf. Vasile Maciu, "La Roumanie et le Pacte Dualiste austro-hongrois de 1867," ed. Holotík, pp. 264–265.

103. See, among others, F. R. Bridge, *From Sadowa to Sarajevo: The Foreign Policy of Austria-Hungary, 1866–1914* (London and Boston, 1972), p. 41.

104. Beust insisted that now was the time to defeat Russia. Gramont to La Valette, Dec. 24, 1868, *ODG,* XXIII, No. 7116.

105. Reporting the excessive tone of the Prussian press, Wimpffen concluded that Bismarck's efforts to appease the Hungarians were designed to "disturb the good understanding between Vienna and Pest, between Your Excellency and Count Andrássy." Wimpffen to Beust, Tg., Berlin, Nov. 27, 1868, *APP,* X, No. 253. Beust's answer reflected apprehension: "The Emperor was very disagreeably impressed by the flirtation with Hungary." Beust to Wimpffen, Tg., Pest, Nov. 27, 1868, *ibid.*

106. Ladenberg to Thile, Vienna, Nov. 3, 1868, GHAA, Austria, File 56, V, No. A 3474.

107. Wimpffen to Beust, Berlin, Dec. 5, 1868, HHSA, PA, III, 99. Cf. Wimpffen to Beust, Berlin, Dec. 18, 1868, *ibid.* It was generally believed that Bismarck's aim was to discredit and thus unseat Beust. Wimpffen to Beust, Berlin, Jan. 2, 1868, *ibid.,* p. 101.

108. To the outside world Beust kept denying the existence of any serious difference of opinion between himself and Andrássy. Beust to Wimpffen, Vienna, Jan. 6, 1869, HHSA, PA, III, 101. Cf. Gagern to Dalwigk, Vienna, April 15, 1869, SAD, Reports.

109. *Pesti Napló,* Dec. 5 and 12, 1868.

110. Halász, *Egy letűnt nemzedék,* p. 81.

111. Gramont to La Valette, Vienna, Dec. 30, 1868, *ODG,* XXIII, No. 7145.

112. Cf. Tisza, "Wertheimer 'Andrássy'-ja," pp. 337–38.

113. A member of this group, Count Majláth, assured Beust that "the Emperor can count on Hungary in the event of a great conflict." Dalwigk diary, entry of Sept. 16, 1868.

114. Castellane to Moustier, Pest, Dec. 19, 1868, France, Archives des affaires étrangères (hereafter cited as AAE), Dépêches politiques des Consuls (hereafter cited as DC), Autriche XXVIII, No. 11.

115. Gramont to Moustier, Vienna, Nov. 19, 1868, *ODG,* XXII, No. 6996.

116. Castellane to Moustier, Vienna, Nov. 19, 1868, AAE, DC, XXVIII, No. 11.

117. Halász, *Bismarck és Andrássy,* p. 105.

118. Orczy diary, entry of Dec. (n.d.), 1868, Wertheimer, *Andrássy,* I, 572–73.

119. Halász, *Egy letűnt nemzedék,* p. 82.

120. Orczy diary, entry of Dec. (n.d.), 1868, Wertheimer, *Andrássy,* I, 574.

121. *Ibid.*

122. See especially, Falk, *Kor és jellemrajzok,* pp. 273–74. Wertheimer maintains that Falk went too far. Wertheimer, *Andrássy,* I, 574. Falk makes clear that his article was the subject of a detailed discussion between himself, Andrássy and Eötvös. Halász supports Falk's claims: "Andrássy had seen the manuscript of this article, and in fact so had Eötvös." Cf. Halász, *Egy letűnt nemzedék,* p. 82.

123. *Pester Lloyd,* Dec. 24, 1868.

124. Report of a Hungarian agent to Bismarck, Dec. 6, 1868, *APP,* X, No. 234, n. 1.

125. Wäcker-Gotter to Bismarck, Pest, March 30, 1869, DHAA, Austria, File 58, I, No. 1369.

126. *Pester Lloyd,* Dec. 24, 1868.

127. See, for instance, Wäcker-Gotter to Bismarck, Pest, May 15, 1869, DHAA, Austria, File 58, I, No. A 1930.

128. Orczy diary, entry of Dec. (n.d.), 1868, Wertheimer, *Andrássy,* I, 576. Cf. Forth-Rouen to La Valette, Dresden, Jan. 22, 1869, *ODG,* XXIII, No. 7189.

129. Potthoff, *Die deutsche Politik Beusts,* p. 249.

130. Quoted in Halász, *Egy letűnt nemzedék,* p. 83.

131. Andrássy and Wäcker-Gotter alluded to such a suspicion in their conversation. Wäcker-Gotter to Bismarck, Pest, May 15, 1869, DHAA, Austria, File 58, I, No. A 1930.

132. Orczy diary, entry of Dec. (n.d.), 1868, Wertheimer, *Andrássy,* I, 577.

133. Orczy diary, entry of Jan. (n.d.), 1869, *ibid.*

134. Gramont to La Valette, Vienna, Jan. 3, 1869, *ODG,* XXIII, No. 7157. Since his audience with Francis Joseph, Andrássy was taking a large share in the conduct of Austria's foreign policy. Beust, *Aus drei Vierteljahrhunderten,* II, 226.

135. Andrássy himself related it to the Prussian consul general. Wäcker-Gotter to Bismarck, Pest, Nov. 10, 1869, DHAA, Austria, File 58, I, No. A 6314. Cf. Kállay diary, XXXI, entry of April 13, 1869, MNA.

136. Gramont to La Valette, Vienna, Jan. 3, 1869, *ODG,* XXIII, No. 7157.
137. *Ibid.*
138. Graf Scherr-Thoss, "Erinnerungen aus meinem Leben," pp. 78–79. Cf. Bismarck to Benstorff, Berlin, Jan. 18, 1869, DHAA, Austria, File 41, XII, No. A 4132.
139. *Ibid.*
140. Wimpffen to Beust, Berlin, Jan. 15, 1869, HHSA, PA, III, 100. Andrássy's intervention in Berlin to stop the press polemics coincided with the pressure applied by Lord Clarendon, the British foreign secretary. Cf. Bernsdorf to Bismarck, London, Jan. 14, 1869, DHAA, Austria, File 41, XII, No. A 220; and Loftus to Clarendon, Berlin, Jan. 16, 1869, *APP,* X, No. 448.
141. Werther to Thile, Vienna, Jan. 6, 1868, DHAA, Austria, File 41, XII, No. A 148.
142. Following his meeting with the Prussian ambassador, Andrássy described the substance of his conversation with Werther to Gramont. The premier's communication to Gramont strongly indicates that he used it as an indirect warning to Paris that Hungary's participation in any compact could not be counted on. Gramont to La Valette, Vienna, Jan. 13, 1869, *ODG,* XXIII, No. 7173.
143. Rosen to Bismarck, Belgrade, Jan. 15, 1869, DHAA, Austria, File 41, XII, No. A 271. Cf. Kállay diary, XXXI, entry of Jan. 15, 1869, MNA.
144. Bismarck to Rosen, Tg., Berlin, Jan. 19, 1869, DHAA, Austria, File 41, XII, A 271.
145. Rosen to Bismarck, Belgrade, Jan. 22, 1869, *ibid.,* No. A 416. Cf. Kállay diary, XXXI, entry of Jan. 21, 1869, MNA.
146. For an excellent account, see Gonda, *Bismarck,* pp. 125–26. In order to allay the suspicions of the Hungarian leadership, Beust was continually stressing the peaceful aims of his policy both publicly and privately. Speaking in the *Reichsrat* in support of the army reorganization bill, he emphasized that its passage was necessary so that the monarchy might be strong enough to preserve its neutrality in case of a Franco-Prussian showdown and to prevent other powers from intervening. Gramont to Moustier, Vienna, Oct. 30, 1868, *ODG,* XXII, No. 6956. Cf. Ladenberg to Thile, Vienna, Nov. 4, 1868, DHAA, Austria, File 56, V, Nos. A 3475, A 3478.
147. Note by Rouher, Paris, Dec. 30, 1868, enclosed in a communication from Metternich to Beust, Paris, Dec. 31, 1868, HHSA, PA, IX, 177. Rouher put his ideas in writing at the insistence of Beust. Beust to Metternich, Vienna, Dec. 20, 1868, *ibid.* Two days later, in a memorandum, Beust argued again for an entente in the east and stressed that Austria had not renounced its claims in Germany and aimed to reassert itself there by indirect means. With the support of France, he went on, Austria could closely control Hungary. Thus Beust unwittingly admitted that the Hungarians were a major obstacle to realizing an alliance with the Second Empire. Beust to Metternich, Vienna, Dec. 22, 1868, Oncken, III, 83–87.
148. Beust to Metternich, Vienna, Jan. 13, 1869, *ibid.*
149. The French treaty-project of March 1, 1869, with four draft treaties, Oncken, III, 120–34.
150. Metternich to Beust, Paris, March 21, 1869, Oncken, III, 137–41.
151. In his reply, Metternich assured Beust with unconcealed irony that the Hungarians would find nothing in the treaty about the restoration of Austrian

power in Germany and the Austro-Germans no mention of the Rhine. Metternich to Beust, Paris, March 1, 1869, Oncken, III, 117–20.
152. Wertheimer, *Andrássy,* I, 477. Cf. Wäcker-Gotter, Pest, Nov. 22, 1869, DHAA, Austria, File 58, I, No. A 4005.
153. See Rothenberg, *The Military Border in Croatia,* pp. 169–70.
154. Beust, *Aus drei Vierteljahrhunderten,* II, 257.
155. Beust to Francis Joseph, Agram, March 12, 1869, HHSA, PA, IX, 177. Vitzthum reported that "Count Vimecarti [the Italian military attaché in Paris] pretends that he acquired proof in Florence [Italy's capital until 1870] that Count Andrássy has worked in a manner hostile to the alliance since Your Excellency sounded him out in Agram." Vitzthum to Beust, Paris, May 30, 1869, *ibid.*
156. Orczy diary, entry of April 11, 1869, Wertheimer, *Andrássy,* I, 585. The entry is based on Andrássy's letter of early April in which the premier reiterated his position of strict neutrality in case of a Franco-Prussian war, and instructed Orczy to make sure that Beust stayed within the bounds of their mutual agreement.
157. Kállay diary, XXXI, entry of April 4, 1869, MNA.
158. *Ibid.* Andrássy's opposition exasperated Beust. "Kein Minister mehr behindert sein kann als ich durch Andrássy," lamented Beust bitterly. Beust to Metternich, Gastein, June 9, 1869, Oncken, III, 201.
159. *Ibid.,* entry of April 11, 1869.
160. French draft of May 10, 1869, enclosed in report, Metternich to Beust, Paris, May 20, 1869, HHSA, PA, IX, 94.
161. Napoleon to Francis Joseph, St. Cloud, Sept. 24, 1869, *ibid.;* Francis Joseph's reply to Napoleon III has vanished.
162. The argument that Napoleon III was utterly foolish not to have obtained Italy's aid by evacuating Rome is advanced by Bourgeois and Clermont, *Rome et Napoléon III,* pp. 231–35.
163. General Barthélemy Louis Joseph Lebrun, *Souvenirs Militaires 1866–1870* (Paris, 1895), pp. 69–173.
164. *Ibid.*
165. Report of General Lebrun's audience with Francis Joseph, June 14, 1870, Oncken, III, 376–78.

Chapter V

1. See in particular, Jochen Dittrich, *Bismarck, Frankreich und die spanische Thronkandidatur der Hohenzollern* (München: R. Oldenbourg Verlag, 1962), pp. 43, 71 ff. Cf. Lawrence D. Steefel, *Bismarck, the Hohenzollern Candidacy, and the Origin of the Franco-German War of 1870* (Cambridge, Mass.: Harvard University Press, 1962), pp. 101–64.
2. On June 30, Ollivier had said in answer to a parliamentary question that his government was in no way disturbed: "At no period has the maintenance of peace seemed better assured." Cited by Michael Howard, *The Franco-Prussian War* (New York: The Macmillan Co., 1962), p. 48. Ollivier was not alone in his optimism. When Lord Granville took over the foreign office on July 6, he was told by the permanent under secretary, Mr. Hammond, that "he never had during his long experience known so great a lull in foreign affairs."

Quoted in Lord Edmond Fitzmaurice, *The Life of Granville George Leveson Gower, Second Earl of Granville, 1815–1891* (2 vols.; London: Longmans, 1905), II, 32. In the Dual Monarchy the appearance of calm had been equally complete: "The greatest calmness reigns continuously in the foreign political arena," wrote the *Pesti Napló,* July 2, 1870.

3. Steefel, *Bismarck,* pp. 101–03.

4. The text of Gramont's declaration is printed in Oncken, III, 396–97. For the attitude of the French leaders, see especially Metternich's four dispatches of July 8, Metternich to Beust, Paris, July 8, 1870, HHSA, PA, IX, 95.

5. Gramont told the Austrian ambassador that the French government is fully determined to resist the Hohenzollern candidature "even at the cost of war," *ibid.*

6. Prince Karl Anton to William I, Sigmaringen, July 12, 1870, No. 295. George Bonnin, *Bismarck and the Hohenzollern Candidature for the Spanish Throne* (London: Chatto and Windus, 1957), pp. 250–51.

7. Lederer, *Gróf Andrássy,* II, 313–31.

8. Orczy to his mother, Vienna, July 11, 1870, Wertheimer, *Andrássy,* I, 602–03.

9. Gagern to Dalwigk, Vienna, July 17, 1870, SAD, Reports. Cf. Potthoff, *Die deutsche Politik Beusts,* p. 339.

10. Beust to Metternich, Vienna, July 5, 1870, HHSA, PA, IX, 97.

11. Schweinitz to Bismarck, Vienna, July 6, 1870, No. 243, Bonnin, *Bismarck,* p. 225.

12. Beust to Metternich, Vienna, July 6, 1870, HHSA, PA, IX, 97.

13. Beust to Münch, Vienna, July 7, 1870, *ibid.,* III, 102; Beust to Dubsky, Vienna, July 7, 1870, *ibid.,* XX, 27.

14. Beust to Metternich, Vienna, July 7, 1870, *ibid.,* IX, 97.

15. *Hon,* July 7, 1870.

16. *Pesti Napló,* July 8, 1870.

17. *Neue Freie Presse,* July 6, 1870.

18. Apponyi to Beust, London, July 10, 1870, HHSA, PA, VIII, 74; Bernstorff to Bismarck, London, July 13, 1870, Robert H. Lord, *The Origins of the War of 1870* (2nd ed.; New York: Russell and Russell, 1966), pp. 234–36.

19. Metternich to Beust, Paris, July 8, 1870, HHSA, PA, IX, 95. Following his announcement about sending an Austrian observer corps to the Prussian frontier, Gramont told Metternich that he hoped Austria "would not stop at that." Metternich tried in vain to show the pretext France chose for war would incite German nationalism. *Ibid.* The bellicose French behavior disturbed Beust very much because the prospect of a Franco-Prussian confrontation foreshadowed the peril of a German national war (Dittrich, *Bismarck,* p. 231). If this happened, all his efforts "to bring South Germany back under Austrian influence" (Walterskirchen to Beust, Munich, July 18 and 19, 1870, HHSA, PA, VI, 33) would be frustrated and "Austria's German hopes would for all practical purposes" be destroyed. Dittrich, *Bismarck,* p. 231.

20. Metternich to Beust, Paris, July 8, 1870, HHSA, PA, IX, 95.

21. This proved unfortunate for France. Cazaux constantly read more into Beust's statements than actually was there. The Austrian chancellor found Cazaux a "little young for his taste," and anxiously awaited his replacement. Beust to Gramont, Vienna, July 21, 1870, *ibid.,* p. 177.

22. Cazaux to Gramont, Vienna, July 9, 1870, *ODG,* XXVIII, No. 8349.

23. Cf. Potthoff, *Die deutsche Politik Beusts,* p. 340.

24. Beust to Metternich, Vienna, July 9, 1870, HHSA, PA, IX, 97.

25. *Ibid.*

26. Cazaux to Gramont, Vienna, July 10, 1870, *ODG,* XXVII, No. 8393.

27. *Ibid.*

28. Orczy diary, entry of July 10, 1870, Wertheimer, *Andrássy,* I, 604. The Bourgoing mission caused considerable consternation in Paris. Metternich deemed it unwise and untimely. Metternich to Beust, Paris, July 13, 1870, HHSA, PA, IX, 95.

29. Vitzthum to Passetti, Paris, Dec. 10, 1892, HHSA, PA, IX, 177.

30. Metternich reported shortly before 6 p.m. of July 11 that "Gramont is somewhat at odds with Ollivier, who would like to join 'other questions' with the Hohenzollern issue in order to make war inevitable, while Gramont desires peace if the King of Prussia yields." Metternich to Beust, Paris, July 11, 1870, *ibid.,* p. 95.

31. Beust to Metternich, Vienna, July 11, 1870, *ibid.,* p. 177.

32. Gramont to Beust, Paris, Jan. 8, 1873, *ibid.*

33. Beust later admitted that his original intention was to publish it in the *Rothbuch.* Beust, *Aus drei Vierteljahrhunderten,* II, 352. In spite of Beust's own disclosure, some historians made use of this letter as supporting evidence of the chancellor's peaceful intentions. See, for example, Harold Temperley, "Lord Acton on the Origins of the War of 1870 with Some Unpublished Letters from the British and Viennese Archives," *Cambridge Historical Journal,* II (1926), 77, 79; and Schmitt, "Count Beust and Germany," p. 30.

34. Count Alfred Potocki (1817–1889), wealthy Polish nobleman, minister of agriculture (1868–1870), Austrian minister president (April to November, 1870).

35. Beust to Metternich, Vienna, July 11, 1870, HHSA, PA, IX, 177.

36. The foreign minister had to carry out his duties "in accordance with the ministries of both halves [of the Monarchy] and with their consent." See *Corpus Juris Hungarici, 1836–1868,* p. 335.

37. Curtopassi to Visconti-Venosta, Vienna, July 12, 1870, No. T 2496, MAE, AS, Serie politica (1867–1888), Austria-Ungheria, busta, 1253: 1867–1870.

38. To avoid exposing Austria too early, Archduke Albrecht had also cautioned Beust to avoid anything provocative, including concentration of troops. Wéninger to Csengery, Vienna, July 13, 1870, Országos Széchenyi Könyvtár Kézirattár (National Széchenyi Library Archives — hereafter cited as NSLA), Quart. Hung. 2421, Csengery hagyaték (Csengery Papers — hereafter cited as CSP).

39. Beust to Metternich, Vienna, July 13, 1870, HHSA, PA, IX, 97.

40. For details, see Steefel, *Bismarck,* pp. 188–94; and the text of the "Ems Telegram" see *ibid.,* pp. 257–58.

41. Potthoff, *Die deutsche Politik Beusts,* p. 343.

42. Beust to Metternich, Vienna, July 15, 1870, HHSA, PA, IX, 97.

43. Wertheimer, *Andrássy,* I, 612.

44. Orczy diary, entry of July 9, 1870, Wertheimer, *Andrássy,* I, 604.

45. Orczy diary, entry of July 11, 1870, Wertheimer, *Andrássy,* I, 612.

46. Schweinitz to Bismarck, Vienna, July 12, 1870, No. A 2296, Lord, *The Origins of the War of 1870*, p. 211.

47. Curtopassi to Visconti-Venosta, Vienna, July 12, 1870, No. T 2496, MAE, AS, Austria-Ungheria, busta 1253.

48. Orczy diary, entry of July 14, 1870, Wertheimer, *Andrássy*, I, 613.

49. *Ibid.*, p. 605.

50. Lederer, *Gróf Andrássy*, II, 309.

51. See particularly *supra*, pp. 31–32.

52. Bülow, *Memoirs*, IV, 169.

53. Lederer, *Gróf Andrássy*, II, 310.

54. *Ibid.*

55. *Ibid.*, p. 311.

56. *Ibid.*

57. Curtopassi to Visconti-Venosta, Vienna, July 14, 1870, No. 2619, MAE, AS, Austria-Ungheria, busta 1253.

58. Schweinitz to Bismarck, Vienna, July 12, 1870, No. A 2296, Lord, *The Origins of the War of 1870*, p. 211.

59. See especially Steefel, *Bismarck*, pp. 208–13.

60. Vitzthum to Andrássy, Brussels, Jan. 16, 1873, Oncken, III, 440–44.

61. "Andrássy arrived yesterday," Orczy wrote. "He is in a good mood, he hopes the best for us and that we avoid war." Orczy to his mother, Vienna, July 17, 1870; and his diary, entry of July 16, 1870, Wertheimer, *Andrássy*, I, 617.

62. *Pesti Napló*, July 16, 1870.

63. Italian Foreign Minister Visconti-Venosta's instructions to his special emissary, Knight Artom, stressed strongly that, following his arrival in Vienna, he was to seek the views of both "Beust and Andrássy." Visconti-Venosta to Artom, Firenze, July 15, 1870, private and unnumbered, MAE, AS Archivi di gabinetto, busta 219, fascicolo 4.

64. Magda Kégl, *Die Beurteilung der deutsche Frage in der ungarischen Presse, 1866–1871* (Budapest, 1934), pp. 33ff.; Diószegi, *Ausztria-Magyarország*, pp. 30–32.

65. Kégl, p. 34.

66. Diószegi, *Ausztria-Magyarország*, p. 30.

67. Schweinitz, *Denkwürdigkeiten*, I, 263.

68. Bülow, *Memoirs*, IV, 169.

69. *Ibid.*

70. Diószegi, *Ausztria-Magyarország*, p. 31.

71. *Hon*, July 16, 1870. There is no doubt that, besides foreign political considerations, the sentiment of the Left Center party was accentuated by the sympathy of its predominantly Calvinist members toward protestant Prussia. Lederer, *Gróf Andrássy*, II, 308.

72. Wäcker-Gotter to Bismarck, Pest, Jan. 29, 1870, DHAA, Austria, File 58, I, No. A 364.

73. *Reform*, July 16, 1870.

74. Halász, *Egy letűnt nemzedék*, pp. 87–88.

75. *Ibid.*

76. See *supra*, pp. 63–65.

77. Halász, *Egy letűnt nemzedék*, p. 88.

78. Halász writes in his memoirs that, in the days immediately before the

outbreak of the war, among his friends (mostly newspapermen) he was as usual alone in the opinion that Prussia would triumph over France. *Ibid.*, pp. 92–93. According to Sir Robert Morier, one of England's German experts, a French victory was not unlikely. "There is little doubt that the Prussians are not yet ready and that a great portion of Germany will be occupied." Roslyn Wemyss, *Memoirs and Letters of Sir Robert Morier, 1826 to 1876* (2 vols.; London, 1911), II, 159.

79. *Pesti Napló,* July 8, 1870.

80. *Ibid.,* July 12, 1870.

81. *Ibid.,* Jan. 16, 1868. The Leitha is a small river which then formed the boundary between Austria and Hungary.

82. Wäcker-Gotter to Bismarck, Pest, Dec. 21, 1869, DHAA, Austria, File 58, I, No. A 4243.

83. Curtopassi to Visconti-Venosta, Vienna, July 16, 1870, private and unnumbered, MAE, AS, Archivi di gabinetto, busta 219, fascicolo 3.

84. *Pester Correspondenz,* July 20, 1870.

85. *Pesti Napló,* Oct. 28, 1866.

86. See especially, Ministerrath, July 18, 1870, HHSA, PA, XL, 285.

87. See, for instance, Wertheimer, *Andrássy,* I, 546; Bamberg to Bismarck, Paris, Sept. 12, 1867, *APP,* IX, No. 167, n. 2; and Orczy diary, entry of Oct. 31, 1868, and April 11, 1869, Wertheimer, *Andrássy,* I, 570 and 585.

88. Bülow, *Memoirs,* IV, 169.

89. Schweinitz to Bismarck, Vienna, July 12, 1870, Lord, *The Origins of the War of 1870,* p. 211.

90. Cazaux to Gramont, Vienna, July 14, 1870, *ODG,* XXVIII, No. 8512.

91. Orczy diary, entry of July 11, 1870, Wertheimer, *Andrássy,* I, 612.

92. *Pesti Napló,* July 14, 1870.

93. *Pester Lloyd,* July 15, 1870.

94. *Hon,* July 16, 1870.

95. *Reform,* July 17, 1870.

96. See *supra,* pp. 63–64.

97. Lederer, *Gróf Andrássy,* I, 92. Cf. Wäcker-Gotter to Bismarck, Pest, May 15, 1869, DHAA, Austria, File 58, I, No. A 1930.

98. John Jay to Hamilton Fish, Vienna, July 16, 1870, National Archives, Washington, D.C. (hereafter cited as NA); dispatches from U.S. Ministers to Austria, 1838–1906 (hereafter cited as Reports, Austria), X, No. 136.

99. Halász, *Egy letűnt nemzedék,* pp. 80–81.

100. Deák declared emphatically: "The government has only one organ: the official gazette [*közlöny*]; the party has no designated organ." Kónyi, *Deák,* VI, 192.

101. There is much truth in Tisza's assertion that his Left Center party was the decisive force behind Andrássy "to realize, in spite of a good part of his own party," his policy of neutrality. Tisza to Pál Móricz, Geszt, July 21, 1898, cited by Kondor, *Az 1875-ös pártfúzió,* p. 64.

102. Orczy diary, entry of April 11, 1869, Wertheimer, *Andrássy,* I, 585.

103. *Pesti Napló,* July 14, 17, 1870.

104. *Pester Lloyd,* July 15, 1870.

105. John Jay to Hamilton Fish, Vienna, July 16, 1870, NA, Reports, Austria, X, No. 136.

106. Cazaux to Gramont, Vienna, July 17, 1870, *ODG,* XXIX, No. 8626.

107. Engel-Jánosi, "Austria in the Summer of 1870," p. 336.

108. Przibram, *Erinnerungen,* I, 268.

109. Bose to Nostitz-Wallwitz, Vienna, July 22, 1870, quoted in Diószegi, *Ausztria-Magyarország,* pp. 29–30.

110. *Ibid.,* p. 30.

111. Heinrich Pollak, *Dreissig Jahre aus dem Leben eines Journalisten* (3 vols.; Wien, 1894–98), II, 207.

112. *Neue Freie Presse,* July 13, 1870.

113. Cazaux to Gramont, Vienna, July 17, 1870, *ODG,* XXIX, No. 8674.

114. This was a constant preoccupation of foreign diplomats and Austrian officials alike. See, for example, Cazaux to Gramont, Vienna, July 17, 1870, *ODG,* XXIX, No. 8626; Beust to Gramont, Vienna, July 21, 1870, HHSA, PA, IX, 177; Curtopassi to Visconti-Venosta, Vienna, July 18, 1870, No. T 2666, MAE, AS, Archivi di gabinetto, busta 219, fascicolo 3.

115. Bülow, *Memoirs,* IV, 169.

116. Cazaux to Gramont, Vienna, July 16, 1870, *ODG,* XXIX, No. 8596.

117. *Neue Freie Presse,* July 13, 1870.

118. *Ibid.,* July 17, 1870.

119. *Ibid.,* July 21, 23, 24, 26, 1870; Cazaux to Gramont, Vienna, July 17, 1870, *ODG,* XXIX, No. 8674. Cf. Rogge, III, 336.

120. *Ibid.*

121. Palacký to Jan Palacký, Nice, February 16, 1860, cited by Zacek, "Palacký and the Austro-Hungarian Compromise of 1867," p. 15.

122. Revertera to Beust, St. Petersburg, May 30, 1867, HHSA, PA, X, 58.

123. For details, see Petrovich, *The Emergence of Russian Panslavism,* pp. 198–240.

124. See, for example, *Neue Freie Presse,* May 24, 25, 28, and June 2, 3, 1867; and Beust, *Aus drei Vierteljahrhunderten,* II, 426.

125. For details concerning these contacts see Karel Kazbunda, "Dvě Riegrova memoranda" [Two Rieger Memoranda] *Zahraniční politika* [Foreign Policy] (Prague, 1925), pp. 844–70, 954–78.

126. *Ibid.*

127. Otakar Odložilík, "Russia and the Czech National Aspirations," *Journal of Central European Affairs,* XXII (January, 1963), 421; and *Národní listy,* July 16, 18, and August 21, 1870.

128. *Ibid.,* p. 420.

129. *Ibid.,* p. 421; and Zacek, "Palacký and the Austro-Hungarian Compromise of 1867," pp. 19–20.

130. Palacký to Marie Palacký, Prague, September 5, 10, 1870, in Karel Stloukal, ed., *Rodinné listy Františka Palackého dceři Marii a zeti F. L. Riegrovi* [František Palacký's Family Letters to His Daughter Marie and Son in Law F. L. Rieger] (Prague, 1912), pp. 251–52, 254; and Ernest Denis, "Vzpomínky a úvahy o Palackém" [Memories and Studies of Palacký] *Památník* [Diary] (1898), p. 159.

131. Palacký to Louis Léger, Prague, August 13, 1875, in Zacek, "Palacký and the Austro-Hungarian Compromise of 1867," p. 19.

132. Palacký to Marie Palacký, September 5, 1870, in Stloukal, p. 251.

133. *Kraj,* July 16, 18, 1870; *Dziennik Polski,* July 24, 1870; and *Gazeta Narodowa,* July 16, 17, 18, 1870.

134. *Ibid.*

135. *Ibid.; Dziennik Lwowski,* August 22, 1870.

136. Copy of the editorial attached to Kriegsarchiv, Vienna, Kriegsministerium, Präs., 1870, 59–1/7. Cf. Rothenberg, *The Military Border in Croatia,* p. 176, n. 70.

137. See Taylor, *The Struggle for Mastery of Europe,* p. 206. Even during the crisis the French Ambassador at St. Petersburg hoped that Russian support could be won by agreeing to revision of the Treaty of Paris. Fleury to Gramont, St. Petersburg, July 10, 1870, *ODG,* XXIX, No. 8650.

138. Curtopassi to Visconti-Venosta, Vienna, July 12, 1870, No. T 2496, MAE, AS, Austria-Ungheria, busta 1253.

139. Artom to Visconti-Venosta, Vienna, July 20–21, 1870, confidential and unnumbered, *ibid.,* Archivi di gabinetto, busta 219, fascicolo 3.

140. Andrássy to his wife, Vienna (n.d.), 1870, Wertheimer, *Andrássy,* I, 618.

141. Beust to Metternich, Vienna, July 11, 1870, Oncken, III, 420–21.

142. Gramont to Andrássy, Paris, July 17, 1870, Bourgeois and Clermont, *Rome et Napoléon III,* pp. 258–59.

143. Gramont to Beust, Paris, July 17, 1870, HHSA, PA, IX, 177.

144. Cazaux to Gramont, Vienna, July 15, 1870, *ODG,* XXVIII, No. 8548; and Curtopassi to Visconti-Venosta, Vienna, July 15, 1870, No. T 2630, MAE, AS, Austria-Ungheria, busta 1253.

145. Cazaux to Gramont, Vienna, July 17, 1870, *ODG,* XXIX, No. 8626.

146. Taylor, *The Struggle for Mastery of Europe,* p. 207.

147. Diószegi, *Ausztria-Magyarország,* p. 37. The tsar's nervousness about Poland had been stimulated by the appointment of Potocki as premier of Austria in April, 1870, which had been followed by a series of measures designed to satisfy Polish aspirations in Galicia. Chotek to Beust, St. Petersburg, June 29/17, 1870, HHSA, PA, X, 62.

148. Chotek to Beust, St. Petersburg, July 23/11, 1870, *ibid.*

149. Cf. Bridge, *From Sadowa to Sarajevo,* p. 50.

150. Bismarck to Reuss, Berlin, Feb. 13, 1869, *APP,* X, No. 517.

151. Oubril to Westman, Berlin, July 14/2, 1870, Chester W. Clark, "Bismarck, Russia and the Origins of the War of 1870," *Journal of Modern History,* XIV (June, 1942), 204–08.

152. Pfuel to Bismarck, St. Petersburg, July 16, 1870, *GB,* VIb, Bismarck's own draft to No. 1652.

153. Mosse, *The European Great Powers and the German Question,* p. 310, n. 1.

154. Bismarck to Reuss, Berlin, July 26, 1870, *GW,* VIb, No. 1709.

155. Bismarck to Schweinitz, Berlin, July 23, 1870, *ibid.,* No. 1701.

Chapter VI

1. The French declaration of war was not formally presented to the Prussian government until July 19, but the July 15 declaration of the French government created a state of war. Cf. *ODG,* XXIX, 11, n. 1.

2. Ministerrath, July 18, 1870, HHSA, PA, XXXX, 285. The cross-section method used in this chapter is employed in Diószegi, *Ausztria-Magyarország,* pp. 57–63.

3. Lónyay had succeeded to this post in May, following the death of his predecessor Carl, Ritter von Becke.

4. Cf. Diószegi, *Ausztria-Magyarország,* p. 40.

5. *Ibid.*

6. Kállay diary, XXXI, entry of August 19, 1869, MNA.

7. Beust to Francis Joseph, Vienna, July 12, 1870, HHSA, PA, XXXX, 53.

8. The special Italian envoy to Vienna reported: "I know from a very trustworthy source that the Austrian Emperor desires to take part in the war." Artom to Visconti-Venosta, Vienna, July 20–21, 1870, private and unnumbered, MAE, AS, Archivi di gabinetto, busta 219, fascicolo 3. On the eve of war, Count Bellegarde, aide-de-camp to the monarch, confided to Cazaux: "His Majesty considered Austria and France jointly and he did not separate the two causes in his mind. In the Emperor's views, a failure of our aims on the banks of the Rhine would be a greater disaster for Austria than Königgrätz was." Cazaux to Gramont, Vienna, July 17, 1870, *ODG,* XXIX, No. 8626.

9. Thiers, *Memoirs,* p. 29.

10. See *supra,* p. 23.

11. Lónyay to Csengery, Vienna, July 13, 1870, NSLA, Quart. Hung. 2421, *CSP.*

12. The London *Times,* July 20, 1870.

13. Potthoff, *Die deutsche Politik Beusts,* p. 354.

14. Srbik, *Aus Österreichs Vergangenheit,* pp. 192–93.

15. "The Defense Minister [Kuhn] has declared this morning . . . that in three weeks he could put 300,000 men, including the National Guards [of Austria and Hungary], on a war footing," reported the Italian chargé d'affaires. Curtopassi to Visconti-Venosta, Vienna, July 17, 1870, No. T 2659, MAE, AS, Archivi di gabinetto, busta 219, fascicolo 3.

16. See, for example, Potthoff, *Die deutsche Politik Beusts,* p. 356. Cf. Srbik, *Aus Österreichs Vergangenheit,* pp. 168–202.

17. Chotek to Beust, St. Petersburg, June 29/17, 1870, HHSA, PA, X, 62.

18. Ministerrath, Aug. 22, 1870, *ibid.,* XXXX, 285.

19. Orczy diary, entry of July 18, 1870, Wertheimer, *Andrássy,* I, 619. After meeting with Andrássy and Potocki, the American ambassador reported that the views of the two ministers were similar. John Jay to Hamilton Fish, Vienna, July 16, 1870, NA, Reports, Austria, X, No. 136.

20. Cf. Tisza, "Wertheimer 'Andrássy'-ja," p. 336.

21. Lónyay to Csengery, Vienna, July 30, 1870, NSLA, Quart. Hung. 2421, *CSP.*

22. Ministerrath, Aug. 22, 1870, HHSA, PA, XXXX, 285.

23. Cazaux to Gramont, Vienna, July 15, 1870, Telegram, *ODG,* No. 8548.

24. Diószegi, *Ausztria-Magyarország,* p. 45.

25. Artom to Visconti-Venosta, Vienna, July 20–21, 1870, private and unnumbered, MAE, AS, Archivi di gabinetto, busta 219, fascicolo 3.

26. Ministerrath, July 18, 1870, HHSA, PA, XXXX, 285. Hereafter all quotations without a footnote in this chapter will refer to the *Protokoll* of the Council of Common Ministers of July 18, 1870.

27. Cazaux to Gramont, Vienna, July 17, 1870, *ODG,* XXIX, No. 8621.

28. Beust to Francis Joseph, Vienna, July 12, 1870, HHSA, PA, XXXX, 53.

29. Evidently Andrássy made his proposal under the influence of the minister of war, who boasted on July 17 that he could field an army of 300,000 men in three weeks. Cf. *supra,* p. 90.

30. This term became part of military terminology only later.

31. Diószegi argues, to be sure, quite mistakenly, that Andrássy's recommendation "fell little short of general mobilization." Diószegi, *Ausztria-Magyarország,* p. 47. The military laws of Nov. 13 (Austria) and Nov. 28 (Hungary), 1868, increased the war strength of the common army of the monarchy to 800,000 men. In addition, the law set the strength of Austria's *Landwehr* and Hungary's *Honvédség* (National Guard) at 200,000 men each. Thus Andrássy's proposal would have required the mobilization of only one quarter of the available forces — very much within the range of what is now called "partial mobilization."

32. Orczy diary, entry of July 18, 1870, Wertheimer, *Andrássy,* I, 619.

33. Archduke Albrecht's timing appears to have been more accurate than his geography; he expected the decisive battle to be fought on the borders of Saxony.

34. Beust referred emphatically to the experiences of the Crimean War, suggesting that he approved the military policy of Austria at that time, which essentially amounted to general mobilization.

35. Cf. Wagner, "Kaiser Franz Joseph und das deutsche Reich," pp. 54–59; and Potthoff, *Die deutsche Politik Beusts,* p. 358.

36. Orczy diary, entry of Oct. 31, 1868, Wertheimer, *Andrássy,* I, 570.

37. Cazaux to Gramont, Vienna, July 17, 1870, *ODG,* XXIX, No. 8626.

38. This sentence is in Andrássy's own handwriting to replace the one recorded in the *Protokoll* which begins: "One should admit to all who ask, without giving a declaration of neutrality, that...." Curiously, two historians, without any effort whatsoever to learn when Andrássy made the corrections, assumed that the premier made them later to put his subsequent attitude into better light. Cf. Potthoff, *Die deutsche Politik Beusts,* p. 362, n. 160; and Diószegi, *Ausztria-Magyarország,* pp. 50–51. In his excellent study on the Council of Common Ministers, Komjáthy shows that before the final draft of the minutes was resubmitted to the monarch, the foreign minister had to circulate it among the participants to check it for its accuracy, make corrections if necessary and then approve it with their signature. See Miklós Komjáthy, *Az Osztrák-Magyar Monarchia közös minisztertanácsa* [The Council of Common Ministers of the Austro-Hungarian Monarchy] (Budapest: Tempó, 1966), pp. 118–28.

39. Curtopassi to Visconti-Venosta, Vienna, July 15, 1870, No. T2630, MAE, AS, Archivi di gabinetto, busta 219, fascicolo 3.

40. Cazaux to Gramont, Vienna, July 17, 1870, *ODG,* XXIX, No. 8621.

41. Andrássy to Nopcsa, Vienna, May 6, 1871, Wertheimer, *Andrássy,* I, 630.

42. Cazaux to Gramont, Vienna, July 17, 1870, *ODG,* XXIX, No. 8621.

43. Beust to Metternich, Vienna, July 21, 1870, HHSA, PA, IX, 177.

44. See *supra,* p. 96, nn. 39 and 40.

45. Cf. Mosse, *The European Powers and the German Question,* pp. 306–07, n. 5.

46. Taylor's assertion that "they [the Russians] had, in fact, none to mobilize" is remote from the truth. See A.J.P. Taylor, *From Napoleon to Lenin* (New York, 1966), p. 101.

47. Fleury to Gramont, St. Petersburg, Aug. 9, 1870, *ODG,* XXIX, No. 8948.

48. Cazaux to Gramont, Vienna, July 15, 1870, *ODG,* XVIII, No. 8548.
49. Orczy to his mother, Vienna, July 19, 1870, Wertheimer, *Andrássy,* I, 619–20.
50. Andrássy to his wife, Vienna, July n.d., 1870, *ibid.,* p. 618.
51. Cazaux to Gramont, Vienna, July 17, 1870, *ODG,* XXIX, No. 8626.
52. Andrássy to his wife, Vienna, July n.d., 1870, Wertheimer, *Andrássy,* I, 618.
53. Beust to Metternich, Vienna, July 21, 1870, HHSA, PA, IX, 177.
54. Andrássy had expressed this belief on several occasions in the past. See especially, Orczy diary, entry of May 8, 1868, Wertheimer, *Andrássy,* I, 564; and Kállay diary, XXXI, entry of Oct. 15, 1868, MNA.
55. Kállay diary, XXXI, entry of July 29, 1870, *ibid.*
56. Kállay diary, XXXI, entry of Aug. 19, 1868, *ibid.*
57. According to Orczy's diary, Andrássy wanted to move against Russia with the victorious French army. Orczy diary, entry of Aug. 3, 1870, Wertheimer, *Andrássy,* I, 625–26.
58. Diószegi, *Ausztria-Magyarország,* p. 61.
59. Kállay's diary reveals that Andrássy made several steps toward winning the cooperation of Turkey and Serbia. Kállay diary, XXXI, entry of July 29, 1870.
60. Andrássy to his wife, Vienna, July n.d., 1870, Wertheimer, *Andrássy,* I, 618.
61. Several German historians, reading the anti-Prussian remarks of Andrássy in the council of ministers of July 18, 1870, came to question the premier's Germanophilism. Neither of them, however, felt the necessity of raising and solving the problem in its entirety. See especially, Platzhoff, "Die Anfänge des Dreikaiserbundes," p. 305; and Eyck, *Bismarck,* III, 394.
62. Andrássy to his wife, Vienna, July n.d., 1870, Wertheimer, *Andrássy,* I, 618.
63. Lederer, *Gróf Andrássy,* II, 336–37.
64. Eötvös to Andrássy, Karlsbad, Aug. 14, 1870, Báró Eötvös József, *Levelek, életrajz* [Baron Jóseph Eötvös, *Letters, Memoirs*] (Budapest: Révai, 1903), pp. 96–97.
65. Eötvös to Andrássy, Karlsbad, Aug. 22, 1870, *ibid.,* pp. 101–02.
66. Andrássy to Eötvös, Budapest, Sept. 16, 1870, *ibid.,* p. 107.
67. Schweinitz to Bismarck, Vienna, Jan. 5, and July 20, 1870, *GW,* VIb, Nos. 1474 and 1701.
68. Bismarck to Schweinitz, Berlin, Jan. 12, and July 23, 1870, *GW,* VIb, Nos. 1474, 1475, and 1701.
69. Beust to Metternich, Vienna, Aug. 10, 1870, HHSA, PA, IX, 97.
70. Alexander II of Russia had also offered to recognize this. Chotek to Beust, St. Petersburg, July 23/11, 1870, HHSA, PA, X, 62.
71. To support his arguments about the necessity of retaining the friendship of France, Beust pointed out that "if it [France] wishes, it can bring Italy down on our necks again and make difficulties for us in Tyrol, Dalmatia, and Trieste." Ministerrath, July 18, 1870, HHSA, PA, XXXX, 285.
72. Diószegi, *Ausztria-Magyarország,* p. 57.

Chapter VII

1. Orczy diary, entry of July 21, 1870, Wertheimer, *Andrássy*, I, 633.
2. Weninger to Csengery, Vienna, July 20, 1870, in Lorant Csengery, ed., *Csengery Antal hátrahagyott iratai* [Antal Csengery's Posthumous Papers] (Budapest, 1928), p. 558.
3. *Ibid*.
4. (Copy)Beust to Metternich, Vienna, July 20, 1870, HHSA, PA, IX, 97 (Auszug aus den ungedruckten Memoiren) annexed to Vitzthum to Passeti, Paris, Dec. 10, 1892, *ibid*., 177.
5. (Copy) Beust to Metternich, Vienna, July 20, 1870, *ibid*. The original draft of this letter has disappeared from the archives.
6. *Ibid*.
7. Artom to Visconti-Venosta, Vienna, July 20–21, 1870, confidential and unnumbered, MAE, AS, Archivi di gabinetto, busta 219, fascicolo 3.
8. Beust to Metternich, Vienna, July 21, 1870, HHSA, PA, IX, 177.
9. Houston, "The Negotiations for a Triple Alliance between France, Austria, and Italy," pp. 257–59.
10. For details, see S. William Halperin, "Visconti-Venosta and the Diplomatic Crisis of July 1870," *Journal of Modern History*, XXXI (1959), 295–309.
11. Ministerrath, July 22, 1870, HHSA, PA, XXXX, 285.
12. *Ibid*.
13. Ministerrath, July 23, 1870, *ibid*.
14. Chotek to Beust, telegram, St. Petersburg, July 23, 1870, *ibid*., X, 62.
15. Chotek to Beust, St. Petersburg, July 24, 1870, *ibid*.
16. Chotek to Beust, St. Petersburg, July 30, 1870, *ibid*.
17. Ministerrath, July 24, 1870, *ibid*., XXXX, 285.
18. Ministerrath, July 30, 1870, *ibid*.
19. Beust to Chotek, Vienna, August 4, 1870, *ibid*., X, 62.
20. Ministerrath, August 3, 1870, *ibid*., XXXX, 285.
21. Ministerrath, August 4, 1870, *ibid*.
22. Report "Conversation of Chotek with His Majesty the Emperor of Russia," St. Petersburg, August 14, 1870, *ibid*., X, 61.
23. Ministerrath, August 22, 1870, *ibid*., XXXX, 285.
24. *Ibid*.
25. Beust to Chotek, Vienna, August 25, 1870, No. 2, *ibid*., X, 62.
26. Gorchakov's circular repudiating the Black Sea clauses of the treaty of Paris, St. Petersburg, Oct. 31, 1870, *ibid*., 62.
27. Ministerrath, Nov. 6, 14, and Dec. 17, 1870, *ibid*., XXXX, 285.
28. Beust to Chotek, Vienna, Nov. 16, 1870, No. 2, *ibid*., X, 63.
29. Cf. Bridge, *From Sadowa to Sarajevo*, p. 52.
30. *Ibid*., p. 53.
31. For details see, Diószegi, *Ausztria-Magyarország*, pp. 205–214.
32. Memorandum of Beust to Francis Joseph, Vienna, May 18, 1871, HHSA, PA, XL, 54.
33. See Diószegi, *Ausztria-Magyarország*, pp. 253–254.

Bibliography

A. Sources

Archives

Austria. Haus-, Hof-, und Staatsarchiv, Vienna.
Politisches Archiv:
Preussen III, Cartons 95–97, 99–102
Württemberg VI, Carton 33
England VIII, Cartons 74–75
Frankreich IX, Cartons 86, 90–97, 174, 177
Russland X, Cartons 57–58, 62, 204
Spanien XX, Carton 27
Interna XXXX, Cartons 53–54, 285–86
Kabinettsarchiv:
Geheim Akten, Cartons 6, 17
Bavaria. *Geheim Staatsarchiv,* München.
Abt. Gesandtschaftsakten, Berichte aus Wien 1866–70.
Darmstadt. *Staatsarchiv,* Darmstadt.
Abt. Gesandtschaftsakten, Berichte aus Wien 1866–70.
Abt. Nachlass Dalwigk, Briefwechsel Dalwigk-Beust 1866–1870.
Württemberg. *Hauptstaatsarchiv,* Stuttgart.
Abt. Gesandtschaftsakten, Berichte aus Wien 1866–70.
West Germany. *Deutsches Hauptarchiv des Auswärtigen Amts,* Bonn.
I. A. A. 1. (Österreich) 41, Acta betr. die Haltung Österreichs Preussen
gegenüber, XI–XIV. Jan. 1, 1867–Dec. 31, 1870.
I. A. A. 1. (Österreich) 54, Acta betr. Schriftwechsel mit der Kgl. Gesandt-
schaft in Wien, sowie mit anderen Kgl. Missionen und fremden Kabi-
netten über die innere Zustände und Verhältnisse Österreichs, III–IV.
Sept. 1, 1867–Dec. 31, 1867.
I. A. A. 1. (Österreich) 55, Acta betr. den von dem Kaiser und der Kaiserin
der Franzosen dem Kaiser von Österreich in Salzburg abgestatteten
Besuch, I, 1867.
I. A. A. 1. (Österreich) 56, Acta betr. Schriftwechsel mit der Kgl. Gesandt-
schaft in Wien, sowie mit anderen Kgl. Missionen und fremden Kabinetten über die inneren Zustände und Verhältnisse Österreichs, I–V. Jan.
1, 1868–Dec. 31, 1868.
I. A. A. 1. (Österreich) 57, Acta betr. Schriftwechsel mit der Kgl. Gesandt-
schaft in Wien, sowie mit anderen Kgl. Missionen und fremden Kabinetten über die inneren Zustände und Verhältnisse Österreichs, I–V. Jan.
1, 1869–Dec. 31, 1869.

I. A. A. 1 (Österreich) 58, Acta betr. Schriftwechsel mit dem Consulat in Pest über ungarische Zustände, I, 1869–1870.

Italy. *Ministero degli Affari Esteri, Archivo Storico,* Rome.

Archivi di gabinetto (1861–1887), busta 219: guerra franco-prussiana e trattative segrete, 8 luglio–14 settembre 1870, fascicolo 3.

Serie politica (1867–1888), Austria-Ungheria, busta (11) 1253: 1869–1871.

U.S. *State Department, National Archives,* Washington, D.C.

Despatches from U.S. Ministers to Austria, 1838–1906, X, July 8–November 12, 1870.

Hungary. *Magyar Országos Levéltár* (Hungarian National Archives), Budapest.

Kállay Béni, Belgrádi Napló (Béni Kállay, Belgrade Diary), XXXI–XXXIV.

Országos Széchenyi Könyvtár kézirattár (National Széchenyi Library Archives), Budapest.

Fol. Hung. 1733, Kállay Béni: Levélmásolatok, iratok és beszédek (Béni Kállay: Letters, Papers and Speeches).

Quart. Hung. 2421, Csengery hagyaték (Csengery Papers).

Printed Documents

Bismarck-Schönhausen, Otto Prinz von. *Die Gesammelten Werke.* 15 vols. Berlin: Hobbing, 1824–32.

Corpus Juris Hungarici: 1836–1868 évi törvénycikkek [Acts of the Years of 1836–1868]. Budapest: Franklin, 1896.

France. Ministère des affaires étrangères. *Documents diplomatiques français.* 32 vols. Paris, 1929–55.

————. Ministère des affaires étrangères. *Les Origines diplomatiques de la guerre de 1870–71.* 29 vols. Paris, 1910–32.

Kónyi, Manó, ed. *Deák Ferenc beszédei* [Speeches of Francis Deák]. 6 vols. Budapest: Franklin, 1903.

Korrespondenzen des K.u.K. Ministeriums des Äusseren, 1866–71, Österreichisches Rotbuch. Nos. 1–5. Vienna, 1868–71.

Lederer, Béla, ed. *Gróf Andrássy Gyula beszédei* [Speeches of Count Julius Andrássy]. Budapest: Franklin, 1891.

Oncken, Hermann. *Die Rheinpolitik Kaiser Napoleon III, von 1865 bis 1870 und des Ursprung des Krieges von 1870/71* (2nd ed.). 3 vols. Osnabrück: Biblio Verlag, 1967.

Reichsinstitut für Geschichte des neuen Deutschlands. *Die auswärtige Politik Preussens,* ed. Erich Brandenburg et al. 10 vols. Oldenburg, 1933–39.

Memoirs, Letters, Diaries and Correspondence

Bernhardi, Theodor von. *Aus dem Leben Theodor von Bernhardis.* 9 vols. Leipzig, 1893–1906.

Bertrand, Pierre (ed.). *Lettres inédites de Talleyrand à Napoléon.* Paris: Perrin, 1889.

Beust, Friedrich Ferdinand Graf von. *Aus drei Vierteljahrhunderten.* 2 vols. Stuttgart: Cotta, 1887.

Beyens, Baron Napoléon Eugène. *Le second empire vu par un diplomate belge.* 2 vols. Paris: Plon, 1924–26.

Bismarck, Prince Otto von. *The Memoirs.* Translated by A. J. Butler. 2 vols. New York: Howard Fertig, 1966.

Bloomfield, Georgiana, Baroness. *Reminiscences of Court and Diplomatic Life.* 2 vols. London: Chapman and Hall, 1883.

Bourgoing, Jean de (ed.). *The Incredible Friendship: Letters of Emperor Franz Joseph to Frau Katharina Schratt.* Translated by E. M. Kienast and Robert Rie. New York: State University of New York Press, 1966.

Bülow, Prince Bernhard von. *Memoirs.* Translated by Geoffrey Dunlop and F. A. Voigt. 4 vols. Boston: Little, Brown, and Co., 1931.

Delbrück, Hans. *Erinnerungen, Aufsätze und Reden.* Berlin: Stilke, 1902.

Ducrot, Auguste. *La vie militaire du général Ducrot d'après sa correspondance, 1839–1871.* 2 vols. Paris: Plon, 1895.

Freisen, Richard von. *Erinnerungen aus meinem Leben.* Dresden, 1910.

Fröbel, Julius. *Ein Lebenslauf: Aufzeichnungen, Erinnerungen und Bekenntnisse.* 2 vols. Stuttgart: Cotta, 1890–1891.

Gerlach, Leopold von. *Denkwürdigkeiten aus seinem Leben.* 2 vols. Berlin: Wilhelm Hertz, 1891–92.

Hansen, Jules. *Les coulisses de la diplomatie: Quinze ans à l'étranger, 1864–79.* Paris: J. Bandry, 1880.

Karl von Rumänien, König. *Aus dem Leben König Karls von Rumänien.* 4 vols. Stuttgart: Deutsche Verlags-Anstalt, 1894.

Lebrun, Barthélemy L. J. *Souvenirs militaires, 1866–1870.* Paris, 1895.

Loftus, Lord Augustus. *The Diplomatic Reminiscences.* 2 vols. London: Cassell, 1894.

Mednyánsky, Cézár br. *Emlékezései és vallomásai az emigrációból* [Recollections and Confessions of Baron Caesar Mednyánsky from Exile]. Translated by Dr. Károly Óvári-Avari. Budapest: Singer and Wolfner, 1930.

Molisch, Paul (ed.). *Briefe zur deutschen Politik in Österreich von 1898 bis 1918.* Vienna: Braumüller, 1934.

Mollinary, Anton Freiherr von. *Sechsundvierzig Jahre im österreich-ungarischen Heere, 1833–1879.* 2 vols. Zürich: Orell Füsli, 1905.

Plener, Ernst Freiherr von. *Erinnerungen.* 3 vols. Stuttgart: Deutsche Verlags-Anstalt, 1911–21.

Pollak, Heinrich. *Dreissig Jahre aus dem Leben eines Journalisten.* 3 vols. Wien, 1894–98.

Przibram, Ludwig von. *Erinnerungen eines alten Österreichers.* 2 vols. Stuttgart: Deutsche Verlags-Anstalt, 1912.

Schnürer, Franz (ed.). *Briefe Kaiser Franz Josephs I. an seine Mutter 1838–1872.* Munich: Kosel and Pustet, 1930.

Schüssler, Wilhelm (ed.). *Die Tagebücher des Freiherr v. Dalwigk zu Lichtenfels aus den Jahre 1860–71* (2nd ed.). Osnabrück: Biblio Verlag, 1967.

Schweinitz, Hans Lothar von. *Denkwürdigkeiten des Botschafters General von Schweinitz.* 2 vols. Berlin: Verlag von Reimer Hobbing, 1927.

Stloukal, Karel (ed.). *Rodinné listy Františka Palackého dceři Marii a zeti F. L. Riegrovi* [František Palacký's Family Letters to His Daughter Marie and Son in Law F. L. Rieger]. Prague, 1912.

Stoffel, Baron Eugene G. *Rapports militaires, écrits de Berlin, 1866–70.* Paris: Plon, 1871.

Stosch, Ulrich von (ed.). *Denkwürdigkeiten des Generals und Admirals*

Albrecht v. Stosch ersten Chef der Admiralität: Briefe und Tagebücher.
Stuttgart and Leipzig: Deutsche Verlags-Anstalt, 1904.
Thiers, Adolphe. *Memoirs of M. Thiers, 1870–1873.* Translated by F. M.
Atkinson. London: G. Allen and Unwin, 1916.
Vitzthum von Eckstädt, Karl Friedrich Graf. *London, Gastein, Sadowa,*
1864–1866: Denkwürdigkeiten. Stuttgart, 1889.
Wemyss, Roslyn. *Memoirs and Letters of Sir Robert Morier, 1826 to 1876.*
London: A. Arnold, 1911.

B. Secondary Works

Books

Andrássy, Count Julius, Jr. *Bismarck, Andrássy and their Successors.* London: T. Fisher Unwin, 1927.
_____. *Ungarns Ausgleich mit Österreich vom Jahre 1867.* Leipzig, 1897.
Bagdasarin, Nicholas Der. *The Austro-German Rapprochement, 1870–1879.*
Rutherford: Fairleigh Dickinson University Press, 1976.
Beksics, Gusztáv. *A dualizmus története* [The History of Dualism]. Budapest:
Athenaeum, 1892.
Bernatzik, Edmund. *Die österreichischen Verfassungsgesetze* (2nd ed.). Wien:
Braumüller, 1911.
Bezecny, Anton (ed.). *Die Thronrede seiner Majestät des Kaisers Franz*
Josef I. Wien: Braumüller, 1908.
Bibl, Victor. *Der Zerfall Österreichs.* 2 vols. Wien: Rikola, 1922–1924.
Bödy, Paul. *Joseph Eötvös and the Modernization of Hungary, 1840–1870: A*
Study of Ideas of Individuality and Social Pluralism in Modern Politics.
Philadelphia: The American Philosophical Society, 1972.
Bonnin, George. *Bismarck and the Hohenzollern Candidature for the Spanish*
Throne. London: Chatto and Windus, 1957.
Bourgeois, Émile et Clermont, Émile. *Rome et Napoléon III.* Paris: Colin,
1907.
Burián, Count Stephen. *Austria in Dissolution.* Translated by Brian Lunn.
New York: George H. Doran Co., 1925.
Brandenburg, Erich. *Die Reichsgründung* (2nd ed.). Leipzig: Quelle und
Meyer, 1922.
Bridge, F. R. *From Sadowa to Sarajevo: The Foreign Policy of Austria-*
Hungary, 1866–1914. London and Boston: Routledge & Kegan Paul, 1972.
Carrol, E. Malcolm. *Germany and the Great Powers, 1866–1914* (2nd ed.).
Hamden, Conn.: Archon, 1966.
Charmatz, Richard. *Österreichs innere Geschichte von 1848 bis 1907.* 2 vols.
Leipzig: Teubner, 1911–12.
_____. *Geschichte des auswärtigen Politik Österreichs im 19. Jahrhundert.*
2 vols. Leipzig: Duncker and Humbolt, 1912–14.
Clark, Chester W. *Francis Joseph and Bismarck: The Diplomacy of Austria*
before the War of 1866 (2nd ed.). New York: Russell and Russell, 1968.

Cornelius, Friedrich. *Der Friede von Nicholsburg und die öffenliche Meinung in Österreich.* München: E. Reinhardt, 1927.

Corti, Egon. *Elizabeth, Empress of Austria.* Translated by C. A. Phillips. New Haven: Yale University Press, 1936.

Daerr, Martin. *Beust und Bundesreformpläne der deutschen Mittelstaaten im Jahre 1859.* Dresden: Baensch, 1931.

Diószegi, István. *Ausztria-Magyarország és Bulgária a San Stefanoi béke után, 1875–1878* [Austria-Hungary and Bulgaria after the Treaty of San Stefano, 1875–1878]. Budapest: Akadémiai Kiadó, 1961.

———. *Ausztria-Magyarország és a francia-porosz háború, 1870–1871* [Austria-Hungary and the Franco-Prussian War, 1870–1871]. Budapest: Akadémiai Kiadó, 1965.

Dittrich, Jochen. *Bismarck, Frankreich und die spanische Thronkandidatur der Hohenzollern.* Munich: R. Oldenbourg Verlag, 1962.

Eisenmann, Louis. *Le compromis austro-hongrois de 1867: Étude sur le dualisme.* Paris: Société Nouvelle de Librairie et d'Édition, 1904.

Engel-Jánosi, Friedrich. *Geschichte auf dem Ballhausplatz.* Graz: Styria Verlag, 1963.

Erichsen, Ernst. *Die deutsche Politik des Grafen Beust im Jahre 1870: Ein Beitrag zur Geschichte der Reichsgründung.* Kiel: University of Kiel, 1927.

Eyck, Erich. *Bismarck, Leben und Werke.* 3 vols. Zürich: Eugen Rentsch Verlag, 1943.

Falk, Miksa. *Kor és jellemrajzok* [Time and Character Studies]. Budapest: Révai Testvérek, 1903.

Ferenczi, Zoltán. *Báró Eötvös József* [Baron Joseph Eötvös]. Budapest: Magyar Tudományos Akadémia, 1903.

Fischof, Adolf. *Österreich und die Bürgschaften seines Bestandes.* Wien: 1869.

Fitzmaurice, E.G.P. *The Life of Granville George Leveson Grower, Second Earl of Granville, 1815–1891.* 2 vols. London: Longmans, 1905.

Foreign Office. *Foreign Policy of Austria-Hungary.* London: H.M. Stationery Office, 1920.

Foster Arnold, Florence. *Francis Deák Hungarian Statesman: A Memoir.* London: Macmillan, 1880.

Friedjung, Heinrich. *Der Kampf um die Vorherrschaft in Deutschland 1859 bis 1866.* 2 vols. Stuttgart: Cotta, 1916.

———. *Historische Aufsätze.* Stuttgart: Cotta, 1919.

———. *The Struggle for Supremacy in Germany, 1859–1866.* Translated by A.J.P. Taylor. New York: Russell and Russell, 1966.

Galántai, József. *Az 1867-es kiegyezés* [The Compromise of 1867]. Budapest: Kossuth, 1967.

Glaise-Horstenau, Edmund von. *Franz Josephs Weggefährte: Das Leben des Generalstabschefs Grafen Beck.* Wien: Amalthea Verlag, 1930.

Gonda, Imre. *Bismarck és az 1867-es osztrák-magyar kiegyezés* [Bismarck and the Austro-Hungarian Compromise of 1867]. Budapest: Akadémiai Kiadó, 1960.

Gratz, Gusztáv. *A dualizmus kora* [The Age of Dualism]. 2 vols. Budapest: Magyar Szemle Társaság, 1941.

Grob, Ernst. *Beusts Kampf gegen Bismarck.* Turbenthal: Buchdruckerei Rob. Fürrers Erben, 1934.

Hajnal, István. *A Batthyány-kormány külpolitikája, 1848–1849* [The Foreign Policy of the Batthyány Government, 1848–1849]. Budapest: Akadémiai Kiadó, 1957.

Halász, Imre. *Egy letűnt nemzedék* [A Bygone Generation]. Budapest: Nyugat, 1911.

———. *Bismarck és Andrássy* [Bismarck and Andrássy]. Budapest: Franklin, 1913.

Hantsch, Hugo. *Die Geschichte Österreichs* (2nd ed.). 2 vols. Graz: Styria Verlag, 1947–53.

Hegedüs, Lóránt. *Két Andrássy és két Tisza* [Two Andrássys and Two Tiszas]. Budapest: Athenaeum, 1941.

Henry, Paul. *L'Abdication du Prince Cuza*. Paris: Alcan, 1930.

Holotík, Ľudovit (ed.). *Der österreichisch-ungarische Ausgleich 1867: Materialien (Referate und Diskussion) der internationalen Konferenz in Bratislava 28.8.–1.9.1967*. Bratislava: Verlag der slowakischen Akademie der Wissenschaften, 1971.

Homan, Bálint, and Szekfű, Gyula. *Magyar történet* [Hungarian History] (2nd ed.). 5 vols. Budapest: Királyi Magyar Egyetemi Nyomda, 1936.

Horváth, Jenő. *Magyar diplomácia, 1815–1918* [Hungarian Diplomacy, 1815–1918]. Budapest: Pfeifer, 1928.

Horváth, Zoltán. *Teleki László, 1810–1861* [László Teleki, 1810–1861]. Budapest: Akadémiai Kiadó, 1964.

Howard, Michael. *The Franco-Prussian War*. New York: Macmillan, 1962.

Jánossy, Denis. *The Kossuth Emigration in America*. Budapest: Hungarian Historical Society, 1940.

———. *A Kossuth-emigráció Angliában és Amerikában* [The Kossuth Emigration in England and America]. 2 vols. Budapest: Magyar Történelem Társaság, 1942–48.

Jászi, Oscar. *The Dissolution of the Habsburg Monarchy* (4th ed.). Chicago: University of Chicago Press, 1966.

Kann, Robert A. *The Multinational Empire: Nationalism and National Reform in the Habsburg Monarchy, 1848–1918* (2nd ed.). 2 vols. New York: Octagon Books, 1964.

———. *A History of the Habsburg Empire, 1526–1918*. Berkeley: University of California Press, 1974.

Kégl, Magda. *Die Beurteilung der deutschen Frage in der ungarischen Presse, 1866–1871*. Budapest: Pester Lloyd, 1934.

Kemény, G. Gábor. *Iratok a nemzetiségi kérdés történetéhez Magyarországon a dualizmus korában* [Documents on the History of the Nationality Question in Hungary in the Era of Dualism]. Budapest: Tankönyvkiadó, 1952–66.

Kenyeres, Ágnes (ed.). *Magyar életrajzi lexikon* [Hungarian Biographical Encyclopedia]. 2 vols. Budapest: Akadémiai Kiadó, 1967–69.

Kienast, Andreas. *Die Legion Klapka: Eine Episode aus dem Jahre 1866 und ihre Vorgeschichte*. Wien, 1900.

Király, Béla K. *Hungary in the Eighteenth Century: The Decline of Enlightened Despotism*. New York: Columbia University Press, 1969.

———. *Ferenc Deák*. Boston: Twayne Publishers, 1975.

Kohut, Adolf. *Bismarck és Magyarország* [Bismarck and Hungary]. Budapest: Athenaeum, 1915.

Komjáthy, Miklós. *Az Osztrák-Magyar Monarchia közös minisztertanácsa* [The Common Council of Ministers of the Austro-Hungarian Monarchy]. Budapest: Tempó, 1966.

Kondor, Victória. *Az 1875-ös pártfúzió.* [The Party Merger of 1875]. Budapest: Akadémiai Kiadó, 1959.

Kónyi, Manó. *Beust és Andrássy 1870 és 1871-ben* [Beust and Andrássy in 1870 and 1871]. Budapest, 1890.

Kosáry, Dominic G. *A History of Hungary.* Cleveland: The Benjamin Franklin Bibliophile Society, 1941.

Kovács, Endre. *Ausztria útja az 1867-es kiegyezéshez* [Austria's Road to the Compromise of 1867]. Budapest: Kossuth, 1968.

Krones, Franz von. *Moritz von Kaiserfeld, Sein Leben und Wirken.* Leipzig: Duncker, 1888.

La Gorce, Pierre de. *Histoire du second empire.* 7 vols. Paris: Plon, 1899–1905.

Langer, William. *European Alliances and Alignments, 1871–1890* (2nd ed.). New York: Alfred A. Knopf, 1950.

MacKenzie, David. *The Serbs and Russian Pan-Slavism, 1875–1878.* Ithaca, N.Y.: Cornell University Press, 1967.

Marczali, Henrik. *Ungarisches Verfassungsrecht.* Tübingen: Mohr, 1911.

May, Arthur J. *The Habsburg Monarchy, 1867–1918.* Cambridge, Mass.: Harvard University Press, 1960.

Millman, Richard. *British Foreign Policy and the Coming of the Franco-Prussian War.* Oxford: Oxford University Press, 1965.

Mosse, W. E. *The Rise and Fall of the Crimean System, 1855–71.* London: Macmillan and Co. Ltd., 1963.

_____. *The European Powers and the German Question, 1848–1871.* Cambridge: Cambridge University Press, 1958.

Ollivier, Emile. *L'Empire libéral.* 18 vols. Paris: Garnier, 1895–1918.

Petrovich, Michael B. *The Emergence of Russian Panslavism, 1856–1870.* New York: Columbia University Press, 1956.

Pflanze, Otto. *Bismarck and the Development of Germany: The Period of Unification, 1815–1871.* Princeton: Princeton University Press, 1963.

Potthoff, Heinrich. *Die deutsche Politik Beusts, von seiner Berufung zum österreichischen Aussenminister Oktober 1866 bis zum Ausbruch des deutsch-französischen Krieges 1870/71.* Bonn: Ludwig Rohrscheid Verlag, 1968.

Przibram, A. F. *The Secret Treaties of Austria-Hungary.* Translated by D. P. Myers and J. G. D'Arcy Paul. 2 vols. New York: Howard Fertig, 1967.

Redlich, Joseph. *Emperor Francis Joseph of Austria* (2nd ed.). Hamden, Conn.: Archon, 1965.

Réz, Mihály. *A kiegyezésről* [About the Compromise]. Budapest: Pátria, 1905.

Riker, T. W. *The Making of Rumania.* London: Oxford University Press, 1931.

Ritter, Gerhard. *Staatskunst und Kriegshandwerk.* 3 vols. Munich: Oldenbourg, 1954–60.

Rogge, Walter. *Geschichte Österreichs von Világos bis zur Gegenwart.* 3 vols. Leipzig-Wien: Brockhaus, 1872–73.

Rothenberg, Gunther E. *The Military Border in Croatia, 1740–1881.* Chicago: University of Chicago Press, 1966.

_____. *The Army of Francis Joseph.* West Lafayette: Purdue University Press, 1976.

Schüssler, Wilhelm. *Bismarcks Kampf um Süddeutschland.* Berlin: Stilke, 1929.

Seton-Watson, R. W. *History of the Rumanians.* Cambridge: Cambridge University Press, 1934.

_____. *Disraeli, Gladstone and the Eastern Question* (2nd ed.). London: Frank Cass and Co., 1962.

Sosnosky, Theodor von. *Die Balkanpolitik Österreich-Ungarn seit 1866.* 2 vols. Stuttgart und Berlin: Deutsche Verlags-Anstalt, 1913–1914.

Srbik, Heinrich von. *Deutsche Einheit: Idee und Wirklichkeit vom Heiligen Reich bis Königgrätz.* 4 vols. Munich: F. Bruckmann, 1935.

_____. *Aus Österreichs Vergangenheit von Prinz Eugen zu Kaiser Franz Joseph.* Salzburg: Otto Miller Verlag, 1949.

Steed, Henry W. *The Habsburg Monarchy* (2nd ed.). London: Constable and Co., 1915.

Steefel, Lawrence D. *Bismarck, the Hohenzollern Candidacy, and the Origin of the Franco-Prussian War of 1870.* Cambridge, Mass.: Harvard University Press, 1962.

Stern, Alfred. *Geschichte Europas von 1848 bis 1871.* 10 vols. Berlin: W. Hertz, 1924.

Stoyanovich, M. D. *The Great Powers and the Balkans, 1875–1878.* Cambridge: Cambridge University Press, 1939.

Sybel, Heinrich von. *The Foundation of the German Empire by William I.* Translated by H. S. White. 7 vols. New York: Thomas Y. Crowell & Co., 1890–98.

Szekfű, Gyula. *Három nemzedék: Egy hanyatló kor története* [Three Generations. Story of a Declining Age]. Budapest: Élet, 1922.

Taylor, A.J.P. *The Struggle for Mastery of Europe, 1848–1918* (2nd ed.). Oxford: Oxford University Press, 1963.

_____. *The Habsburg Monarchy, 1805–1918.* New York: Harper and Row, 1965.

_____. *From Napoleon to Lenin.* New York: Harper and Row, 1966.

Tschuppik, Karl. *The Reign of Emperor Francis Joseph, 1848–1916.* Translated by C.J.S. Srigge. London: G. Bell & Sons, 1930.

Turba, Gustav. *Die Pragmatische Sanktion mit besonderer Rücksicht auf die Länder der Stefanskrone.* Wien: Manz, 1906.

Valentin, Veit. *Bismarcks Reichsgründung im Urteil englischer Diplomaten.* Amsterdam: Elsevier, 1937.

Waldapfel, Eszter. *A független magyar külpolitika, 1848–1849* [The Independent Hungarian Foreign Policy, 1848–1849]. Budapest: Akadémiai Kiadó, 1962.

Wertheimer, Ede. *Gróf Andrássy Gyula élete és kora* [Life and Times of Count Julius Andrássy]. 3 vols. Budapest: Magyar Tudományos Akadémia, 1910–13.

_____. *Bismarck im politischen Kampf.* Berlin: Hobbing, 1930.

Zacek, Joseph F. *Palacký: The Historian as Scholar and Nationalist.* Paris: Mouton, 1970.

Zechlin, Egmont. *Bismarck und die Grundlegung der deutschen Grossmacht.* Stuttgart: Cotta, 1960.

Zöllner, Erich. *Geschichte Österreichs: Von den Anfängen bis zur Gegenwart.* Wien: Verlag für Geschichte und Politik, 1961.

Articles and Periodicals

[Andrássy, Count Julius.] "The Present Position and Policy of Austria," *The Eclectic Review,* XXVIII (November, 1850), 604–29.

Barany, George. "Hungary: The Uncompromising Compromise," *Austrian History Yearbook,* III, Pt. 1 (1967), 235–59.

Berend, Iván, and Ránki, György. "Hungarian Manufacturing Industry, Its Place in Europe, 1900–1938," *Nouvelles études historiques.* 2 vols. Budapest: Akadémiai Kiadó, 1965, II, 423–36.

Blowitz, M. G. de. "Austria and the Congress," *The Times* (London), July 26, 1878.

Clark, Chester W. "Bismarck, Russia and the Origins of the War of 1870," *Journal of Modern History,* XIV (June, 1942), 195–208.

Denis, Ernest. "Uzpomínky a úvahy o Palackém [Memories and Studies of Palacký]," *Památník* [Diary] (1898), 159.

Diószegi, István. "Honvédőrnagy Metternich íróasztalánál: 150 éve született Andrássy Gyula" [A Major at Metternich's Desk: Julius Andrássy Was Born One Hundred Years Ago], *Élet és Irodalom,* 1973, No. 9, p. 7.

Dziennik Lwowski, July and August, 1870.

Dziennik Polski, July, 1870.

Eisenmann, Louis. "Austria-Hungary," *The Cambridge Modern History.* 12 vols. London: Macmillan, 1910, pp. 174–212.

Engel-Jánosi, Friedrich. "The Roman Question in the Diplomatic Negotiations of 1869–70," *The Review of Politics,* III (1941), 319–49.

———. "Austria in the Summer of 1870," *Journal of Central European Affairs,* V (January, 1964), 336–53.

Fremdenblatt, 1866, 1870.

Fügedi, Elek. "The Losses of Hungarian Private Archives," *Journal of Central European Affairs,* VIII (October, 1948), 282–84.

Gazeta Narodowa, July, 1870.

Hanák, Péter. "Hungary in the Austro-Hungarian Monarchy: Preponderance or Dependency?" *Austrian History Yearbook,* III (1967), 260–302.

Hegedüs, Roland. "The Foreign Policy of Count Andrássy," *The Hungarian Quarterly,* III (Winter, 1937/38), 627–42.

Kállay, Béni. "Gróf Andrássy Gyula emlékezete" [Remembrance of Count Julius Andrássy], *Akadémiai Értesíto,* II (June, 1891), 326–50.

Kann, Robert A. "Hungarian Jewry During Austria-Hungary's Constitutional Period (1867–1918)," *Jewish Social Studies,* VIII (1945), 357–86.

Kazbunda, Karel. "Dvě Riegrova memoranda" [Two Rieger Memoranda], *Zahranični politika,* 1925, pp. 844–70, 954–78.

Kónyi, Manó. "Visszaemlékezés Andrássy Gyula grófra" [Recollections of Count Julius Andrássy], *Nemzet,* February 19–21, 1890.

———. "Andrássy Gyula gr. politikai első fellépése" [Political Debut of Count Julius Andrássy], *Budapesti Hírlap,* February 19, 1890.

Kraj, July, 1870.

Matolay, Etele. "Emlékezés Andrássyról" [Remembrance of Andrássy], *Zemplén* (Sátoraljaújhely), March 30, 1890.

Meyendorff, Baron A. F. "Conversation of Gorchakov with Andrássy and Bismarck in 1872," *Slavonic and East European Review*, VIII (December, 1929), 400–408.

Michaelis, Herbert. "Königgrätz, Eine geschichtliche Wende," *Die Welt als Geschichte*, XII (1952), 172–202.

Mosse, W. E. "England, Russia and the Rumanian Revolution of 1866," *Slavonic and East European Review*, XXXIX (1960–61), 73–94.

Mowat, R. B. "Andrássy," *The Hungarian Quarterly*, III (Summer, 1937), 268–76.

Národní listy, July and August, 1870.

Neue Freie Presse, 1866–70.

Norddeutsche Allgemeine Zeitung, 1867–68.

Novotny, Alexander. "Aussenminister Gyula Graf Andrássy der Altere," in *Gestalter der Geschichte Österreichs*, ed. Hugo Hantsch. Innsbruck: Tyrolia Verlag, 1962, pp. 457–71.

Okolicsányi, Sándor. "Adalékok Gróf Andrássy Gyula jellemrajzához"[Additional Data to the Character Study of Count Julius Andrássy], *Budapesti Szemle*, LXII (1890), 116–20.

Odlozilík, Otakar. "Russia and the Czech National Aspirations," *Journal of Central European Affairs*, XXII (January, 1963), 407–39.

Papp, Tibor. "A magyar honvédség megalakulása a kiegyezés után, 1868–1890" [Establishment of the Hungarian Army after the Compromise, 1868–1890], *Hadtörténelmi Közlemények*, II (1967), 302–338.

Pester Correspondenz, July, 1870.

Pester Lloyd, 1868, 1870.

Pesti Napló, 1866–1870.

Platzhoff, Walter. "Die Anfänge des Dreikaiserbundes," *Preussische Jahrbücher*, CLXXXVIII (June, 1922), 283–306.

Prange, Gordon W. "Beust's Appointment as Austrian Foreign Minister," *Iowa Studies in the Social Sciences*, II (1941), 205–31.

Reform, 1870.

Reiner, B. "Graf Julius Andrássy als Diplomat der Revolution," *Neue Freie Presse*, February 21, 22, 23, 1890.

Ritter, Gerhard. "Das Bismarckproblem," *Merkur*, IV (1950), 657–64.

Scherr-Thoss, Graf Arthur. "Erinnerungen aus meinem Leben," *Deutsche Rundschau*, XXVIII (July, August and September, 1881), 1–80.

Schmitt, Hans A. "Count Beust and Germany, 1866–1870: Reconquest, Realignment or Resignation?" *Central European History*, I (March, 1968), 20–34.

———. "Prussia's Last Fling: The Annexation of Hanover, Hesse, Frankfurt, and Nassau, June 15–October 8, 1866," *Central European History*, VIII (December, 1975), 316–347.

Seton-Watson, R. W. "Les relations de l'Autriche-Hongrie et de la Serbie entre 1866 et 1874: La mission de Benjamin Kállay à Belgrade," *Le Monde Slave*, I (January, 1926), 210–30; II (May, 1926), 186–204; III (August, 1926), 273–88.

———. "The Emperor Francis Joseph," *History*, XVII (July and October, 1932), 11–121, 220–30.

Srbik, Heinrich von. "Zur gesamtdeutschen Geschichtsauffassung," *Historische Zeitschrift*, CLVI (1937), 229–62.

_____. "Deutsche Führung – der Segen des Böhmischen Raums," *Völkischer Beobachter*, March 19, 1939.

Szekfű, Gyula. "Andrássy," *Napkelet*, I (1923), 418–22.

Taffs, Winifred. "Conversation Between Lord Odo Russell and Andrássy, Bismarck and Gorchakov in September, 1872," *Slavonic and East European Review*, VIII (March, 1930), 701–707.

[Takács, Sándor.] "Andrássy az 1847–48-iki országgyűlésen" [Andrássy at the Diet of 1847–48], *Budapesti Hírlap*, November 29, 1906.

Temperley, Harold. "Lord Acton on the Origin of the War of 1870 with Some Unpublished Letters from the British and Viennese Archives," *Cambridge Historical Journal*, II (1926), 68–82.

The Times (London), July, 1870.

Thumann, H. H. "Beusts Plan zur Reform des deutschen Bundes von Oktober 1861," *Neues Archiv für sächsische Geschichte*, XLVI (1925).

Tisza, Count István. "Wertheimer 'Andrássy'-ja" [Wertheimer's 'Andrássy'], *Magyar Figyelő*, I (January–March, 1911), 321–39.

Wank, Solomon. "Foreign Policy and Nationality Problem in Austria-Hungary, 1867–1914," *Austrian History Yearbook*, III (1967), 37–56.

Way, Count Sándor. "Az Andrássyak" [The Andrássys] in *Magyarország Vármegyéi és városai: Gömör-Kishont vármegye* [Counties and Cities of Hungary: Gömör-Kishont County], ed. Sándor Borowsky. Budapest, n.d., VIII, 593–613.

Wertheimer, Eduard von. "Francis Joseph u. Napoleon III in Salzburg; nach ungedruckten Acten," *Österreichische Rundschau*, LXII (1920), 164–74, 224–29.

_____. "Zur Vorgeschichte des Krieges von 1870," *Deutsche Rundschau*, CLXXXV (1920), 1–26, 220–41, 342–56.

Wiener Zeitung, May, 1867.

Zatočník, July, 1870.

Reports

Kann, Robert A. *The Austro-Hungarian Compromise of 1867 in Retrospect: Cause and Effect*. Report to the International Conference on the *Ausgleich* of 1867, Bratislava, Slovakia, Aug. 28 to Sept. 2, 1967. Princeton, N.J.: By the Author, 1967.

Zacek, Joseph F. *Palacký and the Austro-Hungarian Compromise of 1867*. Report to the International Conference on the *Ausgleich* of 1867, Bratislava, Slovakia, Aug. 28 to Sept. 2, 1967. Los Angeles, Calif.: By the Author, 1967.

Unpublished Material

Berger, Margaret. "Österreichs auswärtige Politik (Die Ministertätigkeit des Grafen Beust 1866–1870/71) und das Vaterland." Unpublished Phil. dissertation, University of Vienna, Vienna, 1947.

Houston, Douglass W. "The Negotiations for a Triple Alliance between France, Austria, and Italy, 1869–70." Unpublished Ph.D. dissertation, University of Pennsylvania, 1959.

Schoenhals, Kai Peter. "The Russian Policy of Friedrich Ferdinand von Beust, 1866–1871." Unpublished Ph.D. dissertation, University of Rochester, 1964.

Wagner, Walter. "Kaiser Franz Joseph und das Deutsche Reich von 1871–1914." Unpublished Phil. dissertation, University of Vienna, 1950.

Index of Names

Albrecht, Archduke, 2, 23, 69, 89, 90, 92–95, 106, 108.
Alexander II, 21, 51–53, 87–88, 97, 110–111.
Andrássy, Count Gyula, 1–8, 10–12, 14–23, 27–50, 53–69, 72, 74–77, 79, 81–82, 86–92, 94–96, 98–105, 107–116.
Artom, Isacco, 31, 34.
Auersperg, Count Anton Alexander, 9.

Beck, Colonel Baron Friedrich von, 90.
Belcredi, Count Richard von, 25, 137 n. 2.
Bellegarde, General Count August von, 159 n. 8.
Benedetti, Count Vincente, 74, 145 n. 7.
Berchtold, Count Leopold von, 33.
Beust, Count Friedrich Ferdinand von, 1–8, 11, 23–27, 37–70, 72–77, 86–87, 89–99, 103–105, 107–112, 114–116, 129–130 n. 20.
Bibl, Victor, 4.
Biegeleben, Baron Ludwig Maximilian von, 9, 24.
Bismarck-Schönhausen, Prince Otto von, 1–3, 5, 7, 9, 20, 24, 28–31, 40–45, 48–49, 52–53, 61–67, 74, 76, 78, 81, 83, 87–88, 102–103, 112–114, 134 n. 68.
Blome, Count Gustav von, 131 n. 29.
Bloomfield, Lord John Arthur Douglas, 130 n. 21.
Blowitz, M. G., de, 20.
Bonaparte, Prince Jerome Napoleon, 35, 38–39, 55.

Bourgoing, Baron O., 73, 75.
Brabdenburg, Erich, 3.
Brătianu, Ion, 59, 62, 120 n. 2, 148 n. 72.
Breda, Count Paul, 134 n. 73.
Burián, Count István, 14.
Bülow, Prince Bernhard von, 20.

Castellane, Marquis C. de, 63–65.
Cazaux, Marquis Joseph-Aime-Louis de, 73, 75, 83, 91–92, 95–98.
Charles, Prince of Hohenzollern-Sigmaringen, 9, 61–62, 120 n. 2.
Charles V, Holy Roman Emperor, 71.
Charmatz, Richard, 1, 3.
Chotek, Count Boguslav, 87, 110.
Clarendon, Lord George William Frederick Villiers, 58.
Crenneville, Count Franz Folliot de, 23.
Csáky, Count Tivadar, 75.
Csengery, Antal, 108.
Curtopassi, Count Francesco, 31, 74, 76, 97.
Cuza, Alexander Ion, 120 n. 2.

Deák, Ferenc, 6, 11–12, 16–17, 20, 32, 38, 82, 108, 126 n. 81.
Delbrück, Hans, 3.
Dalwigk zu Lichtenfels, Baron Reinhard von, 26, 142 n. 98.
Danielik, Bishop János, 63, 65.
Der Bagdasarin, Nicholas, 119 n. 28.
Diószegi, István, 1, 6, 25, 39, 41, 77–79, 100, 106.
Ducrot, General Auguste Alexander, 50.